T0396841

Resilience as Heritage in Asia

International Institute for Asian Studies

Publications

The International Institute for Asian Studies (IIAS) is a research and exchange platform based in Leiden, the Netherlands. Its objective is to encourage the interdisciplinary and comparative study of Asia and to promote (inter)national cooperation. IIAS focuses on the humanities and social sciences and on their interaction with other sciences. It stimulates scholarship on Asia and is instrumental in forging research networks among Asia Scholars. Its main research interests are reflected in the four book series published with Amsterdam University Press: Global Asia, Asian Heritages, Asian Cities, and Humanities *Across* Borders (H*A*B).

IIAS acts as an international mediator, bringing together various parties in Asia and other parts of the world. The Institute works as a clearinghouse of knowledge and information. This entails activities such as providing information services, the construction and support of international networks and cooperative projects, and the organization of seminars and conferences. In this way, IIAS functions as a window on Europe for non-European scholars and contributes to the cultural rapprochement between Europe and Asia.

IIAS Publications Officer: Mary Lynn van Dijk

Asian Heritages

The Asian Heritages series explores the notions of heritage as they have evolved from European based concepts, mainly associated with architecture and monumental archaeology, to incorporate a broader diversity of cultural forms and value. This includes a critical exploration of the politics of heritage and its categories, such as the contested distinction 'tangible' and 'intangible' heritages; the analysis of the conflicts triggered by competing agendas and interests in the heritage field; and the productive assessment of management measures in the context of Asia.

Series Editors
Adèle Esposito, CNRS Géographie-cités, France
Michael Herzfeld, Harvard University, USA, and Leiden University, the Netherlands

Editorial Board
Sadiah Boonstra, Vrije Universiteit Amsterdam, The Netherlands, and Melbourne University, Australia
Min-Chin CHIANG, Taipei National University of the Arts, Taiwan
Yew-Foong HUI, ISEAS-Yusof Ishak Institute, Singapore
Ronki Ram, Panjab University, India

Resilience as Heritage in Asia

Edited by
Michael Herzfeld and
Rita Padawangi

Amsterdam University Press

Cover illustration: *Rumah Besar Pecinan Tambak Bayan*, Surabaya, Indonesia, by Rita Padawangi, March 2023.

The cover image portrays the interior of *Rumah Besar Pecinan Tambak Bayan Surabaya* (the Big House of Tambak Bayan), located at the heart of an old settlement in Surabaya that has undergone several waves of land tenure crisis over the past seven decades. Inside, several art installations and paintings by local artists materially express solidarity with the residents. Residents believe that the house was built in 1866 as a stable when Surabaya was under Dutch colonial rule. The Dutch landowner returned to the Netherlands in 1928 and left it to his wife, a local person of Chinese ethnicity. The surrounding area eventually developed into a Chinese immigrant settlement. Known as Kampung Tambak Bayan, it is home to many families, some for more than three generations. The current land dispute is with a hotel owner who has been claiming possession for twenty years.

Residents connected with various communities, students, urban activists, social movement organizations, and artists are resisting the hotel expansion through various means, from lawsuits to community events, festivals, and public art. Today, artworks visible in all public spaces and alleyways and the Rumah Besar's role as a space for social and artistic activity interweave with the residents' everyday life as testaments to Kampung Tambak Bayan's resilience.

Cover design: Coördesign, Leiden
Lay-out: Crius Group, Hulshout

ISBN   978 94 6372 856 0
e-ISBN   978 90 4855 499 7 (pdf)
DOI   10.5117/9789463728560
NUR   740

Creative Commons License CC-BY NC ND (http://creativecommons.org/licenses/by-nc-nd/4.0)

© The authors / Amsterdam University Press B.V., Amsterdam 2025

Some rights reserved. Without limiting the rights under copyright reserved above, any part of this book may be reproduced, stored in or introduced into a retrieval system, or transmitted, in any form or by any means (electronic, mechanical, photocopying, recording or otherwise).

Every effort has been made to obtain permission to use all copyrighted illustrations reproduced in this book. nonetheless, whosoever believes to have rights to this material is advised to contact the publisher.

We dedicate this volume to
Mike Douglass,
urbanist and visionary

in gratitude
for his enduring inspiration and leadership in
a complex and contested field.

Table of Contents

List of Illustrations

Acknowledgements

This book is a collective work. We especially wish to thank Mary Lynn van Dijk for her indispensable guidance during the editorial process. We would also like to thank Inge Klompmakers and the entire production team at Amsterdam University Press. We are indebted to two anonymous reviewers for incisive comments that particularly helped us to bring conceptual cohesion to a volume containing a diversity of perspectives and locations. We are grateful to the Asia Research Institute, National University of Singapore for hosting the workshop that brought the authors together for our preliminary explorations of the book's topic. Finally, we thank the International Institute for Asian Studies and the Singapore University of Social Sciences for their material support of Open Access, thereby enabling the theme of "Resilience as Heritage in Asia" to reach a much broader audience.

1. Vernacular Heritage, Vernacular Resilience: Introducing Asian Experiences and Perspectives

Michael Herzfeld and Rita Padawangi

Abstract: Resilience in Asia's urban life is itself a form of heritage. Local social practices have long sustained community identities, although increasingly under pressure from a combination of neoliberal developmentalism and political authoritarianism. We present a small but suggestive sampling of case studies showing that local cultural resources often exceed the imagination of global and nationalistic forces; local communities cope better with disruptions of the natural environment. Yet politically stronger forces do threaten local communities' cultural autonomy, especially where this challenges government authority or elite-driven planning. From the arts to disaster responses, these essays explore the possibilities and the limitations that local communities' resilience faces. Official failures to recognize local resilience tragically wastes human resources and the creative value of human irrepressibility.

Keywords: resistance, developmentalism, community, everyday experience, authenticity, art and music

Heritage and Community: The Threat of Reification, the Promise of Resilience

Mike Douglass, to whose energy and dedication we largely owe the inspiration for this volume,[1] has argued against the tendency of national

---

[1] Mike Douglass generated the ideas that led to the creation of this volume, which we dedicate to him in grateful recognition of his profound and lasting influence. He is one of those rare

Herzfeld, M., and R. Padawangi, eds. *Resilience as Heritage in Asia*. Amsterdam: Amsterdam University Press, 2025.
DOI: 10.5117/9789463728560_CH01

governments, in Asia and elsewhere, to concentrate all capital investment in a single (usually capital) city, thereby creating huge and growing regional economic inequality. This, he argues (see especially Douglass 2002), does not actually constitute genuine resilience, and it virtually guarantees a disastrous future.

In this volume, we have expanded Douglass's vision of the relation between resilience and equality to areas that are far from economics—to the role of small and localized enclaves in contributing to the richness of city life; the place of art and music in enabling cultural identities to thrive in mutual recognition; and the capacity of local and under-recognized social mechanisms to overcome natural and human-induced disasters. These were already embryonically present in Douglass's understanding of resilience, but the essays we have brought together here provide new kinds of empirical evidence for the existence of resilience as well as for the obstacles it must overcome.

Resilience as Resistance

Resilience, then, is much more than a question of communal organizing against larger forces, although that is an important dimension. Resilience is about remaining *different*, about resisting majority oppression and disdain. It appears in the rebellious color scheme of a house that contradicts the ordered uniformity of a so-called historic district. It subsists in the maintenance of foods, rituals, and attitudes that lie outside the nationally sanctioned canon. It intimates itself through the creative riffs that ripple through a jazz jam session, the artistry of graffiti, the impromptu meetings and dances that erupt in the streets. Sometimes it takes the form of obedience to authority when such obedience furthers the social against individual selfishness, as when lockdown and masking are mandated as the most effective measures against a pandemic. Sometimes it simply takes the form of getting on with life and ignoring the impudent disruptions of an insistently homogenizing modernity. Resilience is everywhere. Sometimes it works; sometimes it flutters feebly and flickers out. In each and every situation in which we meet it, however, resilience saves the humanity of social life from the

urban planners for whom one size does not fit all. He brought two major concerns to the Asia Research Institute at the National University of Singapore through his leadership of the Asian Urbanisms Cluster: the over-commercialization of urbanization and the serious environmental challenges that have displaced entire urban neighborhoods and communities.

mechanical operations to which everyday existence is so often subjected. It allows people to become the agents of protecting their own dignity—a dignity widely recognized as starting with the right to a roof over one's head, but also maintained through the respect gained from those with the real capacity to exercise disproportionate and destructive power. In Asia, as elsewhere in the world, we find solace in its infinite variety, drawing ethical and intellectual sustenance from it even when it fails.

In its most visible form, resilience is what halts the growing uniformity of the world's inhabited spaces. The rapid urbanization of much of Asia—with squadrons of skyscrapers marching across landscapes only recently planted with crops and trees, and with glossy new construction wiping old urban communities from the map—has given a particular urgency to our quest for understanding how poor communities will cope with the expansion of neoliberal commerce, the gentrified and gated settlements of the wealthy, the sequestration of residential spaces for the grandiose projects of governments, the destruction of the rural hinterland, and rapidly rising rents and other economic pressures.

If the planners of a particular country elevate one city above all others, moreover, as Douglass presciently warned, within each primate city similar uneven playing fields will continue to tip away from the weak and marginalized who make up a substantial proportion of the total population, and on whom even the wealthiest citizens depend for basic services as well as entertainment and luxury items. Yet there are signs of hope. Even as high-rises sprout everywhere and mall culture seems to offer a cheap and easy substitute for the arcane attractions of antiquity and traditional culture, pockets and patches of older lifestyles and cultural activity appear in many cities in Asia. Some flourish amid the cacophonous disorder of rapid urban change; some disappear with a whimper; some explode in an orgy of demolition and denial. Others, remarkably, just doggedly survive, displaying a resilience that is more than a flash in the pan.

These recrudescences are extremely varied in at least three senses: their national contexts, their local motivations, and the specific type of cultural activity they represent. We have not tried to cover all the possibilities in this relatively short volume, preferring instead to focus on a few cases that should nevertheless give a sampling of the range of scenarios currently playing out. Asia offers a wide variety of cultural, economic, political, and social patterns. Consequently, especially given our modest coverage, we do not attempt generalizations about "Asian resilience." This volume does not cover the entire continent, or even all of its eastern half; nor is it a comprehensive survey. Our goal is the more modest one of selecting a few case studies representative of different kinds of resilience identified by scholars whose Asian focus also leads them to interact intellectually and in terms of regional concerns. What Tessa Guazon says in these pages about resilience and national identity—noting that, even though Filipinos have been praised as resilient, resilience is not the property of a particular nation—is true, a fortiori, for an entire continent: there is no such thing as Asian resilience, even though there is plenty of resilience in Asia.

Our position in this regard is epistemologically consistent. Essentialisms built on already established orthodoxies are not the stuff of which an ethically committed and critical academic inquiry is made. Indeed, we oppose such simplifications. Thus, Motohiro Koizumi's piece on socially engaged art highlights a range of cultural, social, and historical backgrounds of citizens that are more diverse than the usual descriptions—and the internally prevalent stereotype (see Befu 2001)—of a homogenous Japanese society. Official reifications of identity are not a source of resilience; to the contrary, they often suppress the subtly nuanced complexities of social interaction that for millennia have sustained local identities. Today, many of those local identities are threatened by the twin forces of ethnonationalism and globalized neoliberalism, and this, indeed, is evident in several of the studies contained here (De Giosa, Ferzacca, Helmersen, Herzfeld). Selecting a few cases for thinking more constructively about how resilience emerges, what challenges it faces, and why and when it should be encouraged is likely to be more productive, intellectually and socially, than grand predictions or sweeping policy proposals.

Heritage and Collective Resilience

In this volume, we address the strength-in-fragility that defines virtually all forms of collective resilience. We address, in other words, the paradoxical capacity for sociocultural persistence that sometimes sustains fragile identities against all the apparent odds. We especially identify situations in which various forms of heritage have factored into the tussle over whether local communities would survive or be swept away, and recognizable socialities of a seemingly more ephemeral nature have proved to be sustainable. We also maintain that the idea of resilience itself is, or is becoming, a form of heritage in its own right.

To the (limited) extent to which one can legitimately speak of "Asian communities," it would seem that this recognition of resilience is critical for two reasons. First, throughout much of Asia locally rooted resilience—sometimes reinforced by international grassroots networking—has provided the means of resistance to capitalist exploitation and political repression. In the second place, a critical analysis of the phenomenon will also warn us of potential traps for unwary communities seeking to hitch their wagons (or, rather, their houses and their artistic skills) to official models of heritage, or individuals treading the treacherous interstices among received ideas about how to perform vernacular culture.

Ultimately, given the ideologically constructed nature of all heritage (Lowenthal 2015; Meskell 2018; Smith 2006), we must probe some taken-for-granted categories that it might seem decidedly impolitic to challenge. We ask what heritage—the materialization of that collective possession that is so often reified as "a culture" (see Handler 1985)—has to do with resilience. If the question is whether heritage is itself resilient, we first have to ask what "it" actually is. If the question is whether heritage-related activities will help communities to survive, we must also ask another, scarcely less explosive question: what constitutes "a community"? We are not alone in posing such questions, but we do so here by means of the collected case studies in the hope that others will expand the range of contexts in which these questions are recognizably salient.

We hope our collective efforts will help to give increased substance to these questions, replacing the unthinking reification of the three key terms—resilience, community, and heritage—with the specificity of the social, political, and cultural processes that produce the apparent stability these words suggest. Rather than looking to objects that typify a reified and prefabricated notion of collective culture, we can instead seek understanding of the processes of identity formation and protection as these are enshrined in performances such as theatrical or dance events or in artistic happenings. Such events, which display the agency and creativity that create and sustain all identities including those promoted by nation-states, allow us to view heritage as a process-in-action rather than as a collection of inert objects or texts. At the same time, ethnographic perspectives on historic conservation and museum curation allow us to debunk the "methodological nationalism" (Wimmer and Glick Schiller 2002) that treats all nonnational claims to heritage as inferior copies of national models. That attitude, energetically cultivated by national governments and their cultural agencies and to some extent amplified by international agencies such as UNESCO (see, e.g., Labadi 2007, 2013; Meskell 2018; but cf. Bendix et al. 2013), has a trickle-down effect. Helmersen (this volume), for example, demonstrates how Melaka's ethnic enclaves harden over time in response to heavy-handed nationalism in heritage conservation.

Heritage and the Materiality of the Ephemeral

Some observations about "heritage" as a concept are in order. What is to count as heritage is always a vexed and contested question. It is also a debate about something that is by its very nature evanescent, inchoate, and poorly defined—which clearly, if the existing literature and the burgeoning field of critical heritage studies are any indication, has been no impediment to its global significance. The reason is not hard to find. Heritage is not only an arena for state self-glorification and nationalist excess; it is also a space for resistance, rethinking, and, yes, resilience. It is fragile because it is hard to grasp; when national governments seize it, they often squeeze all the life out of it with their clumsy insistence on defining, conserving, and exhibiting it—without ever realizing how evanescent "it" is. Its very "itness" is questionable.

In this context, we should recall Laurajane Smith's (2006) astute observation that all heritage is intangible. By this, she clearly means that we should not be deceived by self-officializing discourses that attribute ontological fixity to the idea of heritage (as in "our heritage") rather than recognizing it as an *attributed quality* of certain cultural items ranging from architecture to proverbs and beyond. Heritage is thus an elusive phenomenon, its status created by performative utterances (often in the form of evaluative statements) and ratified by official organizations. Even its relation to history is problematic. Although we might agree with Valentine Daniel (1996) that some ethnic groups emphasize historicity where others focus instead on the unifying idea of a collective heritage, that schema risks playing the official game of reification. The authors in this collection have moved in a significantly different direction. As Steve Ferzacca perspicaciously notes here, heritage seems to emerge in the space "between historicity and historicide"—a terminological play that puts us in mind of Qin Shao's (2013) use of "domicide," and reminds us that even acknowledgement as "historical fact" is the result of complex processes and sequences of action by key players.

Ferzacca's statement points to the constant struggle around the deceptive appearance of fixity entailed in most officially generated claims to heritage status. Can a sense of heritage be maintained when the physical setting of an older communal entity is being destroyed, or faces imminent destruction? Furthermore, can a sense of heritage be evoked through destruction? Novenanto and Suyadnya's contribution brings out heritage making through the collective memorializing of a place that has been destroyed, and the effort to build resilience as a form of resistance against the destroyer. Is it necessary for elements of the past to be destroyed so that the reified "pastness" we acknowledge as heritage can emerge? Would we even be contemplating heritage at all if such destruction had not awoken a sense of urgency and the need "to do something"? Why, to put the matter in another way, is authenticity so important? And is authenticity a property of material objects, of food systems, of intentions, or of all these and much more (see Brulotte and Di Giovine 2014; Handler 1986)? Who decides what is authentic?

The question of authenticity may turn on that sense of place that emerges over time from collective everyday experiences. The association between authenticity and collective everyday experiences suggests the importance of the vernacular in constructing "authenticity" in heritage making. The term "vernacular" itself originated from a Latin term indicating a slave's birth in the master's house. Fortunately, the term has long since shed all connotations of slavery; it indexes the cultural self-expression of local communities, usually in contrast with an elite cultural ideology (Tjahjono 2014; Werbner 2016; Sand 2013). While we may appreciate ICOMOS's formal acknowledgement of local cultural values as reasons for heritage preservation, that move does not address a major issue—the inequality that so often suppresses local, collective, everyday, and experience-based values. Those are the values that shape what we mean by the vernacular in these pages, and they contest the generalized, top-down notions of national identity and culture sanctioned by nation-state governments and by social elites that often possess power disproportionate to their demographic size.

Urbanizing environments magnify such inequalities since global capitalism as the driving force of development requires all spaces to participate in its plans and therefore transforms social and economic practices that have long shaped the cultural life of the local (Padawangi 2021; see also Yeoh 1996). In such contexts, even when urban heritage is supposedly inseparable from the vernacular character of those spaces, the drive to make all spaces financially valuable makes commercialization the engine and goal of heritage preservation (Padawangi 2015). The over-commercialization of urban spaces becomes a major challenge to the resilience of vernacular heritage; vernacular spaces and practices may survive through resistance or co-optation; they may become ephemeral; or they may at times simply survive by discreetly evading attention. The ephemerality of the vernacular sense of place is a result of its subordination to the state's monopoly of legitimacy in shaping the publicly shared spaces of the built environment, in the context of state politics that do not necessarily represent such place-based communal entities at all.

Heritage—and this, too, is something that national governments conveniently forget or ignore—is social; the status it confers is a social fact.

Anything recognized as heritage must therefore also have a social context. As Ferzacca (this volume) wisely remarks: "without the social, vernacular heritage ceases to exist." A dangerous dichotomy nevertheless lurks in the undergrowth of this statement, because it would be all too easy to ignore the social basis of official heritage as well. Nothing would please officially appointed heritage experts better. Their goal is usually that of creating a sense of perpetuity, whereas what we recognize as vernacular heritage is often celebrated by people who are all too well aware of its fragility—and of the threat that official acceptations of the heritage concept pose to it. Official heritage is no less social than vernacular; it is just far better equipped to hide its contingent character. The distinction between official and vernacular culture runs the risk of reproducing the old high-low culture discrimination, with its attendant colonial and classist implications.

The problems posed by the tangible-intangible binary are perhaps less obviously connected to this ideological and political discrimination, but the possibility of such a link should also be kept in mind; the phenomenon of folklorization discussed by Herzfeld in this volume (see also Denes 2015) tends to merge with a relegation of "intangible heritage" to "mere folklore," privileging what is classified as "tangible" (see also Herzfeld 2014). Recalling the social character of official heritage—the fact that it is created by bureaucratic and political actors with very specific interests at stake—is important if we are not to become complicit in the reinforcement of that same hierarchy, a hierarchy that also channels what various parties understand by "participation" in decisions affecting their futures. Despite warnings about the misuse of the concept of participation from Arnstein's (1969) early and incisive critique to de Cesari and Dimova's (2019) ethnographic and comparative examination of its failed promises and occasional successes, state actors tend to dictate what will be regarded as heritage and are notoriously insensitive to vernacular, minority, and socially dissident interpretations. Their invocations of participation are consequently often empty formalities, designed to assuage anxieties and allow the developers to get on with acts of indescribable insensitivity. In those cases where state actors have shown some willingness to compromise and cooperate, they have also had to contend with internal factionalism and this has furnished an excuse for inaction or repression; we should not overlook factionalism's role in revealing and commemorating the multifaceted politics of all shared heritage (on which, see especially Ginzarly, Farah, and Teller 2019). While some governments may be inclined to invoke a stereotyped cultural aversion to conflict, moreover, recent events in China, Myanmar, Thailand, and Vietnam show clearly that such essentialisms, while extremely convenient for those who articulate them, achieve little beyond silencing or deferring effective protest and demands for a more participatory engagement.

Such reactions, in the name of something called national culture, often serve the interests of dominant ethnic, religious, or linguistic majorities. Here, Kim Helmersen's contribution in the present volume offers an insightful perspective on why such top-down management is so destructive. Helmersen compares that approach to Durkheim's mechanical solidarity, arguing that a dynamic in which minority interests also participate would produce the equivalent of Durkheim's organic solidarity, to the advantage of all concerned. Because Helmersen recognizes the agency of local stakeholders as crucial to such a move, he effectively strips the Durkheimian model of its functionalist implications. He is nevertheless not entirely optimistic. He sees the present situation as encouraging a reversion to the mechanical model, noting that particular styles get linked to particular groups, each contributing to the further reification *both* of other groups *and* of "ethnic" styles. His analysis holds an important message for governments intent on establishing a majoritarian monopoly of resources. In suppressing the complex interplay of ethnic traditions within neighborhoods in favor of culturally more homogenous spaces—a move that renders them more "legible" in Scott's (1998) sense—governments also destroy the on-the-ground cosmopolitanism that might otherwise serve as a rich source of economic as well as cultural resilience. That resilience entails resisting and reshaping the process whereby Melaka seems to be ineluctably sucked into the global, neoliberal market system.

Pierpaolo De Giosa's contribution narrows Helmersen's more panoptic focus on Melaka to a particular community, a "village" of Tamil Chetti who struggled to maintain their distinctive enclave in the face of rapidly encroaching "international" high-rise architecture and nationalistic planning. As with many such communities in Southeast Asia (see, e.g., Elinoff 2021; Harms 2011, 2012, 2013; Herzfeld 2016, 2022; and see Gibert-Flutre in this volume), brief success in staking out a distinctive cultural space ultimately provoked a crushing defeat. Independent self-definition is intolerable to governments intent on national "development." Those authorities are also well aware that the rhetoric of modernization often appeals even to the people who particularly stand to become deracinated by it (see especially Harms 2012); invocations of collective national interest (and even heritage), in contrast to the supposedly narrow desires or cultural localism of a particular community, provide sufficient justification for bringing in the bulldozers. Given a regional cultural pattern in which even the most democratic societies simultaneously harbor powerful authoritarian tendencies (see especially

Day 2002), such localizing efforts often seem predestined to enjoy sadly short lives. Resilience can create the conditions for its own failure.

Melaka cosmopolitanism, as Helmersen points out, is truly vernacular. While this vernacular dimension has been a source of social resilience in the past, that very history makes it unattractive to those who would prefer to nationalize and marginalize, turning their official backs on the fluidity that—as Barth (1969) argued so long ago—made ethnic boundaries important without in the least detracting from the viability of ethnic identity. Cosmopolitan neighborhoods, like ethnic boundaries, can be places of fertile exchange; when they become sources of conflict, it is usually because external forces, often in the form of ethnonationalist governments, deliberately upset delicate but well-maintained balances of local interests embedded in ramified social relations (see Hayden 2002; on Melaka, see also De Giosa 2021).

The Case for Experiential Expertise

Resilience does not necessarily mean robustness; indeed, too robust a local or minority identity can attract attention in precisely the worst way. That was the fate of the Bangkok community of Pom Mahakan. At the very moment when its identity had concretized around its success at getting a sympathetic governor of Bangkok to sign off on a deal to save the community's right to remain in situ, it became a more tangible target of bureaucratic hostility.[2] With the arrival of military rule, its fate was sealed. Today, it no longer exists, its traces mostly erased by a public park that has failed to attract the public for whom it was allegedly designed. The irony of its sad history is that the residents had acquired genuine expertise in self-management and heritage curation. Arguably, this expertise particularly angered the officials and made them dig their heels in still further until they could erase the community from the center of old Bangkok.

As the Pom Mahakan case shows, success is often unwelcome when it appears to challenge the modernist ideology of bureaucrats or the economic interests that confuse planning with "development." Marie Gibert-Flutre has provided an elegant demonstration of these tensions in Ho Chi Minh City, where poor communities, forced to find their own solutions to local flooding, receive punishment for their success and for their failure alike. Their

---

2   Some civil servants appear also to have wanted to undermine a governor who had shown great temerity questioning the wisdom of decades of bureaucratic intransigence.

attempts to forestall flooding damage largely generated by unrestrained development meet with hostility and—as so often happens when local ingenuity encounters entrenched bureaucratic lethargy—accusations of environmental irresponsibility. When they succeed in addressing their local problems, in other words, their methods are found to have violated some formal planning code. When they fail, it becomes self-evident—self-evidence being easily manufactured for an audience long fed on developmentalist ideas—that they need official help, which, more often than not, takes the form of forced eviction and relocation. In Gibert-Flutre's essay, therefore, we find a disturbing intimation that resilience in the short time can have disastrous consequences in the longer haul.

Gibert-Flutre's argument, however, does not favor teleological assumptions. To the contrary, it is meticulously descriptive and ethnographic. Consequently, instead of reading her chapter as a prediction of inevitable doom—we remain sensitive to Douglass's care not to assume that one size fits all—we prefer to see in it a warning that those in authority should not automatically assume that bureaucratic planners know better than local people. Among the locals are those whose genuine expertise is experience based and who are thus able to contribute, in Jennifer Mack's (2017) evocative phrase, in "urban design from below" (see also Nattawut and Chawanad 2010 on "community architects"; Nattawut n.d.). Such initiatives deserve encouragement. Or, to use the terms that Gibert-Flutre derives from the writings of Michel de Certeau (1984), higher authority should learn to see in the resilience evidenced by the *tactics* of local actors the makings of *strategies* that would contribute to a socially more integrated and sustainable urban life. Such a move, once again, would require a critical appraisal of the concept of participation. The reason is obvious: if the discourse is monopolized by bureaucrats who lack any real understanding of the day-to-day problems of the poor, it will at best provide what Arnstein called "placation" and at worst will provoke anger and despair at the renewed failure to recognize *experiential expertise* for what it is.

Structure of the Book

Eight chapters that follow this introduction dive deeper into specific aspects of resilience in understanding resilience as heritage, the importance of recognizing resilience as heritage, as well as understanding resilience as dynamic and ever-changing. Immediately following the introduction is Michael Herzfeld's piece, "When Resilience Becomes Tangible: The Social and Political Challenges to Local Self-Expression in Thailand and Elsewhere." He critically discusses the "myth of intangibility" as the notion of "intangible heritage" becomes an instrument of control utilized by elites to reduce the autonomy of local communities. The study of intangible heritage uncomfortably resembles nineteenth-century European folklore studies, which often served to control the peasant populations by inscribing their values in a demeaning hierarchy; state identification and management of intangible heritage constitute a process of colonizing everyday practices. Official renditions act as gateways for the vernacular to the outer world and thereby subject it to a global cultural hierarchy. The promotion of vernacular culture as intangible heritage frames it as a desirable object, but condemns it to serving "a modernity that originates... from the outside," a modernity shaped by, and reinforcing, global financial and political inequalities. The resilience of local communities that resist such a framing of modernity operates somewhere between resistance against official rhetoric and co-optation by it, but this resilience remains dependent on the existence of physical, social, and political space to flourish.

The draining of life from vernacular everyday practices often comes about as a consequence of official heritage designation and the economic forces that support it. Kim Nørgaard Helmersen's "Social Resilience of the Vernacular Cosmopolitan Heritage of Melaka" follows Herzfeld's chapter by questioning the automatic association of cosmopolitanism with global mobility, an association that would make it inaccessible to ordinary people. The celebrated cosmopolitanism of Melaka, he argues, is inherently vernacular, as a "social competency" in a multiethnic society to traverse fluidly between spatial manifestations that he likens to the twin poles of Durkheim's mechanical and organic solidarity. Vernacular cosmopolitanism is thus the quotidian practice of resilience by Melaka's multiethnic society. The official heritage-themed redevelopments of the city, however, contribute to increasing social tensions by dividing the population in accordance with ethnic categories rather than allowing fluid cross-cultural encounters that have historically formed the cosmopolitanism of Melaka's vernacular life.

Pierpaolo de Giosa's "'Like the Story of the Camel and his Master!': A Melakan Village between Vernacular Heritage and Urban Transformation" concentrates the focus of Helmersen's essay to examine the complexity of resilience as a social practice in Kampung Chetti. While Kampung Chetti is part of the mosaic that shapes the vernacular cosmopolitanism of Melaka, the urban development that has accompanied the city's official heritage designation has taken away a significant portion of the *kampung* space from its users. Such a spatial transformation has often been subject to criticisms of the heritage designation—particularly UNESCO World Heritage—because it allows global economic forces to dominate local communities. The case of Kampung Chetti, however, clearly illustrates the striking resilience of vernacular everyday practices. Residents attempted to ask for inclusion into the World Heritage City delineation—to be a "heritage kampung" as an option to save their neighborhood. That attempt was an appropriation of "World Heritage City" designation and at the same time represented an effort, under conditions of disproportionate restraints, to sustain resilience amid the developmentalist depredations against the community.

Chapters by Steve Ferzacca, Motohiro Koizumi, and Tessa Maria Guazon take the discussion of vernacular resistance against dominant narratives in a somewhat different direction by focusing on artistic practices as alternative spaces of social encounter. Hegemonic nation-state framings of identity that stereotype national traits homogenize heritage within territorial borders, but, at the same time, limit the expression of diversity – in Ferzacca's chapter, this expression refers to music – and this limitation eventually contradicted the very ingredient of ever-elusive common identity and belonging. "Cosmopolitan conviviality," in Ferzacca's chapter, is a manifestation of resistance against such homogenization. For Guazon, artistic practices and interventions are effective and provocative means by which communities survive.

Both Guazon and Koizumi look at "socially engaged art" as interventions to encourage the resilience of individuals and communities as they collaboratively work together in art projects and in the process create productive mutual relationships. The making of these socially engaged arts, while challenging the homogenizing rhetoric of nation-state-based narratives, is also a practice of constructing alternative narratives of empowerment, survival, and diversity as values crafted collectively to evolve along with the dynamics of everyday conviviality. These three chapters contribute to the understanding of vernacular heritage not only through their deep examinations of artistic practices and interventions as resilience, but also through the notion of the constant evolution of social groups as they battle homogenization.

From the creation of alternative spaces of vernacular heritage through the arts, the next two chapters—one by Anton Novenanto and I Wayan Suyadnya, the other by Marie Gibert-Flutre—evoke the process of heritage making in a landscape of hazard and destruction. Guazon's chapter also features the context of a landscape destroyed by typhoons, where acts of resilience became acts of empowerment. Novenanto and Suyadnya's chapter, however, takes on heritage making as one that was prompted by the destruction itself. The living spaces of communities were completely drowned by an ever-expanding mudflow, which left no room for rebuilding but forced displacement on the residents. It was through the rupture of displacement, as people lost their residences, livelihoods, and everyday social spaces, that these communities collectively acted and recollected memories of the place. Collective memory became a tool of resistance against misleading narratives about a disaster made by humans—narratives promulgated by the company responsible for the disaster and by a complaisant government. In other words, collective memory acts both as heritage-making tool and as a means of empowerment, through asserting the "vernacular meaning of the mudflow" against the narratives of the powerful.

Resilience against hazards can also come gradually rather than abruptly, and allow spatial evolution through adaptation. In studying Ho Chi Minh City's alleyways, Marie Gibert-Flutre delves into the pragmatic side of the continuous transformation of vernacular heritage. Adaptation to flooding as a "family and individual matter" manifests itself spatially in the neighborhood as indications of power relationships, as barricading against flood waters in one place would save one house from flooding just to inundate another. In communities with a shared notion of "a common past," there can be collective action against flooding by elevating the whole alleyway, although this does not prevent each family from continuing to employ minor tactics such as sandbag barricades. Gibert-Flutre's chapter reminds us to question the notion of "community" when it comes to vernacular heritage: what constitutes a community, how does it evolve and to what extent does the evolution affect the processes and practices that shape vernacular heritage?

Toward a New Approach: Resilience as Heritage

The radical move that might shift the ground away from bureaucratic ignorance and top-down planning is to recognize local resilience itself as a form of heritage. Celebrating communities' capacity for self-management as a form of heritage would achieve several simultaneous goals. It would accord the residents the dignity to which most national constitutions nominally entitle them. It would draft local expertise in the service of local needs. It would relieve city authorities of the urge to promote expensive and usually counterproductive forms of development that physically and socially marginalize active populations and relegate them to zones of despised marginality. Perhaps most important of all, it would encourage a form of active community participation that might well elicit emulation around Asia and indeed around the globe.

The COVID-19 pandemic in the early 2020s has become a window through which we can observe how communities activate local forms of cultural resilience. Restrictions by nation-states and cities have tremendously affected social and economic activities in areas that have received official heritage designations, and are therefore increasingly reliant on tourism for economic viability. Amid official pandemic approaches that ranged from rigid but reliable to hopelessly chaotic, pockets of civil society responses emerged in various localities in Asia. Responses ranging from self-imposed area quarantines by local communities to citizen-managed food sharing, crowdfunding, and collective farming suggest that socially and culturally active societies have good chances of remaining resilient under such circumstances. Resilience, as this observation should make clear, is cultural (Padawangi 2020). The bottom line of this resilience is the ability to function autonomously—socially, economically, and culturally—in the local context. The pandemic is also a timely reminder that the treatment of cities as engines of economic growth has resulted in environmental degradation and the displacement of marginalized communities. This same paradigm has driven urban development and the official acceptance of heritage in a direction diametrically opposed to that of recognizing cultural resilience as vernacular heritage.

Promoting resilience itself as heritage is also an effective answer to the neoliberal monopoly of heritage architecture. The emergence of "old city" and "historic center" enclaves around the world has spurred a rapid and socially destructive rise in property values that had rarely hitherto been subject to rent control (see, e.g., Herzfeld 2009). This abrupt shift has allowed ambitious developers to evict the poor and replace them with wealthy tenants, while the aesthetics of both antiquity and the modernity that replaces it are also controlled by bureaucrats and developers (see Ghertner 2010, 2015). So we ask what might happen if, instead, local aesthetics and local practical knowledge—the substance of the tactics described by Gibert-Flutre—were allowed to determine what would constitute acceptable changes. What if local operators joined forces with forward-looking historians and archaeologists to produce attractive neighborhoods redolent of their locally experienced pasts and invested with the legal right to resist challenges to their cultural autonomy? Recognizing their resilience as a significant feature of their cultural heritage would be an important start.

At the same time, it is important to resist the temptation to reify that heritage and turn local communities into museum-like spaces, little better than the old colonial expos in which hapless "natives" performed exotic behaviors for the benefit of bemused metropolitan publics all over Europe and North America (see, e.g., Rydell 2017). To treat resilience as heritage is to acknowledge that it has a place in national planning and that it represents many generations of acquired knowledge and tactical savvy. By contrast, treating it as an object of condescending curiosity undermines the very point of acknowledging it in the first place. In Asia, various social and cultural hierarchies—many of them created by the backwash from colonialism, but others grounded in ancient traditions—continue to make local engagement in social and urban action extremely problematic. A concerted effort to show that local, tactical, nonconformist resilience has a long history of its own, largely as a result of the frequent inability or unwillingness of hierarchical systems to care for the poor and marginal, would be a substantive first step in making the case for greater social justice in the region.

References

Arnstein, Sherry R. 1969. "A Ladder of Citizen Participation." *Journal of the American Institute of Planners* 35: 216–24.

Barth, Fredrik. 1969. Introduction to *Ethnic Groups and Boundaries: The Social Organization of Culture Difference*, 9–38. Boston: Little, Brown.

Befu, Harumi. 2001. *Hegemony of Homogeneity: An Anthropological Analysis of "Nihonjinron."* Melbourne: Trans Pacific Press.

Bendix, Regina F., Aditya Eggert, and Arnika Peselmann, eds. 2012. *Heritage Regimes and the State*. Göttingen: Universitätsverlag Göttingen.

Brulotte, Ronda L., and Michael A. Di Giovine, eds. 2014. *Edible Identities: Food as Cultural Heritage*. Farnham, Surrey: Ashgate.

Daniel, E. Valentine. 1996. *Charred Lullabies: Chapters in an Anthropography of Violence*. Princeton: Princeton University Press.

Day, Tony. 2002. *Fluid Iron: State Formation in Southeast Asia*. Honolulu: University of Hawai'i Press.

de Certeau, Michel. 1984. *The Practice of Everyday Life*. Berkeley: University of California Press.

De Cesari, Chiara, and Rozita Dimova. 2019. "Heritage, Gentrification, Participation: Remaking Urban Landscapes in the Name of Culture and Historic Preservation." *International Journal of Heritage Studies* 25: 863–9.

De Giosa, Pierpaolo. 2021. *World Heritage and Urban Politics in Malaysia. A Cityscape Below the Winds*. Amsterdam: Amsterdam University Press.

Denes, Alexandra. 2015. "Folklorizing Northern Khmer Identity in Thailand: Intangible Cultural Heritage and the Production of 'Good Culture.'" *Sojourn* 30 (1): 1–34.

Douglass, Mike. 2002. "From Global Intercity Competition to Cooperation for Livable Cities and Economic Resilience in Pacific Asia." *Environment and Urbanization* 14 (1): 53–68.

Elinoff, Eli. 2021. *Citizen Designs: City-Making and Democracy in Northeastern Thailand.* Honolulu: University of Hawaii Press.

Ghertner, D. Asher. 2010. "Calculating without Numbers: Aesthetic Governmentality in Delhi's Slums." *Economy and Society* 39: 185–217.

Ghertner, D. Asher. 2015. *Rule by Aesthetics: World-Class City Making in Delhi.* Oxford: Oxford University Press.

Ginzarly, Manal, Jihad Farah, and Jacques Teller. 2019. "Claiming a Role for Controversies in the Framing of Local Heritage Values." *Habitat International* 88: 101982. https://doi.org/10.1016/J.HABITATINT.2019.05.001.

Handler, Richard. 1985. "On Having a Culture: Nationalism and the Preservation of Quebec's Patrimoine." In *Objects and Others*, edited by G. Stocking, 192–217. Vol. 3 of *History of Anthropology.* Madison: University of Wisconsin Press.

Handler, Richard. 1986. Authenticity. *Anthropology Today* 2 (1): 2–4.

Harms, Erik. 2011. *Saigon's Edge: On the Margins of Ho Chi Minh City.* Minneapolis: University of Minnesota Press.

Harms, Erik. 2012. "Beauty as Control in the New Saigon: Eviction, New Urban Zones, and Atomized Dissent in a Southeast Asian City." *American Anthropologist* 39: 735–50.

Harms, Erik. 2013. Eviction Time in the New Saigon: Temporalities of Displacement in the Rubble of Development. *Cultural Anthropology* 28: 344–68.

Hayden, Robert M. 2002. "Antagonistic Tolerance: Competitive Sharing of Religious Sites in South Asia and the Balkans." *Current Anthropology* 43: 205–31.

Herzfeld, Michael. 2009. *Evicted from Eternity: The Restructuring of Modern Rome.* Chicago: University of Chicago Press.

Herzfeld, Michael. 2014. "Drunken Noodles and Prostitutes' Pasta: The Intangible Delicacy of Cultural Embarrassments in International Policy Settings." *Ethnologies* 36: 47–62.

Herzfeld, Michael. 2016. *Siege of the Spirits: Community and Polity in Bangkok.* Chicago: University of Chicago Press.

Herzfeld, Michael. 2022. *Subversive Archaism: Troubling Traditionalists and the Politics of National Heritage.* Durham: Duke University Press.

Labadi, Sophia. 2007. "Representations of the Nation and Cultural Diversity in Discourses on World Heritage." *Journal of Social Archaeology* 7: 147–70.

Labadi, Sophia. 2013. *UNESCO, Cultural Heritage and Outstanding Universal Value.* Walnut Creek: AltaMira Press.

Lowenthal, David. 2015. *The Past is a Foreign Country – Revisited*. Cambridge: Cambridge University Press.

Mack, Jennifer. 2017. *The Construction of Equality: Syriac Immigration and the Swedish City*. Minneapolis: University of Minnesota Press.

Meskell, Lynn. 2018. *A Future in Ruins: UNESCO, World Heritage, and the Dream of Peace*. Oxford: Oxford University Press.

Nattawut Usagovitwong. n.d. "Towards Community Participation in Housing Design: Experience from Low-Income Waterfront Communities, Bangkok." https://www.codi.or.th/downloads/english/Paper/community%20participation%20in%20housing%20design.pdf

Nattawut Usagovitwong, and Chawanad Luansang. 2010. "Housing by People: Performance of Asian Community Architects." Bangkok: Asian Coalition for Housing Rights.

Padawangi, Rita. 2015. "The Vernacular and the Spectacular: Urban Identity and Architectural Heritage in Southeast Asian Cities." In *Asian Cities: Colonial to Global*, edited by G. Bracken, 261–77. Amsterdam: Amsterdam University Press.

Padawangi, Rita. 2020. "Questioning Normalcy: Rethinking Urbanisation, Development and Collective Action through the COVID-19 Moment." *LSE Southeast Asia Blog*. 20 July 2020. Accessed 8 December 2020. https://blogs.lse.ac.uk/seac/2020/07/20/questioning-normalcy-rethinking-urbanisation-development-and-collective-action-through-the-covid-19-moment/.

Padawangi, Rita. 2021. *Urban Development in Southeast Asia*. Cambridge: Cambridge University Press.

Rydell, Robert, ed. 2017. *World's Fairs: A Global History of Exhibitions*. London: Adam Matthew Digital.

Sand, Jordan. 2013. *Tokyo Vernacular: Common Spaces, Local Histories, Found Objects*. Berkeley: University of California Press.

Scott, James C. 1998. *Seeing Like a State: How Certain Schemes to Improve the Human Condition Have Failed*. New Haven: Yale University Press.

Shao, Qin, 2013. *Shanghai Gone: Domicide and Defiance in a Chinese Megacity*. Lanham: Rowman & Littlefield.

Smith, Laurajane. 2006. *Uses of Heritage*. London: Routledge.

Tjahjono, Gunawan. 2014. "Rajin as Heritage: The Value of Craftsmanship in Shaping Indonesia's Vernacular Built Environments." Paper presented at The Resilience of Vernacular Heritage in Asian Cities. Singapore: Asia Research Institute, 6–7 November 2014.

Werbner, Pnina. 2016. "Vernacular Cosmopolitanism." *Theory, Culture & Society* 23 (2–3): 496–8.

Wimmer, Andreas, and Nina Glick Schiller. 2002. "Methodological Nationalism and Beyond: Nation-State Building, Migration and the Social Sciences." *Global Networks* 2: 301–34.

Yeoh, Brenda. 1996. *Contesting Space in Colonial Singapore: Power Relations and the Urban Built Environment*. Oxford: Oxford University Press.

About the Authors

Michael Herzfeld is the Ernest E. Monrad Professor of the Social Sciences *Emeritus*, Department of Anthropology, Harvard University, and IIAS Professor of Critical Heritage Studies *Emeritus*, Leiden University. His fourteen books include *Siege of the Spirits: Community and Polity in Bangkok* (2016) and *Subversive Archaism: Troubling Traditionalists and the Politics of National Heritage* (2022). His current research addresses heritage politics, crypto-colonialism, and artisans' practices of competition and cooperation.

Rita Padawangi is Associate Professor (Sociology) at Singapore University of Social Sciences. Her research is on social movements, community engagement, and environmental justice. Rita coordinates the Southeast Asia Neighborhoods Network (SEANNET), a collaborative urban research and education initiative. She is the author of *Urban Development in Southeast Asia* (Cambridge University Press, 2022).

2. When Resilience Becomes Tangible: The Social and Political Challenges to Local Self-Expression in Thailand and Elsewhere

Michael Herzfeld

Abstract: This chapter explores the possibilities and limitations of resilience. Resilience itself is heritage; community resilience affects its public standing and thus the outcome of its struggles. Initial success renders a previously despised community more visible as a target for bureaucratic hostility, in which materialization of its unique identity becomes mere obduracy. Where dominant cultural discourses effectively infantilize local communities, local claims meet condescension or worse. At Pom Mahakan (Bangkok), eviction of the entire population and the destruction of fine Thai vernacular architecture demonstrated that the agency of karmically based hierarchical class structures constrains cultural independence and even survival. An exportable example of self-governance was thus suppressed, illustrating what makes cultural resilience insufficient to overcome the constraints inhibiting sociopolitical resilience.

Keywords: agency, vernacular architecture, folklore, aspiration, resistance

Resilience, Cultural Hierarchy, and Class

Poor people are realists; they have few choices. This often makes them practical ethnographers of their own condition. Despite occasional support from sympathetic journalists, they operate in the face of massive indifference to their plight, an indifference reinforced in those societies by entrenched assumptions that often, in some Asian societies, rest on karmic notions of

Herzfeld, M., and R. Padawangi, eds. *Resilience as Heritage in Asia*. Amsterdam: Amsterdam University Press, 2025.
DOI: 10.5117/9789463728560_CH02

predestination, and elsewhere on comparable forms of vicarious fatalism such as the so-called culture of poverty.[1]

"Good people" (*phu di*) in Thailand, for example, "look good" (*du di*); they look good because they "are" good. They can afford the visible appurtenances that enable them, in circular fashion, to sustain that status. The corollary also holds true: as the poor begin to increase their demands for a better life, their impudence is trumpeted as evidence of their unmeritorious character (Elinoff 2014: 94). Such a self-fulfilling logic sets dispiriting limits on the extent to which authoritarian states and ethnonational bureaucracies are willing to tolerate local resilience. The resilience of cultural distinctiveness carries grave risks for those whose poverty the powerful represent as an inherited or inherent condition, thereby depriving them of the right to be different on their own terms.

A newly prosperous bourgeoisie and a capitalist establishment sustained by global investment parades cosmopolitanism as the justification for the ironic, even cruelly sarcastic, view of the poor. "Happy New Year," trumpeted an ornamental sign in English as well as Vietnamese in January 2011 over the shattered remnants of a Ho Chi Minh City community once inhabited by the state's own lower-level bureaucrats, as high-rise buildings towered in the middle distance, presaging an imagined future modernity. A continuing assumption that "East" and "West" are real entities, the former forever condemned to playing catch-up with the latter, reproduces a global hierarchy of cultural value. That hierarchy perpetuates the inequalities of the colonial era as cultural truths about high and low culture and thereby reproduces itself locally as class differentiation.[2]

Within that same hierarchy, the adulation of modernity by the poor is a reality (Harms 2012: 744–6), but their adulation does not necessarily serve them well and the modernity in question is not often a goal to which they can ever realistically aspire. Dreams of joining such "progress" are always an option, but they may contribute to the perpetuation of inequality (see also Dharia 2021 and Ghertner 2010, 2015, for India). Indeed, as Paul Willis (1981) has demonstrated for working-class youths in England, the behaviors associated with such yearning for consumer goods and the prestige they confer often do serve to confirm the bourgeoisie's contempt for the riff-raff (see Sopranzetti 2012, 2017).

There are always exceptional cases of individual agency leading to escape and personal triumph. Such exceptions, however, fuel the conventional

---

1   For early critiques of the "culture of poverty model," see especially Leacock 1971.
2   On the global hierarchy of value, see Herzfeld 2004; Salemink et al. 2022.

view that the remaining poor deserve their poverty precisely because they
have failed to escape it. When we speak of resilience, we are not writing
about those exceptions, or about the successful and powerful whose wealth
has allowed them to cherry-pick among the appurtenances of a modern
life. We are instead contemplating the ways in which individuals, groups,
cultural traditionalists, and even small groups devoted to a particular form
of cultural activity pursue the survival of what is most precious to them and
gives them a sense of individuated worth amid all the blaring cacophony
of capital accumulation and its discontents: their lifestyles, their social
identities, their aesthetics, their entertainments, their hobbies.

Even in the West, itself a conglomeration of widely divergent cultural and
economic topoi, there are countries and local places where "getting by" is the
order of daily business (de Certeau 1984; Reed-Danahay 1987: 87; Scott 1998:
328). This is no less true of bureaucrats and politicians, or of the wealthy,
than it is of slum dwellers and rural residents such as those studied in a
range of countries from France to Brazil and Greece to India. The constant
reproduction of the East-West binary in Asian discourse is itself a sign that
the global hierarchy of value continues to infiltrate its insidious poison of
self-disregard into many areas of Asian life.[3]

Such attitudes are an ongoing continental expansion of "methodological
nationalism" (on which, see Wimmer and Glick Schiller 2002). In a book about
Asian heritages, therefore, it is important to insist, not that "there is no such
thing as 'the West'" but that its reality, as a self-reproducing performative
utterance, a conceptual virus for which no strong antidote yet exists, is a
part of the problematic background against which we recognize certain
actions and mobilizations as resilient. A complementary part of that same
background is the rigidity of ethnonational models of culture promoted by
many nation-states—often, ironically, following European models.

The capacity for getting by and making a practical virtue of it is noticeably
more visible among the poor than among those who, after all, have no
self-evident need of it. One may suspect that this is partly because the
poor have fewer resources for "covering up," which may well be part of
the story—a part that explains why the poor often embarrass an elite
ostensibly committed to the rule of law even though its members may in
fact be capable of particularly heinous violations. But there is also a sense
in which the strategies poor people use to stake a claim to a decent life, or
a place in the cultural sun, are themselves a source of embarrassment to

---

3   For my coinage of the term "global hierarchy of value," see Herzfeld 2004. See now also
Salemink et al. 2022.

the power brokers. One of these is the active pursuit of highly localized cultural identity, using what used to be called "folklore" and is now often called "intangible heritage." While such tactics are usually imitations of official discourse, their use as tools of distinctiveness and resistance marks them out, in the eyes of officialdom, as potential trouble.

Condescending Discourses

"Folklore," in nineteenth-century Europe, was a respectable elite pursuit designed to subject peasant populations to elite control through a system of values that appeared to glorify the natural life of the peasantry and their capacity for preserving those cultural goods that the corrupt urbanites had destroyed (see Cocchiara 1952; Herzfeld 2020; Wilson 1976; for an Asian version, see Janelli 1986). The history of Europe is rife with such stories; in Asia, scholars both local and colonial followed the pattern established by European romantic nationalists. Gloria Raheja (1996) has documented how British colonial folklorists created a taxonomy of Indian proverbs as a way of textually generating a hierarchy of the different cultural groups, castes, and tribes in order to justify placing the British themselves at the pinnacle. This bit of transference of the logic of nineteenth-century European folklore to the Indian context shows, in her cogent analysis, that folklore, for all its apparent innocence and association with the pristine and the rural, was actually a robust political instrument. In the postcolonial era, its uses have not appreciably changed.

"Intangible heritage" looks, on the face of it, innocent of such subterfuges. It is the device created by UNESCO and other bodies to deal with the fact that significant areas of a people's culture are not, at least in the everyday sense, material. The framing of UNESCO's position, however, is rife with conceptual difficulty. No amount of pointing to Japanese and Korean models of refusing to allow the material substance rather than the aesthetic form be the determinant of what counts as heritage architecture, or those countries' recognition of "living national treasures," will ever convincingly dispel the frequently voiced criticism of UNESCO's Cartesian heritage. The term *intangible heritage* has usually served as little more than a proxy for "folklore" in the old sense. That sense is of an instrument whereby a national elite controls minority interests and dictates to the ethnic majority what its culture may legitimately contain, although individual functionaries have managed to be relatively creative in finding new ways of framing the practices in question (see Bortolotto 2024; Bortolotto et al. 2020; Karampampas 2021). Especially

where nationalist strategies are buttressed by authoritarian rule, such creativity is constrained by the politics of ethnic identity and belonging. Thus,
for example, Alexandra Denes (2015) has demonstrated for Khmer-speaking
communities in Surin Province, Thailand, that their traditional music and
dance performances subsist on the basis that these people are "our Khmer,"
a view that deliberately encourages them to reject what lies on the other
side of the Thai-Cambodian border as alien, communist, and dishonest.
Ethnic Khmer cultural performances in Surin express fealty to the throne
and respect for the state, the domestication of an otherness that may expect
genial (if condescending) tolerance as long as it does not try to create bridges
across the border.

In this sense, the encouragement of local traditions belongs to a category
of infantilizing policies that restrict the political and economic autonomy
of local communities; it works in tandem with the restrictive, top-down
application of the sufficiency economy in Thailand. Elinoff (2014), moreover,
shows in another context how poor Thai working-class citizens take back
the rhetoric of sufficiency to lay claims of their own. This important insight
underscores the point, central to my argument in this chapter, that cultural
resilience only benefits local communities when it is accompanied by an
equally strong form of *social* resilience (perhaps more recognizable under
the term *collective agency*). One way to achieve this, as Elinoff describes,
is to set up collective savings accounts, or rotating credit systems, that
allow people to tap into a national economy officially defined by the goal
of keeping most of the population content with sufficiency. This tactic is
a double-edged sword, and its outcome usually depends, as Elinoff shows,
on external political developments.

In the three-hundred-strong settlement at Pom Mahakan in the heart
of Rattanakosin Island, the old dynastic capital, local leaders strove in
vain to demonstrate their capacity for survival in terms that theoretically
ought to have satisfied the criteria of the sufficiency economy. The evident
resilience of the community at maintaining its cultural visibility and
financial independence while also resisting official attempts to evict
it wholesale did not make it appear to be a national cultural asset in
the eyes of the bureaucracy. The condescension with which some officials expressed admiration for its arts and crafts did not prevent them
from pursuing the goal of eviction, which finally occurred in 2018. One
bureaucrat dismissed the residents' claim to community status on the
basis of a spurious, bureaucratically inspired definition of community as
necessarily all centered on a single occupation (such as making monks'
begging bowls or paper umbrellas)—a concept that is itself, in the Thai

term *chumchon*, of notoriously recent and ideologically driven coinage, its most recent cousin being Thaksin's and successors' OTOP policy. That policy, not incidentally, was problematic from the start, since it rested on this same assumption—a Taylorist factory image of the country as a whole, its cultural heritage conveniently organized to serve the managerial instincts of its bureaucrats.[4]

There are other markers of social weakness in the face of state repression. Where poverty has been significantly alleviated in the last decade or two, people nevertheless continue to *think* of themselves as poor. The more they struggle to define themselves in terms of what they see as the cultural capital of the nation but their elite detractors regard as peasant or corrupted urban travesties of "true" culture, the more they risk locking themselves into an identity that is as politically ignominious and factually untrue as it appears to be culturally glorious. I have seen how this process works with Greek artisans (Herzfeld 2004), where the transmission of social attitudes simply reaffirms, generation after generation, a generally despised status. In Thailand, socially robust forms of resistance to authority do entail the risk of confirming the elite view that local communities are too rambunctious to be treated as civilized—or, even, as Thai. The more they fight, the implicit argument goes, the less right they have to insist on their cultural identities as true representatives of the national culture.

Officialdom's cultural strategy for addressing such impertinence can be characterized as a strategic folklorization of everyday life. Folklore entextualizes the vernacular as "local knowledge"—a term sometimes adopted by its presumed bearers themselves—and inserts it into a global hierarchy of value that, in postcolonial and crypto-colonial states, extends outward from ideals of national culture grounded in "tradition" and "national spirit" (Herzfeld 1996). It nonetheless embeds that concept of tradition in a modernity that originates—as Erik Harms (2012) has so well argued for Vietnam—from the *outside*, from sources of power that are cultural, financial, and political all at once. Ordinary people can also call on outside resources to legitimize political actions of their own—tactically, as Gilbert-Flutre argues in this volume. In the long haul, however, the transient agency of tactics, of making do rather than following an established plan, is rarely a match for the concerted agency of official strategy, which subordinates folklore, tradition, and heritage to bureaucratic modernism in the form of organized displays: museums, performances, and glossy publications. In

---

4   On Pom Mahakan, see Thanaphon 2007; Herzfeld 2016a: 104–5, 185, et passim, and 2021; Sirinya 2018, 2020.

the most extreme cases, this strategy includes the erection of state symbols and stereotypically "national" architecture, along with labels "celebrating" the former existence of traditional crafts, over the ruins of the homes of the evicted. That is what happened at Pom Mahakan,

Resilience or Subservience

With this in mind, we should now ask whether cultural traditions operating within constraints of this kind, subject to the parallel condescension of local politicians and of foreign observers, really represent resilience. They often instead seem to represent subservience—or, perhaps, mimicry that ill disguises the groveling of the weak. Thus, when we speak of the resilience of vernacular cultural heritage in Asia, as indeed in other parts of the world, we must ask two questions. First, who sets the standards by which cultural items are judged to be heritage? The second question is more complex: to what extent is the persistence of such heritage paralleled by *social* resilience—by a capacity to resist being managed by authorities who tell local people what their culture is, or to fend off the powerful forces demanding adherence to an official line as to what constitutes acceptable—and national—culture?

I have deliberately added the word "cultural" into the phrase "vernacular cultural heritage." "Vernacular heritage" may include a host of social institutions that have been occluded by the pernicious (and authority-driven) distinction between formal and informal settlements, economies, and even religions. To be sure, social institutions are cultural too. Their apparent evanescence, however, driven underground by the formal-informal binary, should prompt the question of why they are so often excluded from the realm of "intangible heritage." They are indeed crucial to survival. As Appadurai (2000) has shown, they are threatened with obliteration by the toxic mixture of harsh neoliberal economics and religiously based ethnonationalism. But they are the essence of what holds people together in the face of such pressures, often through their knowing resistance to its rules and restrictions; they are the space of cultural intimacy.[5] They are rarely even mentioned by the cultural heritage experts, perhaps because they embarrass establishment sensibilities tied to a rigid understanding of culture as "national" and to a reluctance to recognize any social dynamic other than those authorized by the state.

---

5   See Herzfeld 2016b for an extended discussion of this concept.

Culture Against Society: Threats to Social Resilience

The more the resilience of *cultural* heritage is emphasized and praised, the more the resilience of *social* heritage may be threatened. Ethnicity and kinship offer two obvious arenas, but the so-called informal practices are equally important, and, like ethnic and kin relations, they are actually highly patterned albeit in very localized cultural terms. There are extreme examples of this superficially paradoxical situation. The regeneration of prerevolutionary culture that we see in the case of China as described by Li Zhang (2006), for instance, comes at the cost of the destruction not only of old familiar places but also of the sort of genius loci, the "breath of humanity" (*ren qi*) that her informants invoked and that animates social relations and an older social order. What Adam Chau (2008: 197) has called "text acts"—the performative display of the Chinese character for demolish, *chai*—is not merely an announcement of intent, like an eviction notice; it is the sign that puts the entire process of wrecking a particular kind of sociality into motion.

The problem with resilience is that it seems to invite precisely this kind of repressive response. To the admirers of Pom Mahakan, the community offered a wonderful example of collective self-management and the construc-tive use of tradition that might spread throughout Thailand and become an example for other countries. But this, in the end, was also the community's undoing. It is clear that the authorities not only resented what I have come to call the residents' "subversive archaism" (Herzfeld 2022) but also feared that the model would indeed prove contagious. The community leadership plausibly saw this problem as the effect of the too-tangible identity that emerged over years of struggle. They are now "visible," in James Scott's (1998) terms, to a state-like city bureaucracy (and a city bureaucracy obedient to an authoritarian state that currently controls it). The community had come to use cultural heritage as a means of denying its ascribed political identity as a disobedient community. This, to paraphrase Althusser (1971: 162), was a variety of "self-interpellation," and made the community's distinctiveness all the more tangible and disturbing to officialdom. The community's resilience thus became dangerous precisely as its claims on the narrative of historically deep national harmony solidified. Its suitability for imitation only increased the threat it represented to the bureaucracy.

One city official told me that had the people of Pom Mahakan been a distinctive minority group, the administration would have had been less reluctant to accept their separate identity and their right to live on the site (Herzfeld 2016a: 185). This was an extraordinary admission. I was focused on the argument that their multiple origins meant they did *not* constitute a real community; I therefore failed to grasp the full significance of this comparison. An enclave that lays claim to Thainess but does it in a way that defies official authority is a more serious threat than a minority group—such as the Surin Khmer of Denes's account—to the serene face of what is actually a tightly controlled official definition of national culture. A minority can always be airily dismissed as not understanding Thai culture, and, if it misbehaves (and especially if it is considered to be a threat to national security), it can be summarily removed. Mainstream society is unlikely to object very vociferously. An aggressively self-defining, culturally Thai community, by contrast, can only be removed on copiously legal grounds and with a great deal of preparatory public criticism of its actions. Even under military rule, the city authorities had to make their case against Pom Mahakan through a tortuous succession of confrontations in court.

The residents' appeal to notions of heritage and national culture (the community even boasted a "heritage museum"[6]) thus meant that they had in effect allowed a discourse that paid scant respect to their own, very specific sense of place and descent to pronounce, negatively, on their cause. Their stance of subversive archaism, by concretizing their cultural claims, also exposed them to official ridicule and denial. The irony here is that *cultural* resilience thereby became a fatal flaw in their *social* resilience. Indeed, it became their most visible mark of distinctiveness—so much so that, in an extraordinary example of officially sanctioned cultural vandalism, the authorities followed their legally mandated eviction of the entire community with the destruction of even those houses that had been recognized by experts as fine examples of vernacular architecture from the Rattanakosin era.

That this was a vengeful and entirely unnecessary act is clear from the subsequent fate of the Pom Mahakan space. The eviction and final demolitions took place in late 2018. In 2004, the residents had attempted to capitalize on the city's scheme to create a park, playing on the ambiguous meaning of the word *suan* (which means both "park" and "garden"). That attempt to demonstrate the resilience of the residents' own vision, however, was met with immediate and insulting resistance from the authorities, who

---

6   A sign in English as well as Thai pointed to the modest building, which was almost a caricature of the conventional image of a Thai house. A shingle in front of the museum announced that it was a "pavilion of the community's local knowledge (*phumipanya*)"—the latter term being an important element in official displays of respect for local communities (see also below; cf. Elinoff 2014: 94).

had truckloads of garbage dumped on top of the flower garden they had created (and with no risk that they would be accused of insulting Queen Sirikit, whom both the authorities' scheme and the residents' flower garden were meant to honor, because, as far as the authorities were concerned, nothing created by the residents had any legitimacy or legality). When, following the final demolition, the newly created park attracted little interest but abundant criticism, the city bureaucrats decided to create their own flower display.[7] It seems to have evinced little more enthusiasm than their earlier efforts. The bureaucrats no doubt experienced some self-satisfaction at having shown greater resilience than the residents, but the lack of public enthusiasm speaks volumes. At a time when the old hierarchical order is under challenge, such a blatant parody of the earlier community resilience, for those who remember the Pom Mahakan community, underscores the tragedy of wasted opportunity.[8]

Such evacuations of social meaning and historical depth are to a very large extent the problem of all heritage conservation projects, but especially those in which older architectural forms are obliterated and then replaced by a token set of restored examples, as has happened, for example, with the shophouses in Singapore. Indeed, of those gentrified shophouses one may be tempted to say that they are *architecturally* resilient inasmuch as their restoration has provided economic energy for a set of newcomers—but what happened to the social life they sported in their older and shabbier incarnation? It has hardly shown much resilience in the face of neoliberal urban development (see, e.g., Chang 2016).

The refurbishing of old buildings is thus one of a range of officially sanctioned practices that can kill off what little is left of preexisting social relations, and a cynic—or perhaps a well-informed observer—might argue that some municipal and national authorities encourage precisely such developments. Gentrification, if allowed (or encouraged?) to take its course, does this labor all too well, and municipalities reap handsome taxes and other profits as a result (not to speak of under-the-table deals with construction magnates, a well-known phenomenon throughout East and Southeast Asia). But another force is simple mortality, and it is here that the

---

7   See "Visual Feast of Flowers for Bangkokians," *Nation*, November 29, 2020, https://www. nationthailand.com/news/30398764?utm_source=homepage&utm_medium=internal_referral (accessed 29 November 2020). It is significant that *The Nation*, which has been relatively timid in its criticism of the current political regime, mentions nothing of the residents' earlier attempt to create a flower garden on the site. For a contrasting approach, see Sirinya 2018, 2020.

8   I do not intend to imply that it was *intended* as a parody; parody is a form of humor, and humor is in short supply in the city administration.

focus on "intangible culture" becomes especially dangerous. The passing of generations is a nonnegotiable part of the human condition—something that exponents of conservation often forget or ignore. The bearers of certain skills die—during my time of doing research in Pom Mahakan, for example, both the masseur and the kickboxing master passed away—and, because it is directly embedded in the social realities of community life, their special knowledge passes with them, to be replaced by stylized performances that may be pretty or impressive, or even interesting, but usually do not represent locally generated skill. In consequence, the power to judge local performances moves to other hands, and may be subjected to criteria that have little to do with local social values.

How, then, do we prevent a blandly synthetic, nationalized, and historically inaccurate version of cultural heritage from being used to obliterate the social ties that give meaning to people's lives—and even, as happens with gentrification, to obliterate the presence of the people themselves? And how do we prevent the nationalization of so-called intangible heritage from exercising the same kinds of cultural censorship that were cruelly characteristic of nineteenth-century state-sanctioned folklore studies? Let us be quite clear about the terrible damage that was done by that smiling discipline in the name of saving national cultures: the invention of folklore studies destroyed almost as much as it preserved, rejigged, and transmogrified, and left very little intact in any sense in which a local peasant or poor urbanite would have recognized it, even, in well-documented cases, leading scholars to "correct" the performances of the supposedly ignorant locals. With the passing of years, scholarly sensibilities reversed this pattern, but not before a great deal had been consigned to oblivion—often to the advantage of dominant nationalist ideologies.

Folksongs represent an easily documented space for that kind of interference. More difficult to pin down, because more "intangible" in form, are social values and structures. There are many aspects of social life that disappear from view under the kind of censorship that was exercised by nationalist folklore regimes. Sometimes this happens simply because state authorities refuse to recognize these aspects of quotidian experience as either "real" or "respectable" culture; sometimes local communities, fearful of losing hard-won gains in the defense of their territorial or economic rights, act as self-censors no less than journalists and others who avoid trouble in the same way. In the Thai case, a reputation for being *khemkhaeng* ("tough," here in the sense of "resilient"), a source of admiration by the supporters of the Pom Mahakan community, looked more like rebellion and insubordination to the authorities and their bourgeois supporters. Moreover, whereas the damage that journalists' self-censorship does politically can be contested because it is usually obvious to the more vigorous opponents of a political regime, cultural self-censorship is harder to identify. Recognizable as the defense of what I have called "cultural intimacy" (Herzfeld 2016b), it takes the form of affecting attitudes of deep offense that outsiders might consider a community capable of nurturing attitudes and practices so obscene, so disgusting, or so reprehensible in other ways.

Resilience as a term requires some qualification here if it is to serve us well as a conceptual tool. In particular, it needs a qualifying adjective to indicate in which of its different modalities it is operating. Thus, *cultural resilience*—which in some countries appears as "cultural continuity" or "deep attachment to ancient tradition" and the like—can easily become a tool of official policies that are actively hostile to *social* resilience, by which I mean resilience that resists official control of a community's self-management. In the cultural arena, "resilience" runs the same risk of political cooptation as "participation"—a seemingly benign concept that has too often been used as a rhetorical placebo for those suffering from the ills of top-down control (Arnstein 1969; see also de Cesari and Dimova 2019).

This is not to advocate for the preservation of all aspects of an older social order. We may legitimately wonder whether some of the older modalities were dysfunctional, but the question in such cases is always *for whom* they were dysfunctional. One might, for example, assume that the locked and chained boxes placed visibly in front of private low-income homes in Shanghai signify mutual distrust. To some extent, to be sure, that is precisely what they do mean—but for these boxes even to represent a measure of security, there must be a communal understanding that any attempt to remove them will be met with resistance from the owners' neighbors as well as from the owners themselves. In other words, while privacy has a different significance in post-Mao China than it does in Singapore or the United States, respect for ownership is itself a social phenomenon, and collectively accepted means of securing that ownership are signs of *social* resilience. The same, to offer another example, is true of the closed-circuit cameras and elaborate grilles that protect the workshops of jewelers and goldsmiths in the Ban Maw district of Bangkok. These devices do not mean that the neighbors necessarily distrust each other. Goldsmiths also know how to deal decisively with incidents of theft. Those who discover that their own workers are stealing from them—often by secreting on their persons small quantities of the elusive gold dust left over from filing operations—do not hesitate to send them packing and to make sure that they are henceforth debarred from employment anywhere in the vicinity. The ability to isolate miscreants in this way itself bespeaks a social process, a measure of solidarity, that is the logical complement of known patterns of anti-social behavior. While from the outside they may appear to signal social disruption, they trigger well-tried mechanisms that are the source of social resilience.

These marks of distrust may hand cultural crusaders a ready weapon to use against local communities in the name of development. But a deeper probe, ethnographic in focus and of sufficiently long duration or repeated over a long period of time, might give us better insight. In small communities, what Jane Jacobs (1961: 36) and her followers have called "eyes on the street" continues to function as a mark of social resilience in Shanghai, Bangkok, and most other big cities.[9] Such marks of a solidarity that protects communities from crime by both outsiders and insiders tend to disappear when neighborhoods are gentrified or replaced by tower blocks (the latter a common phenomenon in Asian cities).

Persistence and Aspiration

Planners usually show little interest in social relations, deeming them to be intangible or invisible. Their imprint, however, is not really invisible; they generate particular forms of spatial arrangement (see, e.g., Hirschon and Thakurdesai 1970). Moreover, as Zhang (2001, 2002) has cogently demonstrated for China, changes in the spatial arrangements may also signal shifts in subjectivity. Family structure, local modes of social gathering, and class and ethnic relations are often manifested in the shaping of both domestic architecture and urban public space and its uses. People can force rearrangements of official planning in ways that preserve their own social orientations and civic aesthetics (see especially Mack 2017). But assessing the significance of such acts requires the time-consuming and laborious ethnographic accumulation of intimate knowledge that has led me to label ethnography the slow food of the social sciences—an immersive technique that seeks answers hidden beneath the defensive official carapace that hides the cultural intimacy at the heart of social resilience.

Despite all the evidence of the persistence of local values and practices, one effective way of staking a claim to the right to survive as a community is through the adoption of official rhetoric. This tactic is the core of what I have

9   In Rome, one of the most poignant aspects of the gentrification of the Monti district of the central historic area was the breakup of this kind of collective social responsibility. See Herzfeld 2009.

called "subversive archaism"—the adoption of the state's cultural rhetoric in defense of a dissident local way of life (Herzfeld 2022). The people of Pom Mahakan adopted this tactic successfully for over two decades: reproducing Thai official architecture in a key community building (the community museum); dating each "ancient" house by royal reigns; and destroying the most ramshackle houses in order to make way for more stylized renditions of "Thai vernacular architecture." The use of (mostly Chinese) amuletic inscriptions and the preservation of ancestral shrines did not, at least, conflict with such "officializing strategies," as Bourdieu (1977: 37–40) called them, but connected the historicizing rhetoric to vernacular ritual in ways that appealed to the pervasive syncretism of Thai religious praxis.

These elements, and especially the adoption of official discourse about national identity and culture, seem to serve what Arjun Appadurai (2004), in a very different Asian context, has called "the capacity to aspire." This expression represents the core of social resilience. Just as the concept of agency signifies the capacity to act on the social and cultural world, the capacity to aspire signifies an equally proactive imagining of a better future—which, for communities like Pom Mahakan, has meant a future designed in the cultural trappings of a carefully edited past. Poor communities that have survived decades of persecution and contempt have thereby shown that they already possess considerable political and social skill, a skill that includes, as Hans Steinmüller (2013) has perceptively shown for China, covert but widely understood forms of collusion with officials. These officials operate within their own culturally intimate space—a bureaucracy far more flexible than its public face admits.

Appadurai's recognition of the "capacity to aspire" must be read in conjunction with his treatment of the materiality (my term rather than his) of social relations. Appadurai, indeed, was one of the first anthropologists to understand the past as a material resource (Appadurai 1981). To claim the past was to claim a space, a way of life, a set of architectural features. It was not something that was donated from on high, whether by an NGO or a government; and, above all, it was hotly contested. Its value lay precisely in its being scarce; all parties aspired to it, but not all could achieve it.

Aspiration as a concept thus presents us with three problems. First, aspiration does not guarantee its bearers success, and in fact, if unrequited, may intensify the pain of failure. Second, it is often assumed to mean aspiration for modernity and its trappings—and it often is precisely that (see, e.g., Sopranzetti 2012 for Thailand). The third problem is closely related to the second: aspiration implies an always-already existing standard—the object of aspiration, representing some version of the global hierarchy of value that reproduces as a cultural scale the political and economic inequalities of colonialism and Western hegemony. How, then, does a community exhibit resilience in the face of these three issues?

The sad fate of Pom Mahakan illustrates all three dimensions. First, its eventual failure, after what looked like a protracted war of attrition in which the core of the residents remained defiant and creative, will have sent a chill over all other communities fighting the conservative Thai establishment for the survival of alternative visions, however clearly articulated these visions often were in the discourse of that same establishment. On the second point, the residents assured me that they saw no conflict between maintaining a traditional lifestyle while articulating with the modern tourist economy and benefiting from it to the extent of acquiring creature comforts in what were to be their newly constructed homes. Since some of them had "modern" professions, ranging from motorcycle taxi driver to accountant and lawyer, that claim had the ring of truth. The constricted space meant that, as time went on, more members of the rising generation would be forced to move away; inevitably, some thought, those would be the more educated ones, with modernist aspirations with which living in a village-like enclave might have seemed incompatible in the long run. But the third aspect was what killed the community's chances of survival: the hierarchy, a Thai-Buddhist karmic order battening on a cultural hierarchy of value that treats any display of traditionalism as incompatible with the modernity to which the middle class aspires. Add to that unfortunate case of class-based folklorism the irritation of city officials at being lectured about what really constituted Thai tradition, and one can easily see that the community's success in achieving cultural resilience might have spelled eventual failure in terms of sociopolitical resilience.

Aspiration does not necessarily mean wanting to escape from one's current social and spatial context. Cramped and crowded conditions may guarantee the social solidarity that many poor Asian communities treasure, and may even have provided the means of social control that enabled the famous Dharavi community in Mumbai to control the effects of the COVID-19 pandemic on its own population (see Altstedter and Pandya 2020). Western-trained (and all too many Western) commentators nevertheless adopt a pitying attitude to what are often designated as slums primarily on the basis of population density. But even in Europe, as Hirschon and Thakurdesai (1970) demonstrated for Greece, crowded conditions do not necessarily mean self-deprecation as slum dwellers; they may, to the contrary, represent success in imposing values having to do with property inheritance and the care of daughters through dowry practices on an unpromisingly restrictive urban setting. Appadurai, for Mumbai, showed that dowering practices constrain relocation, while Harms, writing of Ho Chi Minh City, has illustrated how people no longer able to build on expanded plots of land simply build upward in order to maintain the patrilocal residential unit—ironically, as he notes, in the name of modernity. Just as some cultural traditions value physical proximity in conversation where others do not (see, famously, Hall's [1966] treatise on proxemics), the same applies to the built environment. Take crowded conditions away from a socially compact group and offer them new materials to build, and they will not necessarily increase the physical spaces, or intensify the boundaries, between their homes.

In Thailand the usual term for a slum, when the English-derived *salam* is not being used, is *chumchon ae-ad* (literally, crowded community). But this fixation on escaping density may not in fact represent the *intimate* aspirations of those who are thought, or educated by NGOs, to aspire to a thinner density, or who are berated by bureaucrats for failing to achieve it. Density may sometimes, though not invariably, be implicitly regarded as an asset; in such cases, only when people adopt middle-class cultural values will they also perhaps decide to seek a large, airy house in the suburbs. By then, however, they will no longer have much interest in community coherence; middle-class communities in the vicinity of Pom Mahakan showed much less cohesive interest in maintaining their communal existence, and in those communities the residents' major concerns seemed to be instead with the inconvenience and expense of moving.

Even today and even in the industrialized countries of Europe and North America, however, density is not in itself a negative feature, if it can be combined with privacy; that appears to be the most important effect of the privatization of social life. For those who live in gentrified older areas, perhaps, if the example of Rome is indicative, historicity and heritage will come packaged as luxurious living regardless of the minuscule size of the elegant bijou apartments that now succeed to less densely packed working-class housing. Crowding is again given value, albeit with mediating conveniences ranging from upmarket fittings to luxurious equipment. In that case, the only social resilience of the erstwhile inhabitants will consist of the ersatz traditions packaged for tourists in such invented spaces as the so-called *hutong* hotels of Beijing, with their Jacuzzis and air-con rooms, or the new upscale "residences" of Rome that have taken over the spaces once inhabited by working-class clusters.

When workers and local dwellers gaze every day on the materializations of inequality that confront them, as Namita Dharia (2021) shows for the migrant workers of Delhi, they cannot aspire—they know that these luxurious dwellings are not for them. In such situations, envy can quickly turn to anger, and even more so when they incorrectly believe plentiful housing to be available—"spectral," in Appadurai's (2000) terms—and it thus easily, fed by the flames of nationalist rhetoric, becomes fuel for interethnic violence (2000: 635), turning the poor against the poor and so revictimizing them by forcing them into situations that superficially appear to justify the moral panic thereby fanned among the wealthy. Community resilience among the poor requires acceptance by the wealthy, and that is a scarce resource in these days of gated communities and walled enclaves (see Caldeira 2000; Low 2003).

A radical difficulty for the poor lies in the tension between wanting a piece of modernity—wanting to climb the global hierarchy of value—and knowing that in practical terms it is unreachable. Even those who suffer from modernity's discontents may agree with its basic premises, as Erik Harms shows for Vietnam, and as my Bangkok materials also suggest. They are seduced by an aesthetic allure that ultimately is also the criterion used for shutting them out (see also Ghertner 2010, 2015). Aspiration is thus not a sufficient goal; indeed, it may be taken as evidence of dangerous insubordination.

For related reasons, the language of cultural rights will not always secure those hidden aspects of daily cultural experience that are nevertheless often surprisingly resilient and certainly deeply important to local people, although the extent to which it does so varies enormously from one country to another (see especially Larsen 2018). In Thailand, that discourse was no match for a judicial system devoted to sustaining the class hierarchy. Moreover, cultural rights tend to be viewed in terms of what national governments accept as the content of culture. Much that anthropologists would regard as cultural practices, especially those of the more intimate spheres of cultural activity, are viewed with loathing by bureaucrats and politicians even (or especially?) when, as in the activation of patron-client links, they are its primary beneficiaries. The list includes the slang and commercial structures that mark the world of prostitution and transvestitism, the daubing of graffiti even in the carefully monitored cities of Vietnam, the production of illicit forms of alcohol, the speech forms of the underworld, the techniques of bribery and petty theft, sexual and political jokes, and underworld deals—many of these practices, many of them deeply resilient (to the eternal annoyance of the bureaucrats), are not protected by the rhetoric of cultural rights. Of course, some protection is necessary where threatened minorities might be in danger of not being able to pursue practices they identify as their own. But cultural rights advocates also often, by ignoring the extent to which the culturally intimate dimensions of everyday life are concealed, miss the sources of the most enduring forms of social and cultural resilience.

The reason for this is straightforward. The cultural rights rhetoric makes no space for the *private* dimensions of culture, those one would not usually reveal to outsiders. That is the conundrum: from the moment that these dimensions show some signs of visible vibrancy, they become a target. Those who want to use culture as a line of defense (for example, against eviction) must largely use the official models of culture in order to gain any traction at all. But these are often not the cultural features that actually hold a community together, except when—as in the case of Pom Mahakan—they can be consolidated as a way of *protecting* the cultural intimacy of a community. Even in such cases, however, they are treated as evidence of failure to achieve the norm. Much as minority children from the slums might be treated as "not quite Thai" so that their wearing of a school uniform is automatically assumed to be slovenly (Bolotta 2021), communities like Pom Mahakan are automatically deemed incapable of producing culturally valuable objects and performances at a level that would justify giving them the recognition they have fought to achieve.

It is nevertheless legitimate to wonder whether the formal face of culture can ever survive as a living entity (as opposed, that is, to a museum display) without the corresponding rootedness of intimate culture. For example, if Buddhist activists make much of formal piety, it is nevertheless on their amulets and spirit shrines that they place particular reliance to protect them from danger; these elements abound, they are the religious equivalent of what Michael Billig (1995) calls "banal nationalism," and what they represent is not music to official ears. It is often the external sign of a deep sense of sin, especially marking underworld practices that are the only means of survival for many poor Thais, Indians, and others. These practices are the anchors by which official norms can attach at least to the surface of ordinary people's everyday lives. Official culture rarely provides resilience of its own; its dramatic failures at Pom Mahakan, having destroyed what arguably *was* a socially resilient community, illustrate the inevitable results of cultural engineering of this mechanistic variety.

What is *not* inevitable, I suggest, is the destruction of all such communities by an uncomprehending and inflexible bureaucratic apparatus. But their resilience will always be dependent on political will, and the challenge for the future—if we are not to succumb to the fatalistic view that social resilience can never win out in the long run—will be the creation of that political will among those charged with administration at the municipal level. Among the bureaucrats of the Bangkok administration, there were certainly some who had a measure of sympathy for the residents of Pom Mahakan, although some of the regret did look suspiciously like crocodile tears. We cannot know for certain whether there was any internal push for a more constructive response to the community; the only governor of Bangkok who openly saw the resilience of the community as a reason to defend it, Apirak Kosayodhin, was rapidly ousted as a result of political and bureaucratic machinations within a civil service he never managed to control and that was perhaps scared by his talk of reform.

I thought at the time that real reform would have to include a period of residence in local slums for all the bureaucrats who held the residents' fate in their hands—a policy that might indeed have generated more respect for that resilience that Governor Apirak had explicitly acknowledged. As long as the majority of the city officials deliberately avoided knowing these communities with any degree of intimacy, the hostility would endure. Direct engagement, however, carries its own risks. The one official who did cultivate close contacts with the community, but remained implacably opposed to the residents' plans and may have used his contacts to insert division and conflict into an otherwise largely harmonious community, was apparently pursuing his own ambitions; these are circumstantially evidenced in his eventual rise to a position of considerable power within the city administration.[10] So even the cultivation of greater mutual knowledge between functionaries and residents does not guarantee mutual trust or mutual respect.

Resilience and its Limits

We usually assume that resilience is a resource; it can also be a trap. Appadurai's work in Mumbai illustrates the ideological dynamic underlying the difficulty of promoting local communities as resilient: any challenge to a state discourse that seeks cultural homogeneity is likely to meet an unsympathetic response. Appadurai argues that the Marathi vernacularization of Bombay as "Mumbai," a claim to local cultural specificity, is in reality an effect of fundamentalist Hinduism and a clear preference for neoliberal economics. Instead of the hoped-for rent-controlled housing for the poor, it has instead generated a cruelly competitive economic

---

10   Out of respect for this individual's privacy and for that of the Pom Mahakan residents with whom he dealt, I am intentionally leaving certain details unspecified.

environment that intensifies the precarious condition of the masses while turning a religious identity into a hegemonic yardstick of belonging. It is hard, under such circumstances, to achieve even minimal resilience for a distinctive social or cultural identity. Only the majority may act in ways that connote resilience.

The specific process he describes may be unique to India and even to Mumbai, but it is important to trace its underlying roots to their European source—a source that is held in common with the invention of *folklore* as an academic discipline. In particular, the association of neoliberal economics with nationalistic, fundamentalist, and sometimes racist ideas of heritage has many European antecedents. Vitriolic right-wing attacks on "ethnic" (usually Asian) food in Italy are tied to precisely such unholy alliances. Let us not forget that in Europe and North America "ethnic" is usually a prefix denoting a lower status in the global hierarchy of value. In Italy, attacks on "ethnic food" are usually disguised as attempts to conserve the local cultural character of the so-called "historic centers" (*centri storici*)—already gentrified zones of housing made expensive by canny speculators and a high valorization of "culture" and "history." In Europe, some of the discourses about heritage have morphed into bitterly exclusionary devices (see, e.g., Niklasson and Hølleland 2023; Poulis 2017). There is no reason for surprise when the same thing happens in Asia, especially under authoritarian regimes. Indeed, those regimes often follow European models. In Thailand, the rhetoric of culture (*watthanatham*) and history (*prawatisat*) illustrates the mimetic qualities of much of this discourse, itself the product of a Pali vocabulary grafted onto Italian Fascist philosophizing (Barmé 1993). The Thai authorities would certainly not expect to use a term like "ethnic" to describe their own "national" food culture, and indeed have frequently tried to control or at least influence its production overseas. At the same time, however, they have made many attempts to limit what they see as the disorder and chaos of traditional vending modes by street hawkers—themselves resilient actors who only now are beginning to experience a more comprehensive defeat. In other cases, notably the dismantling and destruction of working-class communities, their methods have been a great deal less gradual or gentle. Community resilience has its limits.

The kind of cultural homogeneity produced by officialdom stifles the necessary—and, in Thailand and elsewhere, long overdue—recognition that inequality ceaselessly saps society. True community resilience requires physical, social, and political space to flourish. When that condition is satisfied, the powerful should also be willing to learn from the weak. But to create the will of the powerful to go beyond pro forma incantations of ritualistic respect for local knowledge—a common stance in southeast Asia—requires an attitude of humility on the part of the powerful that only a close acquaintance with the poor can generate; and that is something that many bureaucrats studiously avoid. The problem of resilience is thus not only that of infusing cultural resilience with social resilience. It is also a matter of persuading the powerful that inequality and a lack of humility on the part of civil servants—note that in Thailand they are technically "servants of the kingdom" (*kha rajakan*) rather than people devoted to the service of the people (*phu rapchai prachachon*)—does not promise a peaceful future. The demise of Pom Mahakan did not write a definitive conclusion to an already long history of social resentment and failure of imagination. Similar defeats elsewhere in Asia do not spell the end of local resilience. They do draw attention to the difficulties that it faces.

References

Althusser, Louis. 1971. *Lenin and Philosophy and the Other Essays*. Translated by Ben Brewster. London: New Left Books.

Altstedter, Ari, and Dhwani Pandya. 2020. "The Mumbai Slum that Stopped the Virus." *Bloomberg*. 8 October 2020. https://www.bloomberg.com/features/2020-mumbai-dharavi-covid-lockdown/. Accessed 6 December 2020.

Appadurai, Arjun. 1981. "The Past as a Scarce Resource." *Man* (n.s.) 16: 201–19.

Appadurai, Arjun. 2000. "Spectral Housing and Urban Cleansing: Notes on Millennial Mumbai." *Public Culture* 12 (3): 627–51.

Appadurai, Arjun. 2004. "The Capacity to Aspire: Culture and the Terms of Recognition." In *Culture and Public Action*, edited by V. Rao and M. Walton, 59–84. Palo Alto: Stanford University Press.

Arnstein, Sherry R. 1969. "A Ladder of Citizen Participation." *Journal of the American Institute of Planners* 35: 216–24.

Barmé, Scot. 1993. *Luang Wichit Wathakan and the Creation of a Thai Identity*. Singapore: Institute of Southeast Asian Studies.

Billig, Michael. 1995. *Banal Nationalism*. London: Sage.

Bolotta, Giuseppe. 2021. *Belittled Citizens: The Cultural Politics of Childhood on Bangkok's Margins*. Copenhagen: NIAS Press.

Bortolotto, Chiara. 2024. "The Embarrassment of Heritage Alienability: Affective Choices and Cultural Intimacy in the UNESCO Lifeworld." *Current Anthropology* 61(1): 50–51.

Bortolotto, Chiara, Philipp Demgemski, Panas Karapampas, and Simone Toji. 2020. "Proving Participation: Vocational Bureaucrats and Bureaucratic Creativity in the Implementation of the UNESCO Convention for the Safeguarding of the Intangible Cultural Heritage." *Social Anthropology* 28: 66–82.

Bourdieu, Pierre. 1977. *Outline of a Theory of Practice.* Translated by Richard Nice. Cambridge: Cambridge University Press.

Caldeira, Teresa P.R. 2000. *City of Walls: Crime, Segregation, and Citizenship in São Paulo.* Berkeley: University of California Press.

Chang, T.C. 2016. "'New Uses Need Old Buildings': Gentrification Aesthetics and the Arts in Singapore." *Urban Studies* 53: 524–39.

Chau, Adam Yuet. 2008. "An Awful Mark: Symbolic Violence and Urban Renewal in Reform-Era China." *Visual Studies* 23: 195–210.

Cocchiara, Giuseppe. 1952. *Storia del folklore in Europa.* Turin: Einaudi.

de Certeau, Michel. 1984. *The Practice of Everyday Life.* Translated by Steven Rendall. Berkeley: University of California Press.

de Cesari, Chiara, and Rozita Dimova. 2019. "Heritage, Gentrification, Participation: Remaking Urban Landscapes in the Name of Culture and Historic Preservation." *International Journal of Heritage Studies* 25: 853–69.

Denes, Alexandra. 2015. "Folklorizing Northern Khmer Identity in Thailand: Intangible Cultural Heritage and the Production of 'Good Culture.'" *Sojourn* 30 (1): 1–34.

Dharia, Namita Vijay. 2021. *The Industrial Ephemeral: Labor and Love in Indian Architecture and Construction.* Berkeley: University of California Press.

Elinoff, Eli. 2014. "Sufficient Citizens: Moderation and the Politics of Sustainable Development in Thailand." *PoLAR: Political and Legal Anthropology Review* 37: 89–108.

Ghertner, D. Asher. 2010. "Calculating without Numbers: Aesthetic Governmentality in Delhi's Slums." *Economy and Society* 39: 185–217.

Ghertner, D. Asher. 2015. *Rule by Aesthetics: World-Class City Making in Delhi.* Oxford: Oxford University Press.

Hall, Edward T. 1966. *The Hidden Dimension.* New York: Anchor Books.

Harms, Erik. 2012. "Beauty as Control in the New Saigon: Eviction, New Urban Zones, and Atomized Dissent in a Southeast Asian City." *American Anthropologist* 39: 735–50.

Herzfeld, Michael. 1996. "National Spirit or the Breath of Nature? The Expropriation of Folk Positivism in the Discourse of Greek Nationalism." In *Natural Histories of Discourse*, edited by Michael Silverstein and Greg Urban, 277–98. Chicago: University of Chicago Press.

Herzfeld, Michael. 2004. *The Body Impolitic: Artisans and Artifice in the Global Hierarchy of Value.* Chicago: University of Chicago Press.

Herzfeld, Michael. 2009. *Evicted from Eternity: The Restructuring of Modern Rome.* Chicago: University of Chicago Press.

Herzfeld, Michael. 2016a. *Siege of the Spirits: Community and Polity in Bangkok.* Chicago: University of Chicago Press.

Herzfeld, Michael. 2016b. *Cultural Intimacy: Social Poetics and the Real Life of States, Societies, and Institutions*, 3rd edition. New York: Routledge.

Herzfeld, Michael. 2020. *Ours Once More: Folklore, Ideology, and the Making of Modern Greece*, 2nd edition. Oxford: Berghahn.

Herzfeld, Michael. 2022. *Subversive Archaism: Troubling Traditionalists and the Politics of National Heritage*. Durham: Duke University Press.

Hirschon, Renée, and Thakurdesai. 1970. "Society, Culture and Spatial Organization: An Athens Community." *Ekistics* 30 (178): 187–96.

Jacobs, Jane. 1961. *The Death and Life of Great American Cities*. New York: Vintage.

Janelli, Roger L. 1986. "The Origins of Korean Folklore." *Journal of American Folklore* 99: 24–49.

Karapampas, Panas. 2021. "(Re)inventing Intangible Cultural Heritage through the Market in Greece." *International Journal of Heritage Studies* 27: 654–67.

Larsen, Peter Bille, ed. 2018. *World Heritage and Human Rights: Lessons from the Asia-Pacific and Global Arena*. London: Routledge.

Leacock, Eleanor Burke, ed. 1971. *The Culture of Poverty: A Critique.* New York: Simon and Schuster.

Low, Setha M. 2003. *Life, Security, and the Pursuit of Happiness in Fortress America.* New York: Routledge.

Mack, Jennifer. 2017. *The Construction of Equality: Syriac Immigration and the Swedish City*. Minneapolis: University of Minnesota Press.

Niklasson, Elisabeth, and Herdis Hølleland. 2023. "Possessive Pasts: Heritage in Far-Right Rhetoric in Scandinavia." In *Polarized Pasts: Heritage and Belonging in Times of Political Polarization*, edited by Elisabeth Niklasson, 69–87. Oxford: Berghahn.

Poulis, Konstantinos. 2017. "Golden Dawn and the Classics." *Political Critique*. May 30, 2017. https://politicalcritique.org/world/2017/golden-dawn-and-the-classics/. Accessed 15 June 2022.

Raheja, Gloria Goodwin. 1996. "Caste, Colonialism, and the Speech of the Colonized: Entextualization and Disciplinary Control in India." *American Ethnologist* 23: 494–513.

Reed-Danahay, Deborah. 1987. "Farm Children at School: Educational Strategies in Rural France." *Anthropological Quarterly* 60: 83–9.

Salemink, Oscar, Amélia Siegel Correa, Jens Sejrup, and Vibe Nielsen, eds. 2022. *Global Art in Local Art Worlds: Changing Hierarchies of Value.* London: Routledge.

Scott, James C. 1998. *Seeing Like a State: How Certain Schemes to Improve the Human Condition Have Failed*. New Haven: Yale University Press.

Sirinya Wattanasukchai. 2018. "At Fort Mahakan, a Birthday that Shuns the Past." *Nation*. 28 April 2018. https://www.nationthailand.com/perspective/30344180. Accessed 26 February 2024.

Sirinya Wattanasukchai. 2020. "City's History Being Lost to Fake Facade of Beauty." *Bangkok Post.* 5 November 2020. https://www.bangkokpost.com/opinion/opinion/2014143/citys-history-being-lost-to-fake-facade-of-beauty. Accessed 26 February 2024.

Sopranzetti, Claudio. 2012. "Burning Red Desires: Isan Migrants and the Politics of Desire in Contemporary Thailand." *South East Asia Research* 20: 361–79.

Sopranzetti, Claudio. 2017. *Owners of the Map: Motorcycle Taxi Drivers, Mobility, and Politics in Bangkok.* Berkeley: University of California Press.

Steinmüller, Hans. 2013. *Communities of Complicity: Everyday Ethics in Rural China.* Oxford: Berghahn.

Stolcke, Verena. 1995. "Talking Culture: New Boundaries, New Rhetorics of Exclusion in Europe." *Current Anthropology* 36: 1–24.

Thanaphon Watthanakun. 2007. *Kahnmoeang roeang phoen thi: pholawat thang sangkhom khawng chumchon (Koroni soeksah: Chumchon Pom Mahahkahn)* [Politics of place: Social dynamics of a community (Case study: The Pom Mahakan community)]. Bangkok: 14 October Scholarly Institutional Foundation.

Willis, Paul. (1977) 1981. *Learning to Labor: How Working Class Kids Get Working Class Jobs.* Reprint, Morningside Edition. New York: Columbia University Press.

Wilson, William A. 1976. *Folklore and Nationalism in Modern Finland.* Bloomington: Indiana University Press.

Wimmer, Andreas, and Nina Glick Schiller. 2002. "Methodological Nationalism and Beyond: Nation-State Building, Migration and the Social Sciences." *Global Networks* 2: 301–34.

Zhang, Li. 2001. "Migration and Privatization of Space and Power in Late Socialist China." *American Ethnologist* 28: 179–205.

Zhang, Li. 2002. "Spatiality and Urban Citizenship in Late Socialist China." *Public Culture* 14: 311–34.

Zhang, Li. 2006. "Contesting Spatial Modernity in Late-Socialist China." *Current Anthropology* 47: 461–84.

About the Author

Michael Herzfeld is the Ernest E. Monrad Professor of the Social Sciences *Emeritus*, Department of Anthropology, Harvard University, and IIAS Professor of Critical Heritage Studies *Emeritus*, Leiden University. His fourteen books include *Siege of the Spirits: Community and Polity in Bangkok* (2016) and *Subversive Archaism: Troubling Traditionalists and the Politics of National Heritage* (2022). His current research addresses heritage politics, crypto-colonialism, and artisans' practices of competition and cooperation.

3. Social Resilience of the Vernacular Cosmopolitan Heritage of Melaka

Kim Nørgaard Helmersen

Abstract: In 2008, Melaka was granted UNESCO heritage status owing to its unique cosmopolitan heritage. While the UNESCO status has provided protection to the city's historical core, the heritage of local communities located outside the heritage (buffer) zone has fallen out of category—and protection—making it vulnerable to a redevelopment of the city. Catering to demands of the tourism industry and fitting into national heritage narratives, the heritage is being (re)constructed along lines of colonial stereotypes, endangering the vernacular cosmopolitanism. Cross reading Durkheim's social solidarity with literature on cosmopolitanism, I argue that vernacular cosmopolitanism can unfold in local networks, suggesting that the local and the cosmopolitan are not mutually exclusive.

Keywords: Émile Durkheim, Southeast Asia, urban redevelopment, mass tourism, racial politics

Introduction

Southeast Asian cities are well known for their multiethnic populations, which have brought about a rich variety of cultural and religious habits and traditions (Laquian 1996). The sociocultural and ethnic heterogeneity is the foundation for the vibrancy and dynamics that is widely associated with urban Asia, but it also brings a potential social instability (Varshney 2014). Differences between social groups can become challenging during times of abnormal changes in society, such as an economic crisis, and in such situations there is a need for resilient social networks for the city to adapt to rapid change (Yamagata and Sharifi 2018).

Herzfeld, M., and R. Padawangi, eds. *Resilience as Heritage in Asia*. Amsterdam: Amsterdam University Press, 2025.
DOI: 10.5117/9789463728560_CH03

Urban planners and theorists are increasingly interested in vernacular heritage in their search for sources of urban resilience (Yamagata and Sharifi 2018). Vernacular heritage is typically mentioned in relation to *built* vernacular heritage, but it encompasses also "intangible aspects, such as building techniques, lifestyles, territorial connections and transmission of skills from one generation to the next, which are intrinsic to communities" (ICOMOS 1999). It has been described by the ICOMOS Charter on the Built Vernacular Heritage (1999) as a continuing process including necessary changes and continuous adaptation as a response to social and environmental constraints that serves a particular function to a community.

In this chapter, I draw attention to how social skills can be stored as vernacular heritage, and, in turn, be a source of (social) resilience to local communities. This argument unfolds in relation to a more general discussion of urban cosmopolitanism and its relation to vernacular heritage, and takes an urban redevelopment of the city of Melaka, Malaysia, as context for the discussion. Along with George Town, Penang, a number of neighborhoods in Melaka were in 2008 granted UNESCO heritage status in order to protect and preserve the cosmopolitan heritage they showcase(d). However, the question is: How do you preserve a heritage that is lived, dynamic, and interlinked with processes of change and adaptation?

The "inherent character of adaptability and perceived sustainability" ("Vernacular Heritage" n.d.) of vernacular heritage highlights its importance in relation to questions of resilience, and extends an ongoing discussion in regards to heritage preservation. At the core of the vernacular heritage lies the continuous process of adaptation, and this challenges mainstream preservation policies and practices, not least in Melaka.

The Social Resilience of Vernacular Heritage

In July 2008 Melaka was officially declared a UNESCO World Heritage site, branding its value to the world community. In the declaration, UNESCO (2022) places emphasis on the protection and preservation of both tangible and intangible evidence of Melaka's living multicultural heritage, which exemplifies the heritage and tradition of Asia on an exceptional level. However, while the UNESCO heritage stamp is obviously an important recognition of Melaka's heritage and a signature for the city, it is worth questioning if it is good news for the preservation of the city's vernacular heritage. Since gaining UNESCO status, the urban heritage of Melaka has been contested by at least two powerful actors. On the one hand, the local tourism industry is fabricating heritage products to the accelerating demand of both domestic and international tourists. On the other hand, state forces are incorporating Melaka's urban heritage as part of a national heritage story (Worden 2010: 130ff.). Related to these processes, an urban redevelopment is carried out with consequences for the local communities. Multiethnic neighborhoods are being reorganized and communities segregated as part of an urban redevelopment scheme put in motion to cater for the growing tourist mass, but also to make a number of ethnic quarters: Little India, Chinatown, and Malay Village. With that said, Melaka was in no way a "paradise" of vernacular cosmopolitanism before its UNESCO-derived refashioning. For example, Pierpaolo De Giosa (2024) has demonstrated how Malaysia's racial politics has set the ground for frequent episodes of Sino-Malay sectarian violence. In this way, the transformation of Melaka's urban layout should rather be seen as a continuation of colonial frames regarding race than as an entirely new trend (Tajudeen 2012).

While racial tensions are hardly new to Melaka, I argue that the same cosmopolitanism that put the city on the global heritage map is now in danger of diminishing as the communities are being segregated according to ethnicity. This would be unfortunate, not only as a loss of heritage, but because vernacular heritage has a social function. As Yamagata and Sharifi (2018: 15) argue, there has been an increasing awareness within planning theory for the importance of vernacular heritage: "It is especially important to employ effective strategies for preserving functionality of social networks when preparing plans for urban renovation and gentrification in historic neighborhoods. Razing old neighborhoods and districts can destroy social relationships that have been in place for a long time." For example, Wallace and Wallace (2011) argue that policies of urban renewal in Harlem, New York, has promoted ethnic segregation and thus undermined the resilience of the communities and their capacity to respond to negative social and health-related impacts. Building this argument, Wallace and Wallace connect the concept of resilience to vernacular heritage, arguing for a specific social robustness of local communities that has a long-standing, self-grown social organization. Against this background, I argue that there is an urgent need for more knowledge about how vernacular (cosmopolitan) heritage can be preserved and protected.

While I won't provide any final answers to this question in this chapter, I will try to advance the discussion further by linking the notion of social resilience to vernacular cosmopolitan heritage through a sociologist classic by Émile Durkheim. Dusting off his model from *The Division of Labor in Society* ([1893] 1984) and trying to overcome its teleological and evolutionary assumptions, I suggest that the notion of cosmopolitanism has similar attributes to those of organic solidarity.

Vernacular Cosmopolitanism

While the term vernacular typically associates the local, rooted, and culturally specific, cosmopolitanism associates the transnational, transcendent, elitist, enlightened, universalist, and modernist (Werbner 2006, 2013). In fact, vernacular cosmopolitanism has often been called an oxymoron, as it aims to join seemingly contradictory notions of local specificity and universal enlightenment (Werbner 2013: 110). The question is, however, whether the two concepts have simply been too rigidly and narrowly defined, or whether they really form an oxymoron.

Linguistically, the term cosmopolitanism can be traced back to c. 412 BC and Diogenes of Sinope, who referred to himself as *kosmopolitês*, meaning "a citizen of the world" in ancient Greek (Laurtius n.d.). In this way, the story of cosmopolitanism began with the notion of openness to the unknown world. Later, Immanuel Kant ([1795] 1999) formulated cosmopolitanism as a moral universalism in the essay *Perpetual Peace* (Nussbaum 1997). His concept of moral universalism implied the belief that all humans should come under the same moral standards, with boundaries between nations, cultures, or societies becoming morally irrelevant (ibid.).

Since these early notions of cosmopolitanism, the term has been put in use in various contexts and in relation to different phenomena and today it is "multiply defined and variously contested" (Binnie, Holloway, and Millington 2006: 31). With that said, the notion is consistently mentioned in relation to multicultural entities and a number of social characteristics of a well-functioning modern society, such as pluralism, openness, solidarity, networks, and tolerance. In this sense, cosmopolitanism can rightfully be seen as beneficial to societies that are becoming increasingly multicultural following globalization, stepwise replacing segmented local structures with more fluid global structures (Binnie, Holloway, and Millington 2006: 31).

Thus, debates are not so much on whether cosmopolitanism is a positive contribution to society, but rather on the content of the notion, especially in relation to the question of *how* it is achieved. In this connection, there has been a divide in literature between roughly two different views of cosmopolitanism. I call these actor-generated cosmopolitanism, and structure-generated cosmopolitanism: First, actor-generated cosmopolitanism refers to scholarship that associates cosmopolitanism with a certain level of self-reflection in relation to "the other." These scholars emphasize the conscious effort of the individual in acquiring a cosmopolitan mindset. Second, structure-generated cosmopolitanism refers to scholarship that finds that cosmopolitanism can be shaped bottom-up, as part of a person's habitus, rather than necessarily through philosophical education or travels to distant worlds.

Actor-Generated Cosmopolitanism vs. Structure-Generated Cosmopolitanism

Beyond the simple notion of cosmopolitanism as an "openness to difference," the term has often been associated with a form of consciousness, skill set, or attitude to the world acquired through a process of enlightenment, such as philosophical education or travelling (Hannerz 1996). I call this take on cosmopolitanism actor generated, as it requires a self-distancing and self-reflection of the actor. Among others, Ulf Hannerz (1996) and Bryan Turner (2000) reflect this actor-generated position by emphasizing the self-reflective competency of an enlightened actor who puts a set of skills or competences in use when encountering difference or meeting "the stranger." Emphasizing the consciousness of the actor, this notion of cosmopolitanism distances itself from the vernacular by making it inaccessible to the mundane. Instead, it formulates an ideal—something to strive for.

Against this view, there is the belief that cosmopolitanism is not simply a matter of individual choice and reflection, but, rather, it is *socially* produced (Latham 2003; Calhoun 2002). While actor-generated cosmopolitanism emphasizes the self-reflection of an actor "at home in the world," this structure-generated cosmopolitanism argues that individuals can simply be "of the world." The idea is that simple, continuous exposure to difference can form the basis of a sort of cosmopolitan habitus. In this understanding, cosmopolitanism is not a competency you have to leave your comfort zone to acquire; it is a part of your everyday life and inseparable from that. It is part of the habitus (Bourdieu 1987), and in this way structure-based cosmopolitanism seeks to overcome apparently contradictory opposites, such as rooted cosmopolitanism, working class cosmopolitanism, and vernacular cosmopolitanism (Werbner 2006).

In addition, it is worth emphasizing that many poor and marginal people, such as refugees and other migrants, do travel and potentially gain the aforementioned attitude to the world without it being part of any conscious aspiration (De Genova 2002). In the South East Asian context, Charles

Keyes (2012) has, for example, argued that "rural" villagers can become cosmopolitan through their global labor and increasing access to modern information and communications technology. Keyes describes such migrant workers as "cosmopolitan villagers" and contests the relation between rural/urban in relation to cosmopolitanism. This situation is quite different to the one we encounter in Melaka, where the cosmopolitanism rather transfers in and through the local heritage, which is indeed connected to urbanization and to the trading that brought the many cultures together (Widodo 2011). In this way, I suggest two forms of vernacular cosmopolitanism: Firstly, there is a "global-to-local" variety where—through information streams, technological progress, or work migration—"the global" enters the local (perceived "rural") whereby the communities become cosmopolitan. Secondly, there is a "local-to-global" variety where—through vernacular heritage—cosmopolitanism is formed within the local communities. One might argue that the second variety is built on the first variety, in the sense that—as it is the case with Melaka—"the global" entered the local, which over generations layered as heritage. However, when the world came to Melaka it was obviously a very different time before information technologies or the migration streams of today.

In this way, theorists of actor-generated cosmopolitanism and structure-generated cosmopolitanism can also differ from each other in relation to their view of the importance of spatial scale. While notions of cosmopolitanism are generally related to experiences of the global, it is contested at which scale this phenomenon will occur: Can one experience cosmopolitanism in the "glocal" or does one have to leave the local and travel globally? Answers to this question are bound up with a notion of mobility and linked to the actor vs. structure debate. While some would argue that mobility (forced or voluntary) is necessary to acquire a cosmopolitan set of skills, others state that cosmopolitanism can derive from the local milieu—e.g., be vernacular. Notions that emphasize mobility or the competent self-reflective actor are generally criticized for being essentially class based, as they require access to cultural and economic capital (Binnie, Holloway, and Millington 2006; Werbner 1999). Keyes's (2012) migrant workers obviously provide a different case.

In sum, I argue that structure-generated cosmopolitanism opens the possibility that cosmopolitanism—as a social competency—can be transferred through (heritage) practices of the mundane everyday life. When emphases are not placed on the self-reflective ability of the actor, but instead on a structural basis for cosmopolitanism, it becomes possible to see how cosmopolitanism can derive from local culture. In her study of the "Paradoxes of Postcolonial Vernacular Cosmopolitanism in South Asia and the Diaspora," Werbner (2013) argues that Bollywood reflects such vernacular cosmopolitanism as it transcends the spaces of South Asia's cultural and religious diversity, despite its deep divisions. In this way, she emphasizes how there can be found a political capacity in the vernacular cosmopolitanism of Indian popular cinema. This presents "a hybrid mixture of a wide range of traditions and languages within the space of South Asia Bollywood," which she further argues, "does not belong to a single, pure culture. It has created its own imaginary country" (Werbner 2013: 110).

Social Resilience of Cosmopolitanism: The (Urban) Production of Organic Solidarity

Cosmopolitanism is consistently associated with two major socio-spatial transformations of modernity—urbanization and globalization. The changing pattern of the social world coming together in cities brings questions of urban cosmopolitanism to the forefront. Cities known as cosmopolitan have always been surrounded with great mystique as they present a structured chaos and a cultural vibrancy. They confront their visitors with a key question of classic sociology: How can it be that societies, while becoming ever more socially complex and heterogeneous, are also getting more connected and coherent?

This was *the* question for Emile Durkheim in the early parts of his authorship, where he studied the transformation of modernity, particularly regarding processes following the industrialization in European countries. In answer to the question, he found that social solidarity is not a single but a two-stringed phenomenon as it manifests itself in respectively premodern and modern societies. In this way, he found it is a transformation of social solidarity that explains how the increasingly heterogeneous structures of society are held together by ever-stronger ties. Durkheim connects this transformation of social solidarity to the division of labor in society, which brings about new patterns of social interaction (Durkheim [1893] 1984). He describes how "the products of the new industrial system were no longer created by individual craftsmen or by the collaboration of a few, but emerged instead from the coordinated activities of a large number of persons who had been assigned specialized tasks" (Durkheim [1893] 1984: x). To Durkheim, this specialization and dependence on coordination with others leads to an *organic solidarity,* which in short can be described as the social glue between people who are *unlike* each other. As a contrast, Durkheim formulates a *mechanical solidarity,* describing the bonds between people who are *alike.*

Durkheim further linked the transformation of social solidarity to a spatial transformation of society. He suggested that it is an increase in social density and volume of the members of society that is the catalyst for the division of labor. The scattering over land characterizing the segmented social relations of premodern societies is stepwise replaced by dense urbanities and mechanical bonds replaced by organic bonds (Durkheim [1897] 2005: 257–60). In this way, division of labor is brought about by an increased social density and volume, which leads to a more complex social organization. However, Durkheim found that this complexity is not disorganized; rather it is organized in a different way—as organic solidarity. He further argued that this transformation also brings about a development in sensibility and intelligence, which is how, "without having willed it, humanity finds itself prepared to accept a more intense and varied culture" (Durkheim [1893] 1984: 214). In this way, the transformation process from premodern to modern society is not seen as a simple transformation of society, but as a development.

While this thesis has had tremendous influence on sociological theory, it has also received criticism for its teleological argumentation of societies mechanically moving *forward*. However, Durkheim in fact argued that "mechanical solidarity persists even in the most elevated societies" (Collins 2004: 186). Also, critics have argued that organic solidarity existed in the most primitive societies (Sahlins 1974; Adair 2008), and that the substitution of mechanical solidarity by organic solidarity cannot be complete. In other words, mechanical and organic solidarity are not mutually exclusive (Thijssen 2012). This argument opens up the interpretation that the Durkheimian model can be put to use in a more dynamic way, as the changing of solidarity from mechanical to organic (and vice versa) relates to more general patterns of socio-spatial division and integration. To further explain this, however, I need to stretch the argument by looking to a number of interpretations of Durkheim's model.

Spatializing Durkheim's Solidarities

While Durkheim was criticized for the overtly teleological aspects of this theory, I will argue that his model provides an interesting framework for a study of how vernacular cosmopolitanism might generate. If one looks at the meaning of the categories of his model in isolation, they provide a potential for a language for analyzing how ways of social organization might relate to spatial organization. One important example comes from Hillier and

Hanson (1984), who used Durkheim's conceptual framework to develop a social theory of space, which can be applied in actual studies and designs of both architectural and urban spaces. In *The Social Logic of Space* (1984: 18), they formulate Durkheim's theory of social solidarity in relation to actual spaces: "Organic solidarity required an integrated and dense space, whereas mechanical solidarity preferred a segregated and dispersed space. In the work of Durkheim, we found the missing component of a theory of space, in the form of the elements for a spatial analysis of social formations." In their reception of Durkheim, Hillier and Hanson (1984: 18) draw on his social morphology and the concept of "dynamic density" (Durkheim [1893] 1984: 200) formulated in *Division of Labour*: "Durkheim actually located the cause of the different solidarities in spatial variables, namely the size and density of populations."

In a micro-sociological context, Randall Collins has reformulated Durkheim's model in connection with his theory outlined in *Interaction Ritual Chains* (2004). Operationalizing Durkheim's model, he argues that mechanical solidarity is found with "the overlap of high social density and low social diversity (localism)" (Collins 2004: 117). Organic solidarity is found with "a situation of high social diversity (cosmopolitanism, i.e., the modern division of labor, as contrasted to undifferentiated small tribal or rural communities)" (Collins 2004: 117). In this way, he argues that the complex combinations of social density and diversity decide whether a social environment can be associated as more mechanical or organic. While social density is measured in the amount of time that people are spending in each other's presence, diversity is about the cultural differences between the copresent people—e.g., the encounter with "the stranger" (Collins 2004: 117). If we follow this argument and return to the discussion of actor- vs. structure-generated cosmopolitanism, then we find that localism is not necessarily at odds with cosmopolitanism, since highly localized networks can also consist of a diverse social population. Such a proposal challenges Durkheim's model by pointing at a complex combination of mechanical and organic solidarity, since societies characterized by an organic solidarity would normally be associated with individuals covering a wider range of situations and experiencing a higher degree of solitude (Collins 1988: 201).

Leaving the discussion of Durkheim's model here, I would like to add a note of caution, acknowledging the fact that Durkheim himself only commented directly on the notion of cosmopolitanism in one connection, as "the notion of *cosmopolitanisme* to recover Kant's idea of perpetual peace" (Chernilo 2009: 533). When choosing to revisit Durkheim's theory, it is not to state that he developed a theory on cosmopolitanism, or that he intended to do so. It is only to make use of his conceptual framework to help facilitate a discussion about how cosmopolitanism relates to different morphologies and why it is valuable precisely to multicultural urbanities as a source of resilience. In this connection, I repeat that mechanical and organic solidarity are not mutually exclusive, and vernacular cosmopolitanism might in fact portray a situation where the dichotomous relation between the local and the cosmopolitan (the mechanical and the organic) transcends, as vernacular cosmopolitanism can be generated from local networks.

Urban Cosmopolitanism in Southeast Asia

Emile Durkheim associated patterns of organic solidarity with a division and specialization in the labor force that would lead to people exchanging economically and—eventually also—culturally and socially with people who were different from them. Relating this thesis to (Western) modernity, he didn't consider that "premodern" examples of cultures' social and economic organization could be associated with his organic solidarity. Trading has led to cultural exchange for thousands of years, not least along the great maritime routes where strategically located settlements over generations grew into maritime cities of global importance. Widodo (2011: 34) argues that such "maritime cities in Southeast Asia were founded as settlements of immigrants, who came for different purposes. In these cities, people of different traditions intermingled while engaging in bartering and forged new mental and social integration, forming a truly cosmopolitan community."

I argued earlier that cosmopolitanism has been "multiply defined and variously contested" and I would now question the use of the term "truth" in relation to cosmopolitanism. Widodo doesn't define more precisely the mental and social integration that he describes as "truly cosmopolitan," but his argument is interesting to consider in relation to Durkheim's theory. Widodo (2011: 34) describes how the primary element of Southeast Asian coastal cities was the market for commercial exchange, as they developed over centuries as entrepôts, which he defines as "a centre of distribution or exchange of foreign merchandise with little or no local product to export." Rather than a port for the export of local products, Melaka's rise to influence depended on its strategic location on the trading route between India and China, making it an international hub for maritime trade. I argue that the form of social integration Widodo here refers to as cosmopolitan is largely consistent with the social integration Durkheim defines as organic solidarity.

Also, Durkheim associated cosmopolitanism with (urban) spaces of highly differentiated commercial activity bringing about an intercultural exchange.

However, Widodo argues that Melaka's strategic location and commercial activity wasn't enough alone to build an urban cosmopolitanism. Instead, it was the combination of Melaka's location and the efforts of the Ming dynasty's Admiral Zheng He in the early fifteenth century to promote a peaceful coexistence among different religions and racial groups that shaped Melaka's identity as an entrepôt (Widodo 2011: 37). In other words, Melaka's historical urban cosmopolitanism doesn't rest alone on the "natural" forces of social integration that relates to the vibrant life of "the market," but also on its political climate. It was during peacetime that cosmopolitanism flourished. In deference hereto, Durkheim viewed the uprising of organic solidarity as a necessity. To him, process was by definition progress. He found that the social life he was trying to describe held an internal logic to it—an evolutionary logic. From this perspective, Melaka's history of cosmopolitanism would be a great deal different to the one Widodo describes, where the cosmopolitanism can be periodical and rise and decline along with the social and political changes. Whether or not cosmopolitanism is tied to deeper social forces alone or sensitive to political attitudes, Melaka's colonial history needs acknowledgement. The process through which the Portuguese, Dutch, British, Hindu-Buddhist, Chinese, and Japanese each put their stamp on the urban fabric since the days of the Melaka Sultanate has left a trauma that Malaysia continues to maneuver (King 2012). This brings me back to the central question: Is there (still) vernacular cosmopolitanism in Melaka? And if so, how does this cosmopolitanism transfer between people and generations?

Malaka's Heritage Map

In summer 2012, a group of student researchers (myself included) went on a fieldtrip to Melaka looking for answers to the aforementioned questions. The trip was part of a summer school on the topic of Urban Cosmopolitanism in Southeast Asia organized by the National University of Singapore (NUS). Empirical and material experiences and insights gained during this fieldtrip formed the basis for a small exhibition at the NUS Museum and the formulation of further questions explored, for example, in this chapter. In preparation for the fieldtrip, researchers were presented historical and theoretical perspectives on cosmopolitan Melaka, including the ongoing construction of this heritage against the background of national, political, and economic

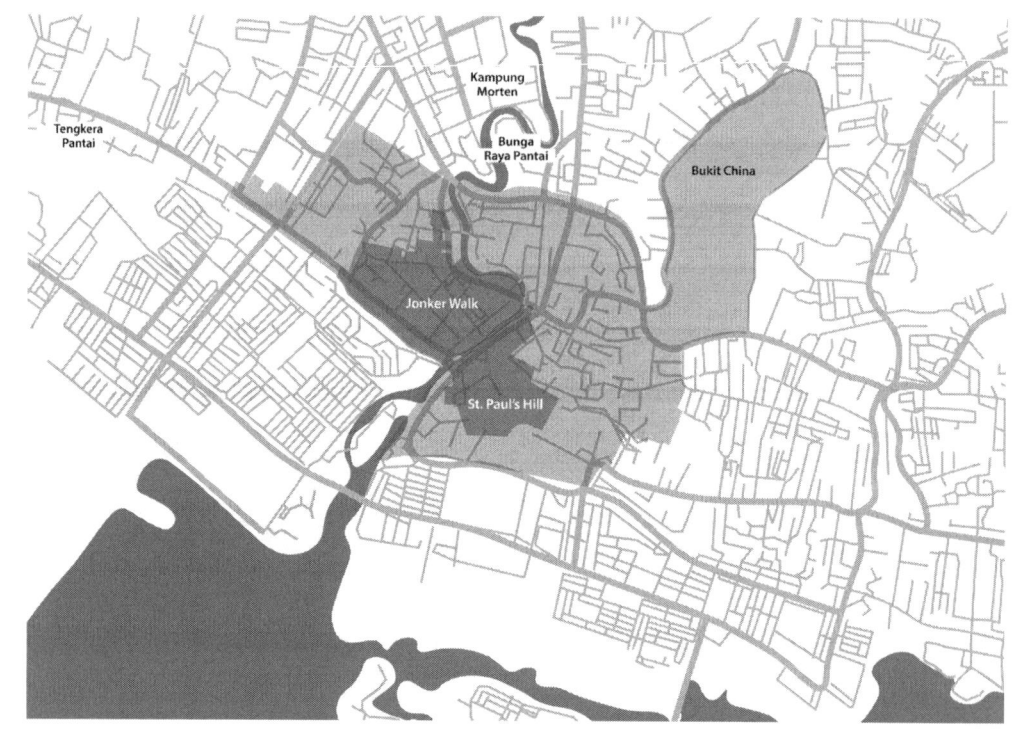

Figure 3.1. Heritage map of Melaka (map by author on Google Maps background. Map based on learning material from the IARU summer program, Southeast Asian Cosmopolitan Urbanism, The National University of Singapore, October 2014)

interests. Attention was given to understanding and analyzing how heritage architecture has been used in the construction of racial discourses, but also how stereotypes can be exposed and deconstructed through genealogical analysis of the architectural heritage. In Melaka, the group was separated into two subgroups, one of which ended up exploring such constructions in the urban neighborhood. At the time, the city was undergoing deep transformation as the urban redevelopment authorities responded to the dramatic increase in tourism following the heritage branding (Widodo 2011; Tajudeen 2012; Worden 2010). More than a regular urbanization, the urban layout was changing along the lines of a heritage map (figure 3.1).

The Melaka World Heritage Site so far has been a project in two stages. First, in 2007, 38.62 hectares of property was included in the UNESCO heritage core zone and 134.03 hectares as a buffer zone. Later, in 2011, this preservation plan was revised as 6.7 hectares was added to the core zone and 108.8 to the buffer zone. The heritage map is based on a map of Melaka (October 2022), with the second stage heritage zones on top. The core zone (dark grey) comprises Bukit Melaka (St Paul's Hill), Jalan Tun Tan Cheng Lock, Jalan Hang Jebat (Jonker Street), Jalan Kg Kuli, Jalan Tukang Emas, Jalan Tokong, Jalan Tukang Besi, and Jalan Kg Pantai. The buffer zone (light grey) consists of Jalan Kubu, Jalan Bunga Raya, Jalan Kg Jawa, Jalan Bendahara, and Jalan Temenggong, encircling the core zone (UNESCO 2022). Beyond this boundary there are the remaining neighborhoods of Melaka, not granted heritage status. These include Kampung Morten and Bunga Raya Pantai, which were the focus areas of my subgroup, and Tengkera Pantai, the focus area of the second subgroup.

The making of the heritage zone is positive in the sense that the heritage within the zone is now granted extraordinary protection. However, heritage existing beyond the zone is falling out of category and runs the risk of being considered "not heritage." As argued by De Giosa (2024), the inscription of the historical core of the city into the World Heritage List resulted in a boom in tourist arrivals, increasing land values and attracting interest for infill development projects (new construction on underdeveloped land within built-up areas). Rather than communicating with the city's existing building stock, these "infill development projects are mostly high-rise luxury hotels, apartment blocks, and shopping malls targeting the middle and upper classes, tourists, and foreigners" (De Giosa 2024: 11). Filling in the townscape roughly along the line of the UNESCO heritage buffer zone, the previously adjacent and connected neighborhoods of the city are being separated, and members of the communities rehoused to different parts of the city. As a concerned official told De Giosa (2024: 11): Melaka will end up as a heritage site with a circle of high-rises around it.

Along the outer edges of this circle lie Tengkera Pantai, Bunga Raya Pantai, and Kampung Morten. These neighborhoods used to house multiethnic populations and are principally *kampung*. The populations come from different ethnic groups (Chinese, Javanese, Bugis, Indians, Arabs, and a Eurasian community) which—during Portuguese rule—began to settle in the area outside the walled town (where the Portuguese resided) (King 2012). Over time these ethnic groups formed their own distinctive kampung, but, by the end of eighteenth century, the ethnic districts were not so clear-cut when the Chinese began to move into the areas (as the Dutch had also done earlier). In this way, the different kampung of Melaka—originally ethnic quarters—over time developed as rather more hybrid wards (King 2012). At the time of the visit in 2012, Bunga Raya Pantai comprised a predominantly Straits-born Chinese population (*peranakan*), Kampung Morten a predominantly Malay-Muslim population and Tengkera Pantai's population ranged from Chettis to Chinese Buddhists to Chinese Christians.

In the present discourse, kampung primarily refers to rural settlements of the Malay ethnic majority (De Giosa 2024), and associated rural Malay (Tajudeen 2012), but "in every-day usage, the word also refers to rural-like neighborhoods absorbed by urban growth, and not necessarily inhabited by Malays" (De Giosa 2024: 2). Beyond the predominantly Malay urban villages such as Kampung Morten, neighborhoods exist that are connected to other ethnic and religious communities such as Kampung Chetti. Also, Bunga Raya Pantai comprised numerous "kampung houses" before the ward got demolished to make way for denser building mass. As history tells, the kampung is more than simply an administrative unit (De Giosa 2024: 2). It is a place of communal solidarity and identity, and its heritage is in some way tied to ethnicity. However, I will suggest in the following section that the ethnic heterogeneities of these neighborhood communities are being glossed over as part of a heritage-making process (Tajudeen 2012).

Heritage Making in Melaka: The Gazetting of Kampung Morten as "Malay Village" and the Redevelopment of Bunga Raya Pantai

The heritage of Melaka's kampungs is woven by heterogeneous patterns and home to the types of mixed ethnic families, traditions, and religious beliefs that are ubiquitous to the "Straits Region" (Tajudeen 2012: 213). However, processes of urban densification that have accelerated in response to the city's increased tourist popularity endanger this vernacular cosmopolitan heritage. I take the recent transformation of two neighboring urban wards in Melaka as a departure point for an analysis of how these densification processes—and different transformations of two kampung—relate to colonial frames and racial stereotypes continued by national policies.

Tajudeen (2012: 213) argues that two typical building types of the region—the "kampung house" and the "shophouse"—have historically been associated with the two diasporic groups, "Malay" and "Chinese." However, his research shows that there was, in fact, "early on developed syntheses that problematize purely 'Malay' or 'Chinese' categorization, and that bear out multiethnic involvement in their production and use" (Tajudeen 2012: 213). He further argues that "despite this complexity of origins, the architectural and socio-cultural narratives constructed for kampung houses and shophouses have tended toward entanglement with colonial assumptions on race that have enjoyed continued currency in national-heritage projects" (Tajudeen 2012: 213). According to these racial stereotypes, the Malay and the Chinese represented rural life and urban life respectively, with the kampung houses being typically Malay, and therefore rural, and the shophouses typically Chinese, and therefore urban. This practice of binary categorization, purifying perceived tendencies in complex social relationships, has later been associated more generally with modernity through such notions as "discursive power" (Foucault 1982, 1995) or even the scientific method at large (Latour 1993). Tajudeen (2012: 213) links this way of framing—and the particular racial frames themselves—to European imperialism. He further argues that these frames have continued currency in national-heritage projects, two of these being the redevelopment and rebranding of Melaka as a national heritage site and role of the kampung in this transformation (Tajudeen 2012: 213).

Kampung Morten and Bunga Raya Pantai are two neighborhoods located next to each other on each side of the Melaka River, right outside the buffer zone. Over the last decades, these two areas have taken vastly different paths. Kampung Morten, comprising a predominately Malay-Muslim population (but also Chinese, Arab, and other ethnic backgrounds), has, since 1998, been gazetted as a "traditional Malay village" and stands today as a tourist attraction (Tuah 2013; Tajudeen 2012: 237). Bunga Raya Pantai was technically a kampung as well, containing numerous kampung houses, of which what remains is only a Taoist temple ("Hǎi Lóng Gōng"). Previously home to a predominately Straits-Born Chinese (*peranakan*) community, which has now been resettled elsewhere, the houses have been demolished to make way for the city's highest building, The Shore.

Despite the dramatic impact this redevelopment and resettlement has had on the urban fabric and its heritage, very little knowledge is accessible about this process and the former community. The relative silence speaks for itself: Why this community? Both areas are located right in the "building zone" on the outer skirts of the circle that separates the buffer zone from the remaining part of the city. The need for more square meters—and a general urbanization—required densification, and the area around the heritage core is the most attractive and thus expensive. While the value of social communities and their heritage cannot be put in formulas or numbers, decisions clearly reflect a choice of weighted benefits. In this regard, it is interesting to consider the role that the kampung plays in Malaysian national heritage making.

Mundane and ubiquitous to the region, the kampung hasn't always been considered valuable heritage. Considered by the state as sites of rural regress, they have been replaced by modern housing, but recently—in response to trends in the World Heritage system—Malaysian heritage politics has developed an interest in vernacular heritage (De Giosa 2024: 2).

With this increased awareness of "the vernacular" and "the cosmopolitan" in relation to heritage, local authorities now label selected vernacular settlements associated with representative Melakan communities as *kampung warisan* (De Giosa 2024: 2)[1]. However, as Tajudeen (2012) has shown, the government's treatment of the kampung heritage relates to racial policies operating within colonial frames. He argues that the history of the architecture and socio-culture of both kampung houses and shophouses speaks against these stereotypes (Tajudeen 2012). In fact, these two building types worked as a lingua franca between the different communities of colonial Melaka's heterogeneous urban landscape (Tajudeen 2012). In this way, it was precisely because of their "commonness" and heterogeneity (in styles and use) that these building types could be a "common ground" in a heterogeneous urban society—a vernacular heritage and a source of social resilience to the urban society that gave form to them (Tajudeen 2012).

Take, for example, the type of kampung house called *rumah limas* of which Melaka's most well-known is Villa Sentosa in Kampung Morten, which was built in 1920 and transformed into a "living museum" in 1991 (Tajudeen 2012). These houses originated from the Straits region but "showed adaptations thought to be derived from Dutch-colonial antecedents in terms of the roof form and overall massing. The structural and ornamental techniques, meanwhile, remained Malay, but the house plan underwent some modification from the Malay Plan" (Tajudeen 2012: 220). In this way, different mixed cultures put their stamp on the building type.

Kampung Morten's history makes an interesting case. The kampung came to existence when the residents of Kampung Jawa in 1920 were relocated by plans for the city's new "Central Market", and they resettled in the area now called Kampung Morten (Tajudeen 2012: 236). Despite the neighborhood's relatively new and rather urban history (and the modern lifestyles of the inhabitants and the materials used in the construction of some of the houses) the area—known as "Malay Village"—has been made to represent the rooted and traditional Malay. "Sandwiched" in the heart of Melaka, it's said to still retain its "rustic charm" (Murali 2018). Yet, it feels more urban than rural, and ironically it never really was rural, as it was built by an urban population.

It appears as though the heritage narratives constructed around Kampung Morten become harder to retain. It is now part of a heritage

---

1   Such settlements included Baba Nyonya Heritage Village (along Heeren Street and Jonker Street), Kampung Chetti, Kampung Morten, and the Portuguese Settlement (De Giosa 2024: 2).

landscape, which, while containing a rich vernacular cosmopolitan heritage, is changing into what Tajudeen (2012: 214) has described as "chinatownification." In 1971, a state-sponsored conference on national culture in Malaysia declared that "national culture must be based on the indigenous culture of the region," meaning that the hybrid layers of Melaka were reduced to a simple division of Malay, Chinese, and Indian (Worden 2010: 133). The city now has its "Chinatown" in the historical core (Upeh), its "Little India" in the area around Jalan Bendara, and its "Malay Village" with Kampung Morten.

While Kampung Morten comprises a predominately Malay-Muslim population fitted into the heritage narratives, Bunga Raya Pantai presented a contradictory and perhaps challenging reality. In 2012, at the time of our visit to Melaka, the redevelopment of Bunga Raya Pantai had already been under way for a while, and the former inhabitants had relocated to other parts of the city. In a Taoist temple surrounded by trees and barely visible from the river, a number of these former inhabitants gathered on weekends to play "Mah Jong." The caretaker of the temple kept a pile of local newspaper articles about the redevelopment of the area on a shelf. To the community, the newspaper articles helped to shape a timeline of the redevelopment, and additionally bear witness to the differential treatment of Kampung Morten, which they viewed as preferential. Over the course of our stay in Melaka, we visited the temple on several occasions, and every time there were new and unfamiliar faces—inhabitants who had lost their home but now tried not to lose their community as well. To them, the temple was more than a community center and a space of shared religious belief. It was a last bastion against the overwhelming—literally and metaphorically—power of the developers and government politics. Apart from the temple, there were only a couple of houses left on the land that used to belong to the kampung. We visited one of them. It belonged to a family which was in the process of relocating. The mother showed us through the house and into the "backyard," which was now a construction site. Theatrically, the dad sat in a plastic chair on the edge of his cadaster overlooking the construction, his head bent forward.

On the grounds of the former kampung now stands the tallest building in Melaka with forty-two stories (De Giosa 2024). The high-rise was completed in 2014 and houses a hotel from which you can overlook Kampung Morten (De Giosa 2024). Why did the two neighborhoods take such different paths? To the former inhabitants of Bunga Raya Pantai, it was clear that this in part was connected to the Malay-Muslim heritage of Kampung Morten, which they linked to a preferential treatment of this ethnic group over the

Sino-Malay in Malaysian racial politics at large.[2] With that said, the caretaker of the Taoist temple emphasized that the two communities used to have a very good relationship, but that the urban redevelopment had made it hard to keep up the good spirit. As compensation, the government paid RM 1.45 million to the forty-two property owners and tenants of Bunga Raya Pantai following the acquisition of the area (*Star* 2012). While being an important economic compensation, the money doesn't cover the loss of a kampung community, and it also doesn't cover the loss of its heritage.

Heritage Lost? Cosmopolitan Melaka's Uncertain Future

In my analysis, I have focused more on understanding and making visible how heritage is being handled and transformed than on describing the heritage itself. However, I would argue that important vernacular heritage was lost with the redevelopment of Bunga Raya Pantai, and with the segregation of the former community that this action involved. The community's heritage used to present something that is (or was!) ubiquitous to Melaka: an urban ward of kampung houses built by individuals belonging to a community that is socially heterogeneous and encapsulated in diasporic histories. While common to Melaka—an urbanism with a distinctively cosmopolitan history—it is special to the world.

It is precisely in the mundane that the source of Melaka's unique cosmopolitan heritage can be found, and thereby also the source of a local (social) resilience. It is found with the kampung. It is found with hybrid cultural and religious practices, such as when a child uses a combination of Hindu and Chinese practices for performing a prayer, or when a woman describes her identity in Malaysia as "Chindian" (Mukhopadhyay 2012). It is found within the everyday stories of people whose ways of "being in this world" are deeply embedded in an urban fabric that comprises layers of knowledge, which, while local, is simultaneously global.

One might argue that Melaka's complex and multicultural urban fabric is inseparably intertwined with its colonial history. Yet, I argue that the vernacular heritage is profoundly decolonizing. It is precisely the fact that the heritage is hard to understand and place within the colonial frameworks that makes it so important to the local communities—and beyond them to the world community. Take, for example, the hybrid identity of the

---

2 Malaysia is "avowedly communitarian, or race-based, in its formula for political representation" (Tajudeen 2012: 242). For more on this topic see Cartier 1993; King 2012.

kampung house. It constituted a resistance to the colonial frames that continues to influence national-heritage narratives along the lines of racial stereotypes. This heritage held a decolonizing potential to release itself from false perceptions: it left traces of resistance.

The pressing question is, how much of this heritage—of this resistance—will be left in the future? And how can we best preserve it? I don't have the final answers to this question, but I will say that there is a danger in considering a "collection" of separated ethnic neighborhoods reflective of an urban cosmopolitanism. Rather than making cosmopolitan heritage, trying to better understand the social conditions of this phenomenon and the role it plays for local communities might be one way forward. This chapter has been a contribution to this endeavor. In this moment, I trust that the members of the former community of Bunga Raya Pantai continue to gather in the Taoist temple on weekends to play mahjong, as they have done for decades.

References

Adair, Stephen. 2008. "Status and Solidarity: A Reformulation of Early Durkheimian Theory." *Sociological Inquiry* 78 (1): 97–120. https://doi.org/10.1111/j.1475-682X.2008.00223.x.

Binnie, Jon, Julian Holloway, and Steve Millington. 2006. "Introduction: Grounding Cosmopolitan Urbanism: Approaches, Practices and Policies." In *Cosmopolitan Urbanism*, edited by Jon Binnie, Julian Holloway, Steve Millington, and Craig Young, 1-34. New York and London: Routledge.

Böhme, Gernot. 1993. "Atmosphere as a Fundamental Concept of a New Aesthetics." *Thesis Eleven* 36: 113–26.

Bourdieu, Pierre. 1987. "What Makes a Social Class? On the Theoretical and Practical Existence of Groups." *Berkeley Journal of Sociology* 32: 1–17.

Calhoun, Craig. 2002. "The Class Consciousness of Frequent Travellers: Towards a Critique of Actually Existing Cosmopolitanism." In *Convincing Cosmopolitanism: Theory, Context, and Practice*, edited by Steven Vertovec and Robin Cohen, 86–109. Oxford: Oxford University Press.

Cartier, Carolyn. 1993. "Creating Historic Open Space in Melaka." *The Geographical Review* 83: 359–73.

Chernilo, Daniel. 2009. "Cosmopolitanism and Social Theory." In *The New Blackwell Companion to Social Theory*, edited by Bryan S. Turner, 533–50. Hoboken: Wiley-Blackwell.

Collins, Randall. 1988. *Theoretical Sociology*. San Diego: Harcourt Brace Jovanovich.

Collins, Randall. 2004. *Interaction Ritual Chains*. Princeton: Princeton University Press.

De Genova, Nicholas. 2002. "Migrant 'Illegality' and Deportability in Everyday Life. *Annual Review of Anthropology 31*: 419–47.

De Giosa, Pierpaolo. 2025. "'Like the Story of the Camel and his Master!': A Melakan Village between Vernacular Heritage and Urban Transformation." In *Resilience as Heritage in Asia*. Amsterdam: Amsterdam University Press.

Durkheim, Emile. [1893] 1984. *The Division of Labour in Society*. New York: The Free Press.

Durkheim, Emile. [1897] 2005. "Review of Antonio Labriola, Essays on the Materialist Conception of History." In *Readings from Emile Durkheim*, edited by Kenneth Thompson, 18-23. London & New York: Routledge.

Foucault, Michel. 1982. "The Subject and Power." *Critical Inquiry* 8: 777–95.

Foucault, Michel. 1995. *Discipline and Punish: The Birth of the Prison*. Translated by Alan Sheridan. New York: Vintage Books.

Hannerz, Ulf. 1996. *Transnational Connections: Culture, People, Places*. Routledge: London.

Hillier, Bill, and Julianne Hanson. 1984. *The Social Logic of Space*. Cambridge: Cambridge University Press.

Kant, Immanuel. (1795) 1999. "Toward Perpetual Peace." In *Practical Philosophy – Cambridge Edition of the Works of Immanuel Kant*. Translated by M.J. Gregor, 311-352. Cambridge: Cambridge University Press.

Laquian, Aprodicio. 1996. "The Multi-Ethnic and Multicultural City: An Asian Perspective." *International Social Science Journal* 48 (147): 43–54.

Latham, Alan. 2003. "Urbanity, Lifestyle and Making Sense of the New Urban Cultural Economy: Notes from Auckland, New Zealand." *Urban Studies* 40 (9): 1699–724.

Latour, Bruno. 1993. *We Have Never Been Modern*. Translated by Catherine Porter. Cambridge, MA: Harvard University Press.

Keyes, Charles. 2012. "'Cosmopolitan' Villagers and Populist Democracy in Thailand." *South East Asia Research* 20 (3): 343–60.

King, Victor. 2012. "UNESCO in Melaka: Cultural Politics, Identities and Tourism in a World Heritage Site." *Leeds East Asia Papers*, New Series No. 4, e-series.

Nussbaum, Martha. 1997. "Kant and Stoic Cosmopolitanism." *The Journal of Political Philosophy* 5 (1): 1–15.

Sahlins, Marshall. 1974. *Stone Age Economics*. London: Tavistock Publications.

Tajudeen, Imran Bin. 2012. "Beyond Racialized Representation: Architectural Linguæ Francæ and Urban Histories in the Kampung Houses and Shophouses of Melaka and Singapore." In *Colonial Frames, Nationalist Histories: Imperial Legacies, Architecture and Modernity*, edited by Mrinalini Rajagopalan and Madhuri Desai, 213–52. Farnham: Ashgate Publishing.

Thijssen, Peter. 2012. "From Mechanical to Organic Solidarity, and Back: With Honneth Beyond Durkheim." *European Journal of Social Theory* 15 (4): 454–70. https://doi.org/10.1177/1368431011423589.

Turner, Bryan. 2000. "Cosmopolitan Virtue: Loyalty and the City." In *Democracy, Citizenship and the Global City*, edited by E. Isin, 129-147. London: Routledge.

Wallace Deborah and Wallace Rodrick. 2011. "Consequences of Massive Housing Destruction: the New York City Fire Epidemic." *Building Research & Information* 39 (4).

Werbner, Pnina. 1999. "Global Pathways. Working Class Cosmopolitans and the Creation of Transnational Ethnic Worlds." *Social Anthropology* 7 (1): 17–35.

Werbner, Pnina. 2006. "Understanding Vernacular Cosmopolitanism." *Anthropology News* 47 (5): 7–11.

Werbner, Pnina. 2013. "Paradoxes of Postcolonial Vernacular Cosmopolitanism in South Asia and the Diaspora." In *Ashgate Research Companion to Cosmopolitanism*, edited by Maria Rovisco and Magdalena Nowicka, 107–24. London: Taylor & Francis.

Widodo, Johannes. 2011. "Melaka – A Cosmopolitan City in Southeast Asia." *Review of Culture -International Edition 40*, Instituto Cultural do Governo da R.A.E. de Macau.

Worden, Nigel. 2010. "National Identity and Heritage Tourism in Melaka." In *Heritage Tourism in Southeast Asia*, edited by Michael Hitchcock, Victor T. King, and Michael Parnwell, 130-148. Copenhagen: NIAS Press.

Yamagata, Yoshiki, and Ayyoob Sharifi. 2018. "Resilience-Oriented Urban Planning." In *Resilience-Oriented Urban Planning*, edited by Yoshiki Yamagata and Ayyoob Sharifi, 3–27. Cham: Springer.

Website Content

Atan, Hamidah. 2000. "Saving Old Kampung Morten." *New Straits Times*. 7 February 2000. http://news.google.com/newspapers?nid=1309&dat=20000207&id=W8wy-AAAAIBAJ&sjid=ZBQEAAAAIBAJ&pg=6758,587872. Accessed 8 October 2014.

ICOMOS. 1999. "Charter on the Built Vernacular Heritage." https://www.icomos.org/en/participer/179-articles-en-francais/ressources/charters-and-standards/164-charter-of-the-built-vernacular-heritage.

Laurtius, Diogenes. n.d. *Lives of Eminent Philosophers.* Translated by R.D. Hicks. Cambridge: Harvard University Press, 1925. *Perseus Digital Library.* http://www.perseus.tufts.edu/hopper/text?doc=Perseus%3Atext%3A1999.01.0258%3A-book%3D6%3Achapter%3D2. Accessed 10 October 2014.

Mukhopadhyay, Ankita. 2012. "Melaka." *Asia Now* (blog). http://asianow2012.blogspot.dk/p/melaka.html. Accessed 12 October 2014.

Murali, R.S.N. 2018. "Kampung Morten is where tourists to the historical city get a taste of local culture." *Star*. 9 July 2018. https://www.thestar.com.my/metro/focus/2018/07/09/melakas-showcase-malay-village-kampung-morten-is-where-tourists-to-the-historical-city-get-a-taste-o. Accessed 17 December 2019.

Star. 2012. "Land for Redevelopment." Accessed 17 December 2019. http://www.thestar.com.my/story/?file=%2f2009%2f12%2f4%2fsouthneast%2f5219010&sec=southneast.

Tuah. 2013. "Kampung Morten – A Living Museum in the Middle of Melaka Town." *MelakaCool*. 19 February 2013. https://melakacool.com/kg-morten-village-middle-melaka-town/. Accessed 19 January 2022.

UNESCO. 2022. "Melaka and George Town, Historic Cities of the Straits of Melacca." https://whc.unesco.org/en/list/1223/multiple=1&unique_number=1871. Accessed 29 October 2022.

Varshney, Ashutosh. 2014. "Ethnic Conflict in Urban Asia." *Items*. 24 June 2014. https://items.ssrc.org/the-cities-papers/ethnic-conflict-in-urban-asia/.

"Vernacular Heritage." *Going Beyond Heritage and Sustainability* (blog). n.d. https://heritageandsustainability.wordpress.com/context/vernacular-heritage/. Accessed 13 January 2020.

About the Author

Kim Nørgaard Helmersen, born 1987 in Denmark, studied sociology at the University of Copenhagen and received his doctorate at the ETH Zurich, department of architecture, in 2023. Kim works as a postdoctoral researcher at the ETH Zurich.

4. "Like the Story of the Camel and His Master!": A Melakan Village between Vernacular Heritage and Urban Transformation

Pierpaolo De Giosa

Abstract: Ten years after UNESCO World Heritage inscription, Melaka displays a key dilemma of such designations for Asian cities. Despite assiduous preservation efforts, surrounding neighborhoods—especially the "heritage villages" (*kampung warisan*) at the fringes of the World Heritage site—face massive transformation. Long neglected by official schemes, these enclaves benefit from global interest in vernacular architecture but remain trapped in a fundamental asymmetry. Kampung Chetti, a creolized Indian community, sought to exploit the liberating effects of "heritage village" status to oppose an adjacent high-rise project, illustrating how local communities mobilize heritage discourses to enhance resilience and envision alternative futures. Although, as in other Malaysian communities, its struggle failed, it illustrates international and national institutions' unpreparedness—despite their participatory rhetoric—to accommodate a human-scale vernacular city.

Keywords: heritage village, infill development, Kampung Chetti, Melaka, Malaysia

Introduction

Ten years after UNESCO World Heritage inscription, Melaka displays one of the dilemmas generated by such designations in Asian cities. While the World Heritage site experiences assiduous conservation efforts, the surrounding neighborhoods face large-scale real estate development catering

Herzfeld, M., and R. Padawangi, eds. *Resilience as Heritage in Asia*. Amsterdam: Amsterdam University Press, 2025.
DOI: 10.5117/9789463728560_CH04

to investors and tourists. Among the most affected by this trend are the tiny low-rise "heritage villages" (*kampung warisan*) at the fringes of the World Heritage site. To Mr. Kumar, a man in his sixties who grew up in one of these villages, namely Kampung Chetti, this situation resembled the fable of the camel and his master. On a cold night, the story tells, the camel asked his master to put his head inside the tent. When the master agreed, the camel asked him to go further until, step by step, there was not enough space for both of them, and finally the camel pushed the master out. Mr. Kumar often referred to this fable to address his concerns about the developments around Kampung Chetti. He feared that, just like the master, his *kampung* would have no space in the city of the future.

The *kampung* is a resilient element of vernacular urbanism in a significant part of Southeast Asia. In Malaysia, Indonesia, and Singapore the word *kampung*, usually translated as "village," holds different layers of meaning. In the contemporary Malaysian discourse, *kampung* as an administrative unit (Shamsul 1996: 142) refers predominantly to the rural settlements of the Malay ethnic majority (Ghazali 2013: 122; Thompson 2006: 79). Nevertheless, in its everyday usage, the word also refers to rural-like neighborhoods absorbed by urban growth, and not necessarily inhabited by Malays. In Melaka, for instance, besides Malay urban villages such as Kampung Morten, we find places connected to other ethnic and religious communities like the abovementioned Kampung Chetti or the Perkampungan Portugis (Portuguese Settlement). Beyond its physical and spatial connotation, the *kampung* as a sociocultural construct bears a strong emotional meaning as "home" and "moral community" (see Shamsul 1996: 142; Thompson 2006: 79), a place of affective bond and communal solidarity for its inhabitants and those who grew up in one of them.

For the greater part of the twentieth century, such urban vernacular neighborhoods have been neglected by historic conservation policies, and often threatened by urban development. Considered by the state an "eyesore" (Goh 2002: 62) and sites of anti-urban backwardness, Malaysian *kampung* have been replaced by high-rises and megaprojects: a global urban developmentalist agenda with parallels in other Asian countries where centuries-old neighborhoods and community spaces have been sacrificed in the name of development and national heritage projects.[1] By focusing on this trend, Douglass (2013: 133–4) notes that in Asia the

---

1   See, notably, studies focusing on other Asian countries, such as, for example, China (e.g. Arkaraprasertkul 2012; Zhang 2006), Thailand (Askew 1996; Herzfeld 2016), or Vietnam (Harms 2011).

"corporate globopolis" of state- and capital-led projects is prevailing at the expense of the vernacular city. Hence the state's conception of city *kampung* as obsolete obstacles to progress rather than as something to preserve for future generations. In this regard, a long-term priority accorded to the preservation of tangible-cum-monumental (and often colonial; see Padawangi 2015) heritage contributed to the exclusion of the vernacular urban fabric and the everyday practices of residents from official heritage schemes. Yet since the 1990s, in the name of global reform responding to criticism of a top-down, Western-derived, and monument-obsessed approach, UNESCO-related bodies and nation-states started to promote "a less elite, more vernacular, and broadly anthropological conception of cultural heritage" (Brumann 2018: 22) together with an emerging interest in the intangible aspect and increasing talk of local community involvement (Brumann 2015).

This chapter is concerned with two main questions. First, how do these global and national shifts affect local heritage-making processes? Second, do the recent vernacular heritage and community participation discourses empower residents who feel vulnerable in the face of urban transformation? By focusing on Kampung Chetti, I will trace first the process of "heritagization" (e.g., De Cesari 2013: 400) of this particular settlement in the context of an increasing interest in vernacular architecture and cultural diversity. Then I will tell the story of the Chetti's struggle against a high-rise project adjacent to their *kampung*. This local specificity helps us to understand the challenges of urban transformation faced by other *kampung warisan* in Melaka (see also Ong 2017). Although recognized by the state of Melaka as heritage sites, they are at the bottom of a patrimonial hierarchy and excluded from UNESCO-derived and national heritage regulations. Fieldwork among the Chetti offers a lens for examining both more intimate understandings of heritage beyond official categorizations—such as tangible/intangible and monumental/vernacular—and the ways in which residents appropriate global idioms of conservation in order to build resilience vis-à-vis urban transformation pressures. But it is not my aim to tell a story of victims and villains, or to build up a tale of heritage conservation versus urban development. As I was often told by those who are concerned with the path of urban transformation in Melaka, "We are not against development! But..." These interlocutors were interested in alternative ways of developing the city without affecting its existing built, natural, and social environments. Resilience here is not understood as bias against urban change but instead points to the willingness of residents in shaping a human-scale city by resorting to a Lefebvrian "right to the city" (Lefebvre 2000).

The ethnographic material presented here draws on fifteen months of fieldwork carried out between 2012 and 2014 for a larger project exploring the global/local nexus of heritage politics.[2] I interviewed bureaucrats and officials from the federal to the municipal level, local politicians, real estate agents, academics, and a wide range of conservationists, from heritage experts and professionals to activists and aficionados. The ethnography presented in this chapter nevertheless relies heavily on participant observation among and conversations with members of the Chetti community.[3] Before dealing with Kampung Chetti between heritage making and urban transformation, let me briefly introduce the site and the people connected to it.

Kampung Chetti: The People and the Setting

The Chetti community is the result of old and new diasporas, resettlements, and interethnic exchanges connecting in the present the *kampung* in various ways to Melaka as a whole, India, Malaysia, and Singapore. The Chetti are the descendants of the Hindu merchants from South India who already settled in Melaka during the sultanate era. After the Portuguese conquest of 1511, colonial accounts report that these merchants were living downtown on the western bank of the Melaka River. Thanks to a land grant obtained by the Dutch, they built their first temple, called Sri Poyyatha Venayagar Moorthi, in the city center at the end of the eighteenth century; it is still the oldest functioning Hindu temple in Malaysia. With the increasing monopolization of trade in Dutch hands, however, the Chetti ventured into new activities such as goldsmithing, masonry, and farming. Furthermore, they moved to the northwestern inland part of the town, around what is now called Kampung Chetti. Since then, and throughout the British and post-independence years, the community has experienced a sort of decline with the more prosperous (as well as many others) moving elsewhere, especially Kuala Lumpur and Singapore.[4]

2   This work has been supported by the Max Planck Institute for Social Anthropology while I was a member of the research group "The Global Political Economy of Cultural Heritage" between 2011 and 2016. I would like to thank the convenors of the conference "The Resilience of Vernacular Heritage in Asian Cities" Mike Douglass and Rita Padawangi. To her and Michael Herzfeld I offer my grateful thanks for their invaluable comments on the chapter.
3   I use pseudonyms in order to ensure the anonymity of my interlocutors.
4   For detailed historical accounts of the Chetti community, see Dhoraisingam 2006; Narinasamy 1983.

Physically, this two-hectare *kampung* does not differ from other districts in the region, but its spatial configuration resembles the strong interrelationship between the residents themselves, the land, and the tutelary village deities (*gramādevatās* [Sanskrit]) as observed in South India (e.g., Fuller 2004: 128). The Chetti are fervent Shaivites and their houses stand around temples devoted to major deities. The main temple, dedicated to Sri Muthu Mariamman and built in 1822, is located in the center of the *kampung*. Two other temples, the Sri Kailasanathar (dedicated to Shiva) and the Sri Anggala Parameswari, are located at the main entrance and the northern side of the village, respectively. Only the Sri Kaliamman Temple is outside the *kampung*, in the northern surrounding area of Bachang once used primarily for agricultural purposes. This area, now occupied mainly by low-cost flats and terraced houses, was associated with wilderness in the past in contraposition to the inhabited village space, and it is still home to shrines, called *grammanggal kuil*, devoted to the deities Sri Iyenar, Sri Katai Amman, Sri Dharma Raja, Sri Amman, and Sri Ganghaderi Amman. The location of these places of worship defines the spiritual and everyday life of the village and, as community elders told me, there would not have been a Kampung Chetti without temples: "We are one *kampung*, one temple!"

There are approximately sixty houses in the village; almost half are inhabited by Chetti, slightly more than one hundred souls, and most of the other houses belong to local Chinese (e.g., PERZIM n.d.). While the houses are private properties, they still stand on land belonging to the Chetti community. As in the past, regardless of ethnicity and religion, each household pays a nominal monthly rent. Made of wood, concrete, bricks, and corrugated zinc or asbestos roofs, the houses are predominantly one or two stories in height. The steep, sloping roofs resemble the design of traditional houses in the region, with gables that allow ventilation in order to cope with the equatorial climate. According to my interlocutors, the most distinctive element of a traditional Chetti house is the *thinnai*, a raised platform on either side of the front door where guests are usually received. Today only a couple of houses have such a permanent platform. Despite this, the verandahs of the other houses still maintain this function with chairs and benches. The front doors are decorated with images of deities. Below those images, the Chetti are also accustomed to hang decorations made of mango leaves tied together in odd numbers with a rattan string. The string symbolizes protection from evil, whereas the leaves embody the unity of the household. The houses are often divided into two main parts: a main hall or core house at the front and the kitchen in the back, a widespread division of domestic space in the region. In the front halls, the Chetti keep an altar for the deities that are used for daily *puja* (worship). About ten houses in the village have a prominent role as *rumah abu* (ancestral houses). Besides the altar to the deities, these houses have a special altar for the departed ancestors. The different descent groups gather, twice every year, at their own ancestral houses for special prayers and food offerings to the ancestors.

Kampung Chetti, together with the places of worship just mentioned, is managed by the Sri Poyyatha Venayagar Moorthi Temple Management Committee (hereafter SPVMT Committee). This committee consists of fifteen democratically elected members, including three trustees who are community elders. It is responsible for the welfare of the community, the maintenance of the temples, and the organization of religious festivals and cultural activities. The most vibrant celebration in the Chetti calendar year is undoubtedly the ten-day festival for the worship of Mariamman. During this period, Kampung Chetti attracts hundreds of people: not just Chetti and other Hindus, but also other devotees, especially local Chinese.[5] But the SPVMT Committee is not the only player in the organization of the community religious and social life, since it can count on the support of *kampung* residents and other Chetti living nearby. Elders and women, especially, play an active role in a wide range of *gotong royong* works (mutual aid), from after-school to cleaning activities.

The concentration of families in this tiny area protected the community from disintegration (Narinasamy 1983: 244) and helped to sustain a way of life rich in traditions and spiritual activities transmitted from one generation to another. Most of my interlocutors are proud of the resulting distinctive character of the *kampung*. The *kampung* thus functions as a gathering place for Chetti living elsewhere and keeps alive a sense of moral community. Nevertheless, Kampung Chetti as a community space has had to face some challenges throughout the years. The scarcity of space and consequently the shortage of housing are, for example, a constraint for other Chetti who wish to live there. Although many decided on their own to leave, or have left Melaka because of job opportunities elsewhere (see Narinasamy 1983: 261),[6] today some of my interlocutors, especially retirees like Mr. Kumar,

---

5   For specific studies on the Mariamman festival and other Chetti rituals, see De Giosa 2016; Dhoraisingam 2006; Mearns 1995.

6   Melaka has experienced decline since the nineteenth century. The British encouraged the transfer of trade and people from Melaka to the two other Straits Settlements (Newbold 1839: 126–7), and many Chetti took government jobs especially in Singapore (Dhoraisingam 2006: 16–17). This trend continued also after independence, with the state of Melaka being "the top state of out-migration" until the 1990s (Saw 2015: 47).

often express their wish to go back to the *kampung*, a wish complicated by the housing shortage.

The most critical challenge, however, comes from the pressures of urban development. To maintain the collective ownership of a residential area in the middle of the city is not an easy task for the SPVMT Committee and for a community with relatively modest financial means. Furthermore, there is always the possibility that some leaders will follow their own interests regardless of the *kampung* status as charity land held in trust by the committee for the community. For example, as Goh observed (2002) in Penang, the Roman Catholic Church launched a joint venture with a real estate company for the development of Kampung Serani at the expense of its long-term ground tenants. I was even told that in the past a Chetti trustee attempted to sell community properties to developers. Thus, the community members have to ensure that the leadership operates in the interest of common goals and needs.

Throughout the years, a couple of projects gave the community cause for concern. On one occasion, for example, the Sri Kaliamman Temple in Bachang was relocated and rebuilt to make space for new shopping complexes. The other project was the extension of a road proposed by the city council in the 1990s. By cutting through the *kampung*, this road was meant to solve the problem of traffic congestion on the way to the city center (see De Giosa 2021; Ong 2017). Such a project, however, would also have meant tearing down some houses and would additionally have involved serious repercussions for ordinary and religious activities. Although this plan was put aside because of community opposition, fear returned with the adjacent high-rise project. Before dealing with the ways in which the community addresses urban transformation pressures, however, I will present the making of Kampung Chetti as a heritage village, a strategy that reevaluates this place vis-à-vis a much more glorified monumental heritage while giving the community the hope of remaining in the city—a vernacular space where the "social time" of everyday life coexists with the "monumental time" of folklore (see Herzfeld 1991).

The Making of a Heritage Village

Place attachment to Kampung Chetti is crucial for the community, even for those living elsewhere and to whom it is the only place to *balik kampung* (a Malay catchphrase literally meaning "going home" and used by migrants returning to their hometowns during festive occasions). Furthermore, while describing the *kampung*, many of my Chetti interlocutors used the words *harta nenek moyang* (or "inheritance of the ancestors"), a choice of wording that designates this place as familial and community heritage par excellence. This conceptualization of heritage, which is strongly intertwined with emotions of respect and fear for the deceased kin, highlights the high sense of the moral responsibility to take care of what has been left by the ancestors. Referring directly to the ancestors, or *nenek moyang*, instead of the more neutral English term "heritage" and its Malay versions (such as *warisan* and *pusaka*), makes a significant difference. As the late Mr. Shanmugam, one of the greatest heritage and history lovers I ever met among the Chetti, told me: "When you tell *pusaka*, you are not afraid. You don't worry. [But] you say *nenek moyang*, I'm scared. If the *nenek moyang* are angry, we are in trouble!"

Besides this more intimate understanding of Kampung Chetti as ancestral and community heritage, the village has acquired a place in the official politics of *warisan*. This is the national form (originally meaning "inheritance," from the Arabic word for "heir," *warith*) used by officialdom to translate the all-encompassing category of heritage. Nevertheless, the cooptation of Kampung Chetti in official heritage-making processes is relatively recent; the site had been somewhat marginal to Malaysian heritage politics until the 1990s.

There are two main reasons behind such a long absence. First, for the greater part of the twentieth century the legal framework concerning the preservation of items of historical relevance was based on European and colonial principles that privileged architectural grandeur and monumental heritage. Melaka is a case in point. From the 1920s on, for example, British administrators, the local elite, and Christian priests have been particularly interested in the restoration of old Dutch buildings and in excavations of archaeological artifacts. After independence, the Antiquities Act (1976) itself inherited the colonial conservation philosophy. There was no reference yet to any concept of heritage or *warisan*, and only objects, sites, and buildings that were at least a hundred years old were considered worthy of protection as antiquities. Thereafter, the federal government mostly listed colonial buildings, and did not yet include ordinary spaces of residence (see Malaysia 2008: 132). Much the same quantitative patrimonial approach still influences part of the old guard among the bureaucrats in heritage-related bureaus. I was told by a local bureaucrat in her sixties, for instance, that most houses in Kampung Chetti cannot be really considered as heritage because they are less than a century old.[7]

---

7   For more details on the official politics of heritage in Melaka and Malaysia, see De Giosa 2020; De Giosa 2021.

Second, the marginalization of such ethnic enclaves was entangled in racial politics. In a country where colonial-derived categories of race are a constant of official discourses and everyday life, the population is divided into four macro-groups: 69.4 percent *Bumiputera* or "sons of the soil" (largely constituted by Malays, in distinction to other indigenous people), 23.2 percent Chinese, 6.7 percent Indians, and 0.7 percent others.[8] The Barisan Nasional (National Front) coalition, which governed without interruption until 2018, follows this division with three major constituent parties: UMNO (United Malays National Organisation) as the dominant one, MCA (Malaysian Chinese Association), and MIC (Malaysian Indian Congress). During the perennial UMNO-led administrations, Malay-focused nationalism also characterized the nation-building process and heritage politics. This was clear when the federal government introduced the National Culture Policy in the 1970s. It mandated that Malaysian Culture would be based exclusively on indigenous cultures and Islam, with the eventual inclusion of suitable elements from other ethnic groups. Again, Melaka, as the glorified seat of the first Malay sultanate, is a case in point. The old civic area in the city center was reclaimed as a symbol of Malay heritage (King 2016: 153; Worden 2001: 204) through a gradual process of museumification and replication (De Giosa 2021). From the 1980s on, former colonial buildings have been turned into museums celebrating Malayness, Islam, and even UMNO, side by side with replicas such as that of the Sultanate Palace (which was destroyed by the Portuguese).

For a long time both the federal government and the local administration considered the World Heritage nomination of Melaka, as the celebrated cradle of the nation, a priority. Previous attempts had been fruitless because of both land reclamation at the seafront and the focus on Malayness to the disadvantage of other ethnic groups (King 2016: 159; Worden 2001: 216). Furthermore, there were still great weaknesses in the conservation bureaucracy, and local legal frameworks were still not compliant with World Heritage standards (De Giosa 2021). In the 1990s, however, a momentous convergence of local interests, the development of tourism products, new directions in the nation-building process, and global shifts in the World Heritage system opened the way to a new era of Malaysian heritage politics.

A significant role in this context was perhaps played by Vision 2020, introduced in 1991 by the then prime minister Mahathir Mohamad. Among the goals to be achieved in the new century, Mahathir called for a united

---

8   Department of Statistics Malaysia, last accessed 14 December 2024, https://open.dosm.gov.my/dashboard/kawasanku.

"Malaysian nation" (*Bangsa Malaysia*), thereby revising former Malay-dominated cultural policies in favor of a much more inclusive Malaysian heritage. While the meaning of *Bangsa Malaysia* remains vague, Vision 2020 opened the way to new modes of representations that more completely satisfied the current demands of cultural tourism. "Malaysia, Truly Asia" campaigns clearly promote the country as a harmonious multicultural mosaic. This vision became the cornerstone in the workings of the Department of National Heritage, the federal body established by the National Heritage Act, which was a brand-new law that replaced the Antiquities Act in 2005. In fact, the department started to list for protection various monuments and other items of importance for each ethnic group. The emphasis on multiculturalism was also one of the main strengths of the nomination dossier that brought Melaka onto the World Heritage List in 2008. The dossier displayed the contribution of the Malays, the Chinese, and the Indians as well as the local creole communities—such as the Chetti, the Baba Nyonya (Straits-born Chinese), and the Eurasians—to Melaka's architectural and cultural heritage (Malaysia 2008). In this context, the state accommodated UNESCO's interests in cultural diversity as a lesson in the harmonious coexistence of different ethnic and religious groups. In addition, the success of the new Malaysian heritage politics in the World Heritage system lies in the accurate appropriation of a global conservation grammar that embraced the most recent international trends, including the interest in vernacular and intangible heritage.

At the local level, the state of Melaka already had a bill on the "Preservation and Conservation of Cultural Heritage" (hereafter Enactment 88) used to identify monuments and historical areas with the assistance of PERZIM (the Melaka Museums Corporation). Riding these waves of change, the state of Melaka started to select other sites under Enactment 88. The sites in question included non-monumental heritage and items associated with non-Malays and non-Muslims. Following a living museum model, local authorities now designate such vernacular settlements as *kampung warisan*. According to Hafstein (2007: 97), while the "Convention Concerning the Protection of the World's Cultural and Natural Heritage" (1972) treats heritage spatially as a territory, the "Convention for the Safeguarding of Intangible Cultural Heritage" (2003) identifies heritage as a community. I see *kampung warisan* as an assembled translation of these two conventions at the local level. The first of these settlements was identified along Heeren Street and Jonker Street as Baba Nyonya Heritage Village in the 1990s (Malaysia 2008: 132). Others associated with representative Melakan communities—such as Kampung Chetti, Kampung Morten, and the Portuguese Settlement—followed.

The reassessment of these settlements in official heritage schemes brings two sets of benefits into play. The first set regards identity politics in the nation-building process. Ethnic groups that had hitherto been marginalized in the national narrative finally found a place in the new pluralist heritage discourse. These designations also bring liberating effects, at least symbolically, to bear on minorities and other groups previously incorporated only with difficulty in the dominant Malay-Chinese-Indian triad. In particular, although the Chetti are officially categorized as Indians and define themselves as "orthodox" Hindus, some resort to a sort of minority complex vis-à-vis the dominant Tamil-speaking Indian Hindus. This is due to their Malay creole language and their limited knowledge of Tamil, their affinity with the Malays and other creole communities (especially the Baba Nyonya), and the blending of other local elements in their traditional cuisine, dress, music, and dance. With the new pluralist narrative, the "Indian-yet-not-so-Indian" preconception that once meant marginalization has become a resource for pride. A few families and troupes enthusiastically take part in festivals organized by the state with cooking activities, traditional ballads, and dance performances.

The second set of benefits deriving from this reassessment is a material one. Until then, the SPVMT Committee had to pay the costs of maintenance of, and restoration work on the temples alone or through fundraising. The designation as a *kampung warisan* gives the committee the opportunity to enjoy the benefits of state-led heritage projects. Furthermore, the heritagization of the *kampung* has led to the construction of attractions such as a gate decorated with two elephants' heads and a stage used for cultural performances and religious activities. Undoubtedly, however, the Chetti Museum, funded by the state of Melaka via PERZIM, remains the most important tourism product. The museum, a restored Chetti house inaugurated in 2003, displays the use of domestic space and introduces visitors to the history of the community, its traditions, and its rituals. The majority of the objects and artifacts making up the permanent exhibit have been donated by members of the community. Furthermore, with the Special Area Plan for heritage sites, the city council embraced the development of *kampung warisan* as attractions through beautification, drainage improvement, and the promotion of tourism-oriented activities such as the homestay program to host tourists, and the so-called village industry (*industri desa*), especially in the food and craft sectors (see MBMB 2008). As things stand at the time of writing, however, these proposals have not been implemented because of the *kampung*'s prevailing function as a place of residence and worship;

another factor in this delay is the lack of housing and space that has already affected the Chetti themselves.

Nevertheless, the making of *kampung warisan* brings constraints too, in the form of restrictions and changes in building maintenance practices. Local heritage bureaucrats often reminded me that nominating a *kampung warisan* is not always an easy process because it needs the consensus of all the landlords. If only one of them does not accept restrictions on renovation mandated by the relevant heritage regulations, the entire selected area cannot be registered under Enactment 88. Kampung Chetti was not an exception to this constraint. In fact, before the designation, the SPVMT Committee had to meet the agreement of all homeowners because, once the zone has been registered as a heritage area, maintenance works to each building require special permissions from PERZIM and the municipality. While, on the one hand, some homeowners displayed unease over the stricter regulations, all were proud of the recognition of their *kampung* as a heritage site.

Conversely, some interlocutors were apprehensive about the new rules to be applied to the temples. It is not unusual to tear down the old structure of a Hindu temple in order to create a new one. Building principles rooted in Hinduism do not preclude this practice on condition that the innermost sanctum of the temple, where the image of the primary deity resides (*garbha-griha* [Sanskrit]), should remain in situ. The substantial renovations of the Sri Muthu Mariamman Temple carried out in the 1990s are a clear example of this procedure. While the *garbhagriha* has been retained, the temple was extended to a remarkable degree to accommodate the increasing number of devotees. Furthermore, the SPVMT Committee commissioned massive beautification works from artisans from India; these alterations changed the temple through the addition of sculptures and a brand-new gatehouse tower (*gopuram* [Sanskrit]). Pictures of the temple before these works show a very simple structure. While such renovations works are in conflict with the current official conservation rules of keeping original forms, all my Chetti interlocutors are very proud of the new look of the temple. "Who wants a temple looking like a badminton court?" Mr. Shanmugam rhetorically demanded of me. Besides different views on aesthetic values, strict principles of conservation associated with official heritage expertise may clash with everyday practical needs and conditions. In 2006, for instance, when the SPVMT Committee asked the Department of National Heritage for help in restoring the Sri Anggala Parameswari Temple, the officials decided to bring it back to its original form. In particular, they replaced the corrugated zinc roof with terracotta tiles, the original material. Although they looked more beautiful, they were nevertheless less resistant and in need of constant maintenance that the department could not afford to finance. As a Chetti devotee pointed out, only two years later the roof was already leaking.

Despite these frictions, most Chetti were happy with the heritagization of their *kampung*, except when they started to realize that, instead of improved protection from urban transformation, the World Heritage designation resulted in an unprecedented boom in high-rise projects.

Infill Development and the Right to the City

"We are living on a gold mine!" Some of my Chetti interlocutors often so reminded me. Strangers who visit the *kampung* for the first time may think rather the opposite given that the state carried out only limited work on open drainage ditches and a retention pond area for flood prevention, and also given the lack of amenities and simple living conditions. But my interlocutors were right. When the historic city center was inscribed into the World Heritage List, the resulting boom in tourist arrivals increased land values and attracted massive interest on the part of real estate developers, especially for the so-called infill development projects (new construction on underdeveloped land within built-up areas). Confirming the "fetish for height and magnitude" (Goh 2002: 59) of the Malaysian developmentalist and modernist dream, these infill development projects are mostly high-rise luxury hotels, apartment blocks, and shopping malls targeting the middle and upper classes, tourists, and foreigners. Such changes in the cityscape represented a source of concern not only for the residents in the areas to be developed, but also for heritage professionals. "If you don't control, you will end up with high-rises around the circle!" I was told by Mr. Osman, an official from the Department of National Heritage. While telling me this, he sketched a circle with, at its center, the World Heritage site surrounded by high-rises. He added, "It's what Melaka is going to be."

When I started fieldwork, the Chetti were already busily opposing a high-rise planned for an adjacent lot. This project, approved in 2008 by the city council for construction on a two-hectare empty plot, consisted of a twenty-two-story commercial-cum-residential block and a twelve-story block for a hotel and a car park. The Chetti complained about the lack of consultation before the project was approved. In fact, they learned about it only in 2009, when the building permit had already been issued. The opposition they started should be framed against the specific Malaysian social and legal backdrop. Instead of open protests, the leadership of the community involved itself in interactions with media, direct communication with politicians and bureaucrats through meetings, phone calls, and SMS texts, and in the preparation of memoranda. The opposition had a measure of unifying effect on some members of the community, thereby suppressing ongoing internal disputes in favor of a common stand. For example, Mr. Shanmugam himself, although marginalized for years by the then leaders of the SPVMT Committee, was asked to prepare a memorandum because of his historical knowledge and his past experience of opposing the road extension in the 1990s. The memorandum he composed indeed contained a general introduction to the history and culture of the community, pictures, a collection of newspaper articles, and a copy of museum visitors' impressions. The central message was an appeal to revoke the high-rise project. The memorandum demonstrated a fair appropriation of the global idiom of heritage conservation and it stated—in the same words that experts such as Mr. Osman would use—that the "tangible" and "intangible" aspects of the *kampung warisan* would have been seriously affected: a high-rise on that location was not suitable for the environs as well as for the social and ritual life of the residents.

Residents feared material repercussions for their living space. First of all, the memorandum underlined that the planned construction would have damaged their houses and the centuries-old temples. Moreover, the residents were concerned about the eventuality of increased urban flooding. While Melaka is a flood-prone area, most of my interlocutors were of the opinion that flash floods had been exacerbated because of an inadequate drainage system and the pressures generated by massive high-rise construction. Some residents displayed a significant knowledge of, and expertise on, the flooding prevention system in the area, and they were of the opinion that a high-rise was not sustainable in that location, dependent as it would have been on the tiny drains of the *kampung* and the retention pond that collects rainwater.

Furthermore, the residents feared that once a high-rise came, many others would follow. A high-rise would also bring more people and cars into a relatively small area, and this would have meant bigger roads. The prospect brought back the old nightmare of the road extension cutting through the *kampung* as had been proposed in the 1990s. For these reasons, the memorandum proposed to change the project from a high-rise to two-story terraced houses and shophouses as an alternative more appropriate for the low-rise surroundings. To back these requests, the memorandum urged local authorities to follow UNESCO-derived regulations imposing a height limit of forty feet for infill development projects in the World Heritage buffer zone (see Malaysia 2011); this usually corresponded to the height of a three-story building. Indeed, the Chetti believed that their *kampung* was located in the buffer zone, whereas in reality—as I was in the uncomfortable position of having to inform them—it was at the doorstep of the World Heritage site, where there was no height control. Nonetheless, as a *kampung warisan* they still had Enactment 88 on their side, although its requirements were quite soft and generic, and they could also look to ongoing attempts to extend height control on tertiary zones around the World Heritage buffer zones.[9] Officials like Mr. Osman, who was one of the biggest supporters of these extensions (he called them "buffer-to-buffer-zones"), would have never issued the approval for such a building. But it takes time for new laws to be drafted, and in the meantime more and more projects were approved by local authorities. For analogous reasons, laws still need to be interpreted and Enactment 88 remains an insufficient protection as it does not mention buffer zones and height control.

Besides the call for heritage regulations, the community turned out to be quite effective in playing the game of local politics. On the eve of the 2013 elections, the memorandum emphasized that most people still supported the ruling coalition. Whether or not this factor played a role, the then Melaka state chief minister Ali Rustam decided to stop the project, saying that the developer would receive an alternative piece of land in another area (Murali 2012). In January 2013, the SPVMT Committee received a letter informing it of the possibility that the government might acquire the land for unspecified public utilities.

Whether this move was premeditated just in time for the pending elections, a mere couple of months after elections the piling works at the site were resumed, leaving the community with a handful of broken promises. According to a bureaucrat from the local heritage and planning offices, the authorities did not have the financial means to acquire the land from the developer (Murali 2014); this person added that it was a private property and that the project had in any case already been approved. At this point, people who had been at the forefront of the struggle, such as Mr. Shanmugam, started to lose hope, but some of the Chetti youth did not give up. They prepared a new memorandum and tried to reach a wider public through online social

---

9   Enactment 88 states in very generic terms that individuals cannot, without the consent of authorities, "erect buildings or walls abutting upon the heritage" (Melaka State Government 1988: 6). For current discussions in the Department of National Heritage on World Heritage "tertiary zones" see Koh 2017, and for proposals on height control around the World Heritage buffer zone at the Melaka level see MBMB 2008.

networks and the organization of solidarity campaigns. Mr. Vannan, a resident in his thirties who was among the most active at the moment, even personally texted the newly elected chief minister, Idris Haron. Since local regulations appeared weak, the leadership requested help from national authorities such as the Ministry of Tourism and Culture and its subsidiary, the Department of National Heritage, and UNESCO-related bodies. It was thought that having the *kampung* recognized in the national register of heritage or included in the World Heritage site would have been the only way to get the high-rise project redesigned. A Chetti delegation even had the once in a lifetime chance of informing UNESCO's director general, Irina Bokova, of the situation when she was in Melaka during her first official visit to Malaysia in 2013. I was told by Mr. Kumar that the Chetti residents asked her to include their *kampung* in the World Heritage site to impede adjacent developments. She politely recommended that they first ask the national government, the only body that could officially nominate a site for inclusion. Her reply diminished their hopes of global support, since it meant dealing with institutions to which they had already appealed in vain in previous years.

The second memorandum offers an even better display of the residents' ease and skill with official jargon. "Cultural Kampung Chetti Melaka," the memorandum stated, "would become a dynamic tourism product through the development of the area and infrastructure of Lot [...] following characteristics based on heritage [*warisan*], tradition [*tradisi*], and culture [*budaya*]" (my translation). By emphasizing that Kampung Chetti is "unique" in the world, the residents were asking local authorities to give the entire space to the community. In this way, the Chetti would have been able to develop the tourism products proposed in the municipal Special Area Plan, plans envisaging homestays and cottage industries that have so far never materialized. The Chetti proposed to build traditional houses that would have brought back community members living elsewhere, while attracting tourists, since, as the residents claimed, visitors came to enjoy the *kampung*-scape, not skyscrapers.

Perhaps unsurprisingly, international agencies did not reply and there was no interference from national institutions. In both cases, the formal basis for this refusal was that these bodies could do nothing for non-World Heritage sites, and that the issue had to be settled with local authorities. It was then that the residents started to realize that there was a double standard in the treatment of heritage sites in Melaka. I have argued elsewhere that World Heritage designations, especially in urban contexts, create a patrimonial hierarchy according to which some places are considered deserving of protection as heritage of humankind while others are excluded (see De Giosa 2021). The Chetti found themselves trapped in this asymmetry. The silence of national institutions, international organizations, and NGOs is symptomatic of the selective governance behind heritage-making processes in which the relevant authorities neglect whatever happens outside the boundaries it has created, thereby ignoring the organic nature of built and social environments.

Some of the residents' practical fears were not unreasonable. Since the resumption of construction work, cracks in the temples have been reported and the *kampung* has experienced an escalation of the flooding problem. Some of my interlocutors even showed me pictures of the contractor pumping rainwater from the construction site directly into the *kampung* drains. To date, some memorandum appeals to consider the state of the drainage system before approving new developments in the area have proved to be legitimate. At the time of writing (July 2018), with a completed high-rise in the background, periodic flash floods still make living conditions increasingly precarious. Much as in Ho Chi Minh City (see Gibert, this volume), poor management of the drainage system and unsustainable development have exacerbated urban flooding. Furthermore, the rather opaque decision-making pertaining to urban planning creates fear and uncertainty. While seemingly the opposite of what Herzfeld (2006: 127) has termed spatial cleansing, or "the creation of open spaces in city contexts," the dense high-rise infill development trend taken in Melaka has very similar effects: "the disruption of fundamental security, and especially of ontological security, for entire groups of people" (Herzfeld 2006: 142).

The story I have told is not unique. Other prominent heritage villages are facing the same fate in Melaka. Kampung Morten is now shadowed by The Shore, the tallest building in town with its forty-two stories completed in 2014, and the Portuguese Settlement is still opposing an ambitious Dubai-like land reclamation project that threatens to change the seafront (see also Ong 2017). Perhaps the lack of success in the opposition to this process of urban transformation is due to the fact that each community has resorted to its own *kampung*-scape in an atomized way, rather than as a collective right to the city (De Giosa 2021). Whether a combined opposition of all the heritage villages would have a better chance of success remains an open question.

"See You on the Thirteenth Floor!": The Place of Vernacular Settlements in the Future City?

When I was back to Melaka in 2014, my friends organized a dinner at Mr. Vannan's house. After I had observed how far the high-rise had progressed,

Mr. Vannan said: "Don't worry! When you will be back next time, we will see you on the thirteenth floor." He added: "Don't you know? The developer is going to give us the flats on that floor." With this triskaidekaphobic joke, he was ironically pointing to their position in the development machine—a place that can be omitted. The politics of urban heritage I have explored in this chapter point to the dilemma faced by vernacular settlements such as the Malaysian city *kampung* and their residents vis-à-vis urban transformation. The state and developers promote new development projects as a gift to the urban community because these projects bring new homes and jobs. But so far, none of the families I met in Kampung Chetti can afford a flat in the adjacent high-rise, nor were they interested in working there.

The case of Kampung Chetti shows that more recent developments in the promotion of vernacular architecture and cultural diversity have liberating effects for neighborhoods and communities that have been marginalized by official schemes and projects of earlier ages. It seems, however, that state and developers alike harshly enclose some selected neighborhoods as glass-cased living museums, isolating them from their environs solely to attract tourists and investors. In opposing the adjacent high-rise, the Chetti appropriated a global heritage vocabulary and, although they struggled in vain, this case study shows that the community has been able to challenge the state on its own ground by showing that the state's promises of a livable heritage city have thus far remained mere words printed on paper. The Chetti were not preemptively opposing any form of development whatsoever, but they were interested in more sustainable alternatives. They were calling for nothing more than a genuine realization of the Melakan local authorities' claims that the city was a "World Heritage City" on the way to acquiring *Resilient* "Green Technology City State" status.[10] As Harms (2011: 184) similarly notes in his ethnography of Ho Chi Minh City, even a modernization project praised by people can be a "double-edged sword" with potential "alienating effects of planning as it separates people from the very social forms they supposedly make up." Residents of centuries-old neighborhoods like Kampung Chetti have proven to be resilient throughout the years. More than resistance, this resilient perseverance resembles what scholars have dubbed "affective urbanism," defined as "an urbanism animated by a conceptual vocabulary specific to affectivity" (see Anderson and Holden 2008: 143). The resilience rhetoric increasingly embraced by the authorities is mostly concerned with issues

10   Since 2016 Melaka is also participating in the "100 Resilient Cities" program sponsored by the Rockefeller Foundation. See https://www.100resilientcities.org/cities/melaka/, last accessed 12 July 2018.

related to natural disasters and climate change. At the same time, however, the authorities themselves approve projects that threaten sustainability, the vernacular city, and the everyday life of residents in such neighborhoods.

The state itself has difficulty in implementing goals expressed in the jargon it employs in policies and plans. In this regard, the mantra of community involvement and participation is truly peculiar. The story I have told unmasks the unpreparedness of international and national institutions alike in facilitating "real and active participation" (Lefebvre 2000: 145) despite their rhetorical support for community involvement in city planning. Perhaps, as Ong (2017: 74) suggests, there is "a need to move from a passive, top-down community involvement to a more active, engaging, participatory bottom-up approach." Community involvement pilot projects continue to be rather sporadic and discontinuous. As Mr. Kumar told me, there is no sense in involving the community in state-sponsored cultural festivals if there is no space for the community itself in the city.

Postscript

In 2018, for the first time in history, Barisan Nasional was defeated by the opposition parties allied under Pakatan Harapan (The Alliance of Hope) led by former long-lasting Barisan Nasional Prime Minister Mahathir, himself the key player in the race towards a corporate globopolis model. The Pakatan Harapan-led Malaysian and Melaka state governments, however, lasted less than two years. In February 2020, the first political crisis in the history of the Malaysian Parliament opened the way for a new majority of a Malay-led government under a brand-new coalition called Perikatan Nasional (the National Alliance). During its short-lived administration in Melaka, Pakatan Harapan attempted to inspect the development projects approved by its predecessor and discussed with resident communities issues affecting their neighborhoods. The Chief Minister Adly Zahari formed a special committee to solve the problem of flash flooding. Its administration has carried out works to implement the sewerage system in some areas, including Kampung Chetti. The media have acknowledged that "floods are common in these areas following the massive developments along the coastline" (Murali 2018) and, while the then chief minister claimed that the issue of flash flooding has been mitigated in Kampung Chetti, he also called for a more sustainable approach on the part of developers (Nor 2019). It remains to be discovered what urban future is foreseen by present and new governments. Will it be just a rehash of the global high-rise model or a rediscovery of vernacular spaces as human-scale urban environments?

References

Anderson, Ben, and Adam Holden. 2008. "Affective Urbanism and the Event of Hope." *Space and Culture* 11 (2): 142–59.

Arkaraprasertkul, Non. 2012. "Urbanization and Housing: Socio-Spatial Conflicts over Urban Space in Contemporary Shanghai." In *Aspects of Urbanization in China: Shanghai, Hong Kong, Guangzhou*, edited by Gregory Bracken, 139–64. Amsterdam: Amsterdam University Press.

Askew, Marc. 1996. "The Rise of *Moradok* and the Decline of the *Yarn*: Heritage and Cultural Construction in Urban Thailand." *Sojourn* 11 (2): 183–210.

Brumann, Christoph. 2015. "Community as Myth and Reality in the UNESCO World Heritage Convention." In *Between Imagined Communities and Communities of Practice: Participation, Territory and the Making of Heritage*, edited by Nicolas Adell, Regina F. Bendix, Chiara Bortolotto, and Markus Tauschek, 273–86. Göttingen: Universitätsverlag Göttingen.

Brumann, Christoph. 2018. "Creating Universal Value: The UNESCO World Heritage Convention in Its Fifth Decade." In *The Oxford Handbook of Public Heritage Theory and Practice*, edited by Angela M. Labrador and Neil Asher Silberman, 21–34. Oxford: Oxford University Press.

De Cesari, Chiara. 2013. "Thinking Through Heritage Regimes." In *Heritage Regimes and the State*, edited by Regina F. Bendix, Aditya Eggert, and Arnika Peselmann, 399–413. Göttingen: Universitätsverlag Göttingen.

De Giosa, Pierpaolo. 2016. *Heritage below the Winds: The Social Life of the Cityscape and UNESCO World Heritage in Melaka*. PhD diss, Martin Luther University Halle-Wittenberg.

De Giosa, Pierpaolo. 2020. "Heritage-*Lah*! A Legacy of a Few Wor(l)ds in Peninsular Malaysia." *Moussons* 36: 163–189.

De Giosa, Pierpaolo. 2021. *World Heritage and Urban Politics in Melaka, Malaysia: A Cityscape below the Winds*. Amsterdam: Amsterdam University Press.

Dhoraisingam, Samuel S. 2006. *Peranakan Indians of Singapore and Melaka: Indian Babas and Nonyas – Chitty Melaka*. Singapore: ISEAS.

Douglass, Mike. 2013. "The Future of Cities in a Post-national Urban Age in Asia – Corporate Globopolis versus Vernacular Cosmopolis." *EWHA Journal of Social Sciences* 29 (1): 101–49.

Fuller, Christopher J. 2004. *The Camphor Flame: Popular Hinduism and Society in India*. Princeton: Princeton University Press.

Ghazali, Suriati. 2013. "Sense of Place and the Politics of 'Insider-ness' in Villages Undergoing Transition: The Case of City *Kampung* on Penang Island." In *Cleavage, Connection and Conflict in Rural, Urban and Contemporary Asia*, edited by Tim Bunnell, D. Parthasarathy, and Eric C. Thompson, 117–42. Dordrecht: Springer.

Goh, Beng-Lan. 2002. *Modern Dreams: An Inquiry into Power, Cultural Production, and the Cityscape in Contemporary Urban Penang, Malaysia*. Ithaca: SEAP Publications.

Hafstein, Valdimar T. 2007. "Claiming Culture: Intangible Heritage Inc., Folklore©, Traditional Knowledge™." In *Prädikat "Heritage" – Perspektiven auf Wertschöpfungen aus Kultur*, edited by Dorothee Hemme, Markus Tauschek, and Regina Bendix, 75-100. Münster: Lit Verlag.

Harms, Erik. 2011. *Saigon's Edge. On the Margins of Ho Chi Minh City*. Minneapolis: University of Minnesota Press.

Herzfeld, Michael. 1991. *A Place in History: Social and Monumental Time in a Cretan Town*. Princeton: Princeton University Press.

Herzfeld, Michael. 2006. "Spatial Cleansing: Monumental Vacuity and the Idea of the West." *Journal of Material Culture* 11 (1/2): 127–49.

Herzfeld, Michael. 2016. *Siege of the Spirits: Community and Polity in Bangkok*. Chicago: University of Chicago Press.

King, Victor T. 2016. "Melaka as a World Heritage Site: Melaka as Malaysia?" In *UNESCO in Southeast Asia: World Heritage Sites in Comparative Perspective*, edited by Victor T. King, 140–68. Copenhagen: NIAS Press.

Koh, Kelly. 2017. "Keeping a 'Clear View' of Heritage Sites." *New Straits Times*. 12 November 2017. https://www.nst.com.my/news/exclusive/2017/11/302332/keeping-clear-view-heritage-sites.

Lefebvre, Henri. 2000. *Writings on Cities*. Translated by Eleonore Kofman and Elizabeth Lebas. Oxford: Blackwell Publishers.

Malaysia. 2008. *Nomination Dossier: Historic Cities of the Straits of Malacca*. Kuala Lumpur: Department of National Heritage.

Malaysia. 2011. *Conservation Management Plan and Special Area Plan for Melaka and George Town World Heritage Site*. Kuala Lumpur: Department of National Heritage.

MBMB. 2008. *Draf Rancangan Kawasan Khas*. Melaka: Melaka Historical City Council.

Mearns, David J. 1995. *Shiva's Other Children: Religion and Social Identity amongst Overseas Indians*. New Delhi: Sage Publications.

Melaka State Government. 1988. *Preservation and Conservation of Cultural Heritage Enactment 1988*. Melaka: Melaka State Government.

Murali, R.S.N. 2012. "Chitty Community Extends Deepavali Celebrations After Condo Project Is Halted." *The Star*. 21 November 2012. https://www.thestar.com.my/news/nation/2012/11/21/chitty-community-extends-deepavali-celebrations-after-condo-project-is-halted#2avDoIwW6p7LKz3A.99.

Murali, R.S.N. 2014. "Kg Chitty Will Remain as Heritage Site." *StarProperty*. 10 January 2014. http://www.starproperty.my/index.php/articles/property-news/kg-chitty-will-remain-as-heritage-site/.

Murali, R.S.N. 2018. "Move to End a Watery Problem in Melaka." *The Star.* 5 July 2018. https://www.thestar.com.my/metro/metro-news/2018/07/05/move-to-end-a-watery-problem-in-melaka-mp-calls-for-special-committee-to-be-set-up-to-resolve-recurr/.

Narinasamy, K. 1983. "The Melaka Chitties." In *Melaka: The Transformation of a Malay Capital c. 1400-1980*, edited by Kernial Singh Sandhu and Paul Wheatley, vol. 2, 239–63. Kuala Lumpur: Oxford University Press.

Newbold, Thomas John. 1839. *Political and Statistical Account of the British Settlements in the Straits of Malacca*, vol. 1. London: John Murray.

Nor Farhana Yaakob. 2019. "Melaka Rancang Atasi Banjir Kilat." *Sinar Harian.* 26 December 2019. https://www.sinarharian.com.my/article/63447/EDISI/YMelaka-NS/Melaka-rancang-atasi-banjir-kilat.

Ong, Puay Liu. 2017. "Community Involvement for Sustainable World Heritage Sites: The Melaka Case." *Kajian Malaysia* 35 (1): 59–76.

Padawangi, Rita. 2015. "The Vernacular and the Spectacular: Urban Identity and Architectural Heritage in Southeast Asian Cities." In *Asian Cities: Colonial to Global*, edited by Gregory Bracken, 261–78. Amsterdam: Amsterdam University Press.

PERZIM. n.d. *Inventori Perkampungan Warisan Masyarakat Chetti, Jalan Gajah Berang, Melaka.* Melaka: Melaka Museums Corporation.

Saw, Swee-Hock. 2015. *The Population of Malaysia.* Singapore: ISEAS.

Shamsul, Amri Baharuddin. 1996. "Promise versus Performance: Formal Organizations in Rural Malaysia." In *The Village Concept in the Transformation of Rural Southeast Asia: Studies from Indonesia, Malaysia, and Thailand*, edited by Mason C. Hoadley and Christer Gunnarsson, 140–61. Richmond: Curzon Press.

Thompson, Eric C. 2006. "Rural Villages as Socially Urban Spaces in Malaysia." In *Globalisation and the Politics of Forgetting*, edited by Yong-Sook Lee and Brenda S.A. Yeoh, 63–82. Abingdon: Routledge.

Worden, Nigel. 2001. "'Where it all Began': The Representation of Malaysian Heritage in Melaka." *International Journal of Heritage Studies* 7 (3): 199–218.

Zhang, Li. 2006. "Contesting Spatial Modernity in Late-Socialist China." *Current Anthropology* 47 (3): 461–84.

About the Author

Pierpaolo De Giosa is a sociocultural anthropologist with fieldwork experience in Malaysia, Indonesia and Timor Leste. He was awarded a Marie Sklodowska-Curie Postdoctoral Fellowship for a research project on coastal land reclamation in Malaysia hosted at the Department of Asian Studies of Palacký University Olomouc (2023–2025). He is the author of "*World Heritage and Urban Politics in Melaka, Malaysia. A Cityscape below the Winds*" (AUP, 2021).

5. Heritage and a Community of Belonging in Singapore

Steve Ferzacca

Abstract: Recently in Singapore, hegemonic, highly institutionalized projects of national commemoration have begun to resurrect a past long hidden from public view. Official heritage projects of national pride and local ones of belonging are equally central to the manner in which a community of rock legends assembles itself from time to time.

Keywords: Singapore, popular music, guitar shops, urban life

Method/Acting

"I have a proposal," I announced to a group of aging Singaporean musicians. We had just finished with an evening of rehearsal at a jam studio located in a recreational center. The band I was performing with included myself—an anthropologist on leave from my university, living in Singapore as a research fellow—and the members of a group that included aging Singapore "pioneers," among others who congregated at a music store in a basement of a shopping mall located in the central business district in Singapore. Lim Kiang, who was managing the guitar shop Guitar 77, was the original bass player of the legendary 1960s rock band The Straydogs. James Tan, the original drummer of the same group, I met not long after. The three of us got to know each other in the shop, and after a few jam sessions we decided to form our own "beats and blues" band known as Blues 77, acknowledging the place of its birth.

While all of this was unfolding, I had the pleasure of meeting Joseph Clement Pereira, a journalist, author, local historian, and collector of Singaporean/Malaysian popular culture. His personal collection of Southeast Asian (and South Asian) 1960s pop music memorabilia is made up mostly

[Herzfeld, M., and R. Padawangi, eds. *Resilience as Heritage in Asia*. Amsterdam: Amsterdam University Press, 2025.
DOI: 10.5117/9789463728560_CH05

of recordings, photographs, promotional materials, and other archival materials that are the artifacts of a cosmopolitan regional popular culture thriving in 1960s Singapore, Malaysia, and elsewhere. Joe published several books on the music and the music scene of the 1960s in Singapore.

I turned to James and Kiang and asked if they would be interested in making "heritage" in an academic setting. "Let's see if Joe wants to get involved with this," I said as we packed up our gear for the evening. The Asia Research Institute (ARI), where I was a fellow at the time, had a call for papers for a two-day symposium on the "resilience of vernacular heritage in Asia." This seemed like an opportunity to present some of the ethnographic work that involved the Singaporean music community relevant to heritage making. But I also saw an opportunity for ethnography, an opportunity to observe heritage making in an academic setting, and an opportunity to engage in a collaborative way the assemblage of various actors from various academic and class backgrounds in our own making of heritage. While a panel presentation in an academic setting seemed an odd place to explore emergent and converging forms of heritage—academic discussions are discussions of heritage not opportunities to live heritage—we believed we could turn an "academic" discussion of heritage into a lived one.

The goal was to highlight our presence and performance as participants in the symposium to illustrate our idea that heritage is neither tangible nor intangible—rather, heritage, vernacular or otherwise, is always social. In fact, distinctions drawn around vernacular and other kinds of heritage obscure the reliance on the relationality of various kinds of heritage. In the case of our presentation, we accented the way in which heritage is dependent upon and entangled in the relation between historicide and historicity. For heritage societies, nationally and locally dependent, these "articulating hidden histories" (Schneider and Rapp 1995) are the grist of their work. Our hope was that the assemblage of people and things that participated that afternoon would stand as witness to an emergent intersectionality present in the room as another example of relationality experienced as heritage. Emergence and relationality are central features of assemblage theory, and it was these features we wanted to emphasize. Finally, we wanted to experience together that resilience exists only in the emergent social considered here as assemblages and networks; in the case of the academic panel, our social work involved the academic paper, the conference organization, and the presence of mediators and intermediaries—the numerous objects participating in this "peculiar movement of re-association and reassembling" (Latour 2005: 7). Rather than a presentation on some *thing*—vernacular heritage—complete with historical and ethnographic facts, the paper and the presentation were to *perform* this reassembling of the social emergent in the context of a research institute and academic event that indexed the peculiarity of place in the social of vernacular heritage.

And so, before turning to the panel, let's explore some peculiar places of vernacular heritage that intersect with the method acting that took place that day.

Crossroads: Basement Guitar Shops and Deep Sounds

Sentient and sensorial anthropology, aural and sonic histories, sounded anthropologies and sonic ethnographies are becoming more common. I ventured into this realm of research prior to my arrival in Singapore. Based upon musical experiences in another place, I work with a concept of deep sound (Ferzacca 2006, 2012). Sonic depth is about relationality, resemblances, correspondences, and consequences rather than merely acoustics. Deep sound extends mimesis from its double layering of "sentience and copying" (Taussig 1993: 80) to include communications in the context of difference, even friction. In this way sound is deepened and is "methectic" (Huizinga 1950: 14) in function and affect. I developed this notion of deep sound while learning how to listen in previous ethnographic work that took place in an urban neighborhood (*kampung*) in the city of Yogyakarta, Indonesia. For example, as I listened to the soundscape of the kampung, I became aware of the depth of certain sounds. In the afternoons, as the heat of the day subsided, kampung residents would begin cleaning up the alleyway before afternoon socializing began. The sound of the first broom sweeping the street was a call to all reminding us of our responsibilities as neighbors. Here the sound of the broom resounded our neighborly responsibilities, providing an opportunity to perform citizenship recognized by others as having social consequences. This is deep sound.

The jingle-jangle noise encountered in the basement of the Peninsula Hotel and Shopping Centre located in the heart of Singapore's business district, especially on weekends, hardly seems to be the kind of deep sound offering insights into the social. Several guitar shops are located in close proximity to each other in this aging shopping mall. The shopping mall and hotel were built in 1971. Across Coleman Street, opposite of the Peninsula Hotel and mall is the Peninsula Plaza, built in 1981. Like many of the "veteran shopping malls" in Singapore, the Peninsula looks aged and perhaps "forgotten by time" compared to the many new, sparkling shopping mall palaces complete with ice skating rinks, cineplexes, and so forth that are necessary for the contemporary shopping experience in this glistening Asian city. The Peninsula is a "strata-titled" mall co-owned by different groups of investors as well as individual shop owners. Often, but not always, such arrangements are made when properties can demand top dollar for square footage, allowing owners the freedom to lease their shops to any tenants who are lured by the relatively lower rents. This is one reason why some many guitar shops, and stores that sell CDs and vinyl LPs, turntables and stereo components are all grouped together in the basement of the mall. The basement retail spaces are cheap, and locating one's music business among a cohort of others ensures customers.

Singapore's emergence as a British colony arose as a cosmopolitan trade depot. Singapore has often been referred to, especially in its early history as a British colony, as a "crossroads to the East." Historically, and in the present, the *crossroads* is a place marked in some way as special among human places. Crossroads (or crossways) are found in the Vedic literatures, the Pali texts, Chinese medical treatises and hagiography, and southeast Asian tales and histories, and are described as places where "meritorious public works" (for example, the building of a stupa) can occur alongside the public flogging of criminals. In Vedic literature, crossroads "housed" mother goddesses ("mother companions") with the ability to speak different languages that localized opportunities for domestic offerings to be made to family deities and ancestors. At the confluences of human movement that include but are not limited to roads and waterways, people often encountered "great harmonizers," gate watchers, keepers, teachers, monks in contemplation, and "guardians of the boundaries," as well as devils and other harmful entities.[1] Attention is paid to crossroads and crossways because of this potential. And, so, such places, in the classic and modern sense, are often located at the outskirts of sedentary human settlement, are envisioned and experienced as inauspicious places where goddesses, devils, enchanters, guides, or gift givers carry on as human movements activate their presence. While crossroads are artifacts and perhaps even maps of and for human movements, crossroads and crossways are always local sites "made to do something" (Latour 2005: 191) among the emergent connections that not only haunt but make up these places.

---

1   The sources on crossroads in Asia and elsewhere are scattered, mostly concentrated in scholarship on Europe and Christian traditions. See, for example, Damodar Dharmanand Kosambi, *Myth and Reality* (Mumbai: Popular Prakashan, 1962); Jacoba Hooykaas, "The Gateway on the Crossroads?" *Bijdragen tot de Taal-, Land- en Volkenkunde* 111, no. 4 (1955): 413–5; "The Crossroads in Hoodoo Magic and the Ritual of Selling Yourself to the Devil," http://www.luckymojo.com/crossroads.html; "Kayagata-sati Sutta: Mindfulness Immersed in the Body" [Pali]. Translated by Thanissaro Bhikkhu (1997), http://www.accesstoinsight.org/tipitaka/mn/mn.119.than.html.

For musicians and connoisseurs of American blues music, the crossroads refers to a mythic tale of Faustian bargains. As the story goes, the father of blues music Robert Johnson received the ability to play the blues on his guitar after selling his soul to the devil at the crossroads. In fact, the story should be attributed to a blues player also from the early twentieth century, Tommy Johnson, who when interviewed provided the basic gist of the story:

> If you want to learn how to make songs yourself, you take your guitar and you go to where the road crosses that way, where a crossroads is. Get there, be sure to get there just a little 'fore 12 that night so you know you'll be there. You have your guitar and be playing a piece there by yourself ... A big black man will walk up there and take your guitar and he'll tune it. And then he'll play a piece and hand it back to you. That's the way I learned to play anything I want.[2]

The devil, in Tommy Johnson's rendition, is a teacher that Tommy "jams" with as he learns to play the blues on his guitar. While this storied version of the crossroads reflects African and African American histories and sensibilities, many features of the crossroads found elsewhere around the world appear. In 1936 Robert Johnson recorded "Crossroads Blues," which is not a story of Faustian bargains but rather begins with a verse that has someone kneeling in despair begging forgiveness, followed by anxious, failed attempts to hitch a ride, expressed with resignation and fear as nightfall approaches. "Crossroads Blues" reveals the potential of the crossroads to harmonize and vex human lives.

The Peninsula's location in the central business district is prime. Its location is on Coleman Street and is the historic center of the British colony. The cosmopolitan nature of Singapore's history is embodied in the buildings, streets, and waterways that surround the Peninsula. The marks left by Chinese, Malay, South Asian, British, and other colonial interlocuters continue today in significant ways. The basement of the mall, where the guitar shops are located, continues to reflect and nurture this cosmopolitan history, present, and future. As we will see, this cosmopolitanism assembled by young teenagers as they formed an English language rock band, The Straydogs, in a seaside neighborhood is a crucial, stable feature in their heritage making—a vernacular heritage that implicates these intimacies of the past specific to groups of teenagers, while at the same time converging with broader efforts to foster heritage.

2   David Evans, *Tommy Johnson* (London: Studio Vista, 1971: 12).

Social media descriptions in the present reveal the current flows of cosmopolitanism that course through this urban place. The shopping mall is said to provide a "slew of pleasant surprises for the shopper looking to garner quality bargains."[3] Mall promotions and advertisements note the mall's "colourful cosmopolitan history."[4] An internet-based travel site offers the following description of this cosmopolitan southeast Asian crossroads:

> At first glance, Peninsula Plaza seems like an unremarkable mix of money changers, travel agencies, and souvenir shops. It's not until you're inside and can see the signs in the beautiful, curving script and get a whiff of the fish sauce that permeates the air it is clear that Peninsula Plaza has become a home-away-from-home for Singapore's Burmese community. The clothing shops sell traditional longyi (a unisex wrap skirt), convenience stores stock Myanmar Lager, and there's even a Burmese-language library.[5]

Customers in online comments characterize the mall as a place "for all your Burmese (Myanmar) needs! All ethnic groups of Burna [sic] congregate here (Shan, Chin, Kayin, etc.) A food court at the basement, ticketing agents for your travels in almost every floor!" (Ted Patrick Boglosa). In fact, the shopping complex is also known as "Little Burma," providing services, food, and shopping to a Myanmar community over fifty thousand strong, making some space in this place as a "home away from home" for this community. While standing at the crossroads of current movements of people in the southeast region—the result of travel benefits for citizens of ASEAN countries that include few visa restrictions and extremely competitive regional airfares among a burgeoning fleet of budget airlines—the mall is also described by some customers online as "a very hobby-centric mall – lots of music, photography & sportswear shops" (Benjamin Ng, 24 July 2011).

The basement guitar shops deal in new and used gear. All major internationally known brands are traded and sold. Among these known and desirable brand names are makes and models specific to the region—for example, from China and Australia. Finally, the Japanese versions of internationally known brands of guitars are in more abundance than, say, North

---

3   http://www.stproperty.sg/articles-property/commercial/peninsula-plaza--bargain-city-at-your-fingertips/a/128557. Accessed 20 October 2014.

4   Ibid.

5   http://www.travelfish.org/blogs/singapore/2011/09/26/peninsula-plaza-singapores-little-burma/. Accessed 20 October 2014.

American ones, given the regional flavor of the overall collection of guitars among all the basement stores, and, of course, the proximity of Japan to the musical instrument market in Southeast Asia.

The density of guitar shops and the outstanding overall collection of new and used gear attracts Singaporeans, Southeast Asians, expat and foreign talent working and living in Singapore, and many from all over the world interested in browsing guitar shops while in town. An afternoon in any of the shops is an afternoon with the world. But this is especially true of two shops: Guitar 77 and Guitar Connection. Guitar Connection deals in "vintage" instruments and boasts one of the most outstanding collections of rare and hard to find examples of classic, globally known makes and models. Guitar 77 also deals in used as well as new gear, which increases interest from a crowd looking for something unique and different compared to the common gear found in the shops that only sell new instruments.

This combination of Southeast Asian regional and global connections of people and things offers space for assemblages—heterogenous movements and reassembling of humans and things that as a local site can be "made to do something." The something here is not only the sale and consumption of musical instruments. The guitar shops provide emergent opportunities for gear, musical genres, famous global musicians whose performances and sounds are embodied in objects (guitars, etc.), people, technologies, and technique that are experienced by each individual and each collectivity that traffics this mall basement of music stores.

And, so, I arrived in Singapore September 2011 and made my way down to this basement oasis for the guitar-minded gear lover in search of the "vitality and periodic capacity for surprise in a variety of nonhuman force-fields"—guitar stores, guitars, guitar accessories—"invested with differing speeds and degrees of agency" in which I wished to be entangled (Connolly 2013: 400). In fact, the lure—as any guitar lover will tell you—is the belief that all of these "objects," which have already lived "clearly multiple and complex lives," will continue to live in these sites and in the hands of others (Latour 2005: 80). In fact, this very "fragility of things" (Connolly 2013: 400) resulting in part from the constant circulation and movement among various "regimes of value" (Appadurai 1986: 15) is vital to the emergent social in this basement oasis. New arrivals of gear and the potential for continued social life imbues expectations as, in the case of happy hour jams, players and others take up the social affordances any guitar, amp, pedal, and so forth can evoke. These new opportunities for the social are at the very heart of someone whose way of knowing the world is sonic. All of these opportunities and possibilities are heard and seen upon entering the basement of the Peninsula.

As we will see, the guitar shops, the basement, the guitar gear, and the people who pass through these spaces on a daily basis afford "situated sources of identity" embodied in the spaces and things, the assemblage of human and nonhuman forces within a constantly shifting (fragile "vernacular milieu" (Pickering and Green 1987: 8) encourages resilience. The constant remaking of these worlds, this kind of worlding situates "everyday practices that creatively imagine and shape alternative social visions and configurations—that is, "worlds"—than what already exists in a given context (Ong 2011: 12). The "given context" here is a vision of a Singapore and a citizenship that is productive, efficient, and meritorious. These "worldings from below" work to "remap relationships of power at different scales and localities" revealing the guitar shops and other urban spaces discussed here as "critical sites" of recognition and resilience (Ong 2011: 12). Along the lines Ong follows, I too consider the city as a milieu, or "a field of intervention" (Ong 2011: 12) in which individuals, populations, and groups put into conjunction elements and events towards what Steven Feld (2012) refers to as an acoustemology—a way of knowing—a way of being in the world sonically.

Fieldnotes: 2011

I arrived on 1 September 2011. Searching for an anchor, a familiarity I could use to settle my arrival anxiety, I headed for some guitar shops I had located using online searches before leaving my prairie home. I had been to Singapore before this trip, and so knew enough to buy a transport pass for use on the trains and buses that network this small island city. Taking nothing with me except a pocket full of guitar picks, I headed "downtown"—entirely on my own. Arising from the subterranean chute of screech and halt through which moving masses of hand-held-deviced "Asians" and "others" assemble and flow, the sun and heat greet me without compromise—at least today.

A whitewashed St. Andrews Cathedral stands just outside the glassy mall from which I ascended. Soon I enter another less glassy, not quite so contemporary shopping mall combined with a hotel of towers that compete with the density of towering buildings, scraping the sky as they say. Big city sounds, traffic, and scores of people are off to somewhere or another.

The guitar shops are in the basement and I find them after filing through corridors of knockoffs—jeans, shoes, cowboy boots, belts, and used camera shops. A tattoo parlor is busy. I turn around the corner and the first shops appear, loaded with guitars. It becomes apparent that the basement holds a cluster of guitar stores, and, before long, familiar sounds, songs, and

Figure 5.1. Davis Guitar, the largest, oldest, and most successful of the Peninsula Shopping Centre guitar stores (photo by Steve Ferzacca)

sights excite me. So far from home I can find all of my favorite guitars and amplifiers, famous and not so famous, conventional and "boutique" brands, in great abundance. It is a feast, and I plan to indulge.

After some time in Davis Guitar (figure 5.1), I venture onward and discover a "vintage" shop with gems from guitar history. There are guitars from all ages representing milestones in music history associated with the amplified, "electric" guitar. Acoustic guitars are available as well, but my interest is in loud and amplified.

I am surprised, and this is an understatement. I had not counted on a treasure hunt, but here I am, looking at some really amazing artifacts in various conditions. Obviously the guitar had history here and a history that I might actually know something of, at least from my native point of view. I spent some time in the Guitar Connection (figure 5.2), looking and then asking to try out those guitars more easily accessed.

Talking with store personnel leads to equally familiar questions and exchanges I have had elsewhere. The language of guitars and amplifiers is global, and gear talk sounds the same, with local history, desires, needs, and contingencies vibrating right along with the steel strings. Here I meet Wayne; he's working on a guitar in a small room towards the back that extends the counter where the cash register greets customers as we enter the shop. He is long haired, young, and skinny, wearing jeans and a tee shirt—a uniform that makes sense, once again, for the electric guitar corps. We strike up a

Figure 5.2. The Guitar Connection, a vintage guitar store with an amazing collection (photo by Steve Ferzacca)

conversation, and Wayne hooks me up with a few antiques I play through equally antiqued amplifiers. I lose track of time and place for a while, but only for brief moments while reflecting on this unexpected encounter. I laugh at myself—well, what did I expect? This is Singapore, and I chuckle as I consider the sense of exotica that informed my own motivations and surprise to find guitar shops stocked with the same guitar "good life" I too desire and know.

Thanking Wayne, and leaving Wayne's world, vowing to return, I head off following the sound of "shredding" pulsating from inside another shop, actually a second shop space of Davis Guitar. Hunched over a purple-blue "Greco" Les Paul solid body guitar, screaming at low volume in complete overdrive is Burn. Bespectacled with chains and marked up with body tattoos, Burn shreds—that is, he plays heavy metal music, dense and thick with distortion, squealing squeezed harmonics, a dark and destructive sound meant to be in your face, ears, and body.

I listen for some time and then strike up a conversation. I expected hearing this genre—I knew metal was popular in Asia from past experience, but also from a proliferating scholarship (e.g., Wallach 2008) on youth and popular culture in Southeast Asia. I ask Burn if he is in a band. He says he is, and I return with "where do you play?" "We don't," he replies. "I hate Singapore," he adds. As quick and sharp as his shredding can be, Burn tells me that

Figure 5.3. Guitar 77 (photo by Steve Ferzacca)

Singapore doesn't allow "noise pollution." It turns out he is in a band for which there are few opportunities for gigs. Burn plays in a band that doesn't perform, at least in public venues.

From this experience to the next, I see a black Gibson with "mini-humbucker" pickups hanging in the window of a shop, Guitar 77 (figure 5.3). I had been looking for a guitar with mini-humbuckers, and here was a used one, and so I now had a nice excuse to play another guitar. Behind the counter standing next to the till was an old rocker, I think to myself, like me. I ask about the guitar in the display window. He gets it down for me, finds a cable, and plugs me into a peddle board with a dizzying array of guitar pedals for producing "effects" that is itself plugged into a small amplifier. I switch it on and I play for a few minutes. It is a beautiful guitar with a great sound, made in the 1990s—a custom shop guitar. The graying tee shirted dude behind the counter announces that I am a "bluesman." I smile and continue to play. After a while I stop, ask the price, and we begin to talk.

He introduces himself to me as "Kiang," a bass player who likes to play the blues. I shouldn't be surprised after all, given what I have seen since arriving to this shopping mall, but I am. Kiang explains he was a member of "The Straydogs," a "beats and blues" group that began playing and later recording in 1966 (figure 5.4).

As we exchange musical influences, a recognizable "cosmopolitanism" was stunning in its degree of resemblances. As youth we listened to much of the same music. Together we were able to determine this immediately,

StrayDogs in the 1960s

Figure 5.4. The Straydogs 1960s (photo by Steve Ferzacca)

and sonically. After plugging in and playing for some time, Kiang and I had communicated—our social was mediated sonically, a thing in and of itself dependent upon the connections and movements of my fingers in relation to the fretboard, the pick used for plucking the strings, the strings, the pickups, the guitar, the amplifier, the electricity, and so on. Kiang and I began to know each other before speaking, or at least we emerged socially for each other in the midst of sonic exchanges mediated entirely by things and our actions with them in hand, in sound.

As Kiang and I got to know each other, I spent more time in the guitar shop. Over time I became acquainted with the music scene of Guitar 77 and some of the other shops in the mall. I discovered that nearly every afternoon, and especially on weekends, a group of regulars gets together in Guitar 77 to drink and jam. Happy hour in the shop, in addition to band rehearsals and performances, follows a structure of experience known in Singapore as "talking cock." Yao (2007: 123) describes, "talking cock" as "garrulous affairs" in which "the visceral and the public" meet and "assume a fetishistic form." Talking cock is a visceral pleasure among men in Singapore. As Yao outlines (2007: 123), talking cock is "exuberant talk and masculine boasting, lubricated by delicious food and abundant alcohol." Intense, sometimes fiery, often explosive language and ideas are conjured mostly in reference to the demands of the Singaporean state. Kiang, The Straydogs, and associates present a foundation for the development of a "community of interest" (Pickering and Green 1987), and a sense of belonging organized around rebellious behavior and "cosmopolitan conviviality" (Mignolo 2000). This vernacular milieu celebrates the "rocker" and the rock and roll lifestyle as it existed and is configured in both the past and present that becomes a focus for interaction and identity formation. And in this vernacular milieu there is a shared commitment to leaning into difference, recognizing and knowing difference in social relations and in music as a source for making community and belonging.

The social that emerges around the afternoon happy hour jam sessions connects with cosmopolitan sonic history that, as Gramsci might say, serves this "community of interests" in their own "way of thinking and feeling." I discovered the centrality of a convivial cosmopolitanism that Mignolo (2000) celebrates. While a local community of interests and of place are clearly assembled and reassembled self-consciously among friends and family, the fluid, permeable, open-ended nature of this group means that on any day at any time, anyone is welcomed, especially if that someone can recognize the not entirely nor always coherent "cultural biography" projected by the activities in the store—drinking, the blues, men talking cock, jamming, heritage is welcomed..

One example of this openness of the activities that take place in the shop is illustrated in the yearly celebration of Chinese New Year at the shop. In the public hallway outside the shop's doors, Kiang organizes the *yusheng*, known as *lo hei yusheng* or simply *lo hei* (Cantonese) in Singapore. This "prosperity toss" of a salad made with fish served with daikon (white radish), carrots, red pepper (capsicum), turnips, red pickled ginger, sun-dried oranges, lime leaves, Chinese parsley, chili, jellyfish, chopped peanuts, toasted sesame seeds, Chinese shrimp crackers (or fried dried shrimp), five spice powder, and other ingredients, and laced with a sauce using plum sauce, rice vinegar, kumquat paste, and sesame oil, for a total of twenty-seven ingredients, celebrates past, present, and future prosperity, mostly in terms of wealth. The tossing occurs as those who have come together each use a pair of chopsticks and, after loud announcements of the coming of prosperity, each person begins tossing the salad ingredients with others into the air above the dish at the same time. All who have joined in after tossing begin to eat a plateful of or portions of the salad.

Lo hei is a strictly regional cultural practice found only in Singapore and Malaysia. While considered a "Chinese" feature of New Year's celebrations, many Singaporeans in homes, offices, and so forth participate in lo hei. For those who assemble at Guitar 77, lo hei is a way to remember themselves as Singaporeans, but, more importantly, the tossing of the salad in the hallways of the mall invites others shopping or working in the other stores located in the basement of the Peninsula. In this way, the salad toss does something in the reassembling of communities of interest and place—the

Figure 5.5. Lo hei toss in the hallway outside of Guitar 77 (photo by Steve Ferzacca)

salad toss is part of the action for the social to occur, and the social in this case is open, attractive, interested in the potential and coincidences that occur at crossroads. Domestic rituals that not only mark local experiences but *are* local experiences forging the crossways of life into places where *local* potencies of prosperity might be encountered, into places where the social is made and remade over and over again, into places where "meritorious public works" can occur alongside vulgar display and action of capitalist reality are all that is involved—the guitars, the customers, the stores, the cash, everything resists the renewal of experience without history so essential to the reproduction of capitalist consumption. At a lo hei toss (figure 5.5), different languages are spoken, localizing opportunities for all participants.[6]

The deflation of history, community, and heritage becomes severely inflated as the social of the jams, happy hours, and activities like the lo hei toss take place. The lo hei salad toss, like the crossroads in the basement of this mall, signals the confluences of human movement in associations, or as assemblages. The lo hei tosses occur in the hallways for pragmatic reasons, but also because the hallways themselves flow in ways that crossroads often do with the social potential involved. For these specific lo hei tosses, The Straydogs' heritage and Singapore's become inseparable, only recognizable together as one, even as these fiercely proud Singaporean pioneers, heart-landers, and others associate with rather cynical feelings surrounding some of Singapore's government policies, programs, and regime.

For Pickering and Green (1987: 8), such communities are organized, and such activities as the lo hei toss occur in a "vernacular milieu" that "can

6   For a complete video, see https://www.youtube.com/watch?v=9CiA4MdjtRU&list=UUDw KnqMO9YQT392GPwnxZCA.

Figure 5.6. Happy hour and jam time at Guitar 77 (photo by Steve Ferzacca)

either be dispersed or relatively confined to particular localities" as "situated sources of identity." From these many afternoons and weekends, Kiang and I had the chance to play together and it was not long before we decided to form a band. Of course, forming a band can mean many things, one of which is that the band never really materializes—the actuality remains an imagined community. As Kiang and I began to play together forming a band named after his shop (Blues 77), the recognizable cosmopolitanism referred to as the "60s" that provided an initial medium through which we could communicate opened up to a historically anchored, locally rich Southeast Asian sonic cosmopolitanism that Kiang and others played a part in resounding during jam sessions and happy hours (figure 5.6).

Walter Mignolo (2000) considers cosmopolitanism as a counter movement to globalization. The Straydogs and a small but energetic host of Singaporean bands sounded Singapore's locally established engagements with global pop culture at the time of national awakening. The vibrant music scene Joe Pereira collects and documents are this island nation's objects in waiting and, when activated, remind us that Singapore has always been at the center of cosmopolitics immersed in a kind of "planetary conviviality"—a conviviality for the cosmopolitan forged across vast global networks, and in this case a conviviality whose *structure of feeling* was formed and remains firmly anchored in the barely postcolonial modernity of 1960s Singapore. The Straydogs and other 1960s Singapore bands represent locally produced sonic studies of global history—then and now—engaged in what anthropologist Steven Feld (2012:10) refers to as "acoustemology"—a "way of knowing the world through sound." The sonic cosmopolitanism I encountered forged from a historically situated conviviality continues to be expressed acoustemologically. This sonic cosmopolitanism remains central to the lives and livelihoods of these guitar shops. Singaporeans who frequent these guitar shops and those I met who participate in Singapore's local music scene ascribed fully to the "cosmopolitan commitment" framed in an intense loyalty to Singaporean identity, even though for many of Singapore's 1960s music legends their nationalist loyalty has been established and nurtured out of a "marginal aesthetic footnote in the Singaporean story."[7]

Singapore Music Scene: Making Sonic Places at the End of Colonialism

Turning to the symposium, Joe provided his rendition of 1960s pop music history based on lived experience of the times, his participation in the music community in various ways and roles over the years to the present as a published chronicler of the "swinging sixties" in Singapore. The 1960s are of course the "pioneer" years in the history of the nation-state. The generation coming of age—the generation Joe, James, and Kiang belong to—forged a new nation. The members of this generation are not only referred to as "pioneers," but are card carrying ones as well.

In his presentation, Joe listed significant events and important venues during those years. The Cliff Richard and The Shadows concert held at Gay World Stadium over two nights in November 1961 is earmarked by Joe as the beginning of Western pop music history in Singapore. In addition to the stadium, a dance hall that could accommodate three hundred couples provided adequate acoustics and a dance floor. In the 30s, entry to the cabaret cost between fifty cents and a dollar and ordering drinks was mandatory. Gay World supported various forms of dancing for a cosmopolitan, diverse ethnic audience that was and is Singapore. Singaporean Malays and Babas alike danced Malay *ronggeng* and *joget*, and Gay World offered a special *ronggeng kiosk* (a bandstand) where Singaporean men could find dance partners.[8]

---

7   Thanks to Liew Kai Khun for this turn of phrase.
8   http://eresources.nlb.gov.sg/infopedia/articles/SIP_1044_2006-06-01.html. Accessed 19 October 2014.

Singapore in the 1960s did not have venues to cater to the burgeoning pop music trend emanating from England and the USA. Promoters had to make do with venues that at least could seat large numbers of people. When the Rolling Stones played Singapore in February 1965 they appeared at the Singapore Badminton Hall in Guillemard Road. Joe explained that the rise of the pop music movement in Singapore in the early sixties resulted in "unlikely places" that became homes to the beat movement. One of them was a basement restaurant called The Cellar, which was located in a banking establishment.

For Joe that afternoon, The Cellar was an important sonic place for the developing music scene. The Cellar began to have Sunday tea dances that featured the legendary Checkmates as the house band. The weekly tea dance sessions held on Sunday afternoons were a hit with foreign military personnel stationed in the region as well as a wide range of local Singaporeans. The tea dances provided the opportunity for Kiang, James, The Straydogs, and an impressive number of Singaporean bands playing English language pop music to practice and perform their craft. Following the closing of The Cellar, another club featuring Sunday tea dances opened, known as the Golden Venus Club—a basement club owned by the Orchard Hotel. Tea dances began in 1965, again featuring the Checkmates as the house band. The Straydogs would come to replace the Checkmates as the house band.

Joe spoke of the significance of the crossroads that was Singapore in the 1960s. He noted that other venues included British Military camps with services clubs where local Singaporean musicians and bands could perform. In fact, The Straydogs in these early years relied on these venues for gigs. In the service clubs, Singaporeans mingled with British soldiers, gathering info about the latest English bands, fashion trends, and "Western" popular culture in general. The buildup of the Vietnam War in the mid-sixties brought the Americans, as Singapore was designated as a rest and recreation (R&R) center for soldiers coming out of the war in Vietnam. A similar process of encounter and appropriation took place. Singaporean musicians encountered rhythm and blues, soul music, and, of course, the blues in the form of British and American blues rock popular at the time. The clubs became the barometer for musical trends, for they featured the latest in music happening in the hip meccas of England, the USA, and Europe.

As Joe ended, he sighed and lamented that by the end of the decade the venues for pop had either "altered" or disappeared. The British clubs dwindled as the British announced their pull out and the bases began to close beginning 1968. The US government took Singapore off the list of designated R&R centers and stopped rotating their troops to Singapore in 1970. Bands had lost two acoustemological spaces, not only as venues for performance, but as sonic ways of knowing their world as a crossroads where, "if you want to learn how to make songs yourself, you take your guitar and you go to where the road crosses that way, where a crossroads is." (Evans, 1971:10).

Heritage Straydogs Style

"Heritage" is often generated as a hegemonic, highly institutionalized project of commemoration that is productive of collective identities—most often in the function of nation building (Smith, Shackle, and Campbell 2011). "Working class heritage" has been characterized as counter to some "shared past of the nation" of institutions and regulations that are set in place as part of the state's bureaucracy to administer its significant, distinctive past and the national cultural objects deemed worthy of preservation (Smith, Shackle, and Campbell 2011: 5). Importantly, Kirshenblatt-Gimblett (1995: 369) characterizes heritage as a "new mode of cultural production in the present that has recourse to the past." This is important because production, distribution, and consumption are intrinsically linked. The cultural productions described above—talking cock, lo hei tosses, happy hour jam sessions—are sonic recourses, and vintage guitar shops filled with gear are simultaneously forms of consumption that are experienced as assemblages of individual and collective actions taken in a historically charged phenomenology of an "all-over-present" (Geertz 1995)—in this case, an all over present dominated by "The Singapore Story," a story in which the pioneers of nation building led the way towards establishing social and personal ideals founded in work ethic, productivity level, efficiency, and prosperity articulated in postcolonial markets, regional and global politics, and equally expansive cultural circulations. It becomes difficult to disentangle official, tangible, intangible, and vernacular forms of heritage. The cosmopolitan values that are formative for this small community of musicians, friends, family, and fans articulate individually and collectively the possibilities brought about by the relationality between local actions, global cultural industries, urban places in Singapore, and, of course, the Singaporean state. A couple of examples reveal these various ways in which heritage in Singapore is a mode of cultural production, revealing what vernacular heritage might be, and how resilience is maintained.

Lily Kong (1999:12), interested in the manner in which "different constructions of heritage converge or diverge," critically examines the official invention of "a popular music heritage" in 1990s Singapore. Kong (1999: 12) notes official inventions of heritage in which Singapore's popular music past was of concern, and interest in "undesirable" elements—drugs and rock and roll—were absent in "partial reclamation" projects, or resided at a "safe distance" in a time without heritage. Kong then proceeds to a collection of oral history material collected by the National Archives in preparation for a 1996 exhibition—Retrospin—that focused on Singapore music. She notes that the recordings "revealed a palpable sense of heritage … comprising the raw material of common identity and belonging" (1999: 14). It is this sense of heritage that Kong (1999: 6) argues is "largely unsung" in official heritage projects of national pride and belonging that, ironically, are central to the palpable sense of belonging Kong refers to that is the heart of this community and, for that matter, the symposium as well.

Kiang's potential for actuating vernacular heritage is built from his social associations. Guitar 77's website describes this veteran rocker in the following way:

> Kiang (aka Dennis or Old Man, sometimes Dirty Old Man) is no stranger to the local music scene. He is the "hot" bassist of recently revived 70's rockers, Stray Dogs (…) yes he is that old! Needless to say he is musically influenced by all the 60's and 70's rock giants in particular Pink Floyd, The Beatles, Led Zeppelin and The Who. He is also a huge fan of local Alternative Funk Rock band, Ugly In The Morning, and can frequently be seen at their shows scaring some of the other fans with his cheering and screeching like a drunken little girl (UITM loves him for this!). Besides teaching himself how to play the guitar and the bass, Old Man learned to play the Conga and the Cajon under the tutelage of Faiser Florez.[9]

Presently, Kiang remains associated with 1960s Singapore, heritage music (1960s rock music), and several currently performing heritage bands. Kiang and James, as well as the other members of The Straydogs, are captured in various degrees and contexts in the jargons within "cultural heritage." Kiang, James, and The Straydogs are of the "intangible" sort. Intangible heritage, sometimes referred to as virtual heritage, is "living heritage," or "the practices, representations, expressions, knowledge, skills—as well as the instruments, objects, artefacts and cultural spaces associated therewith—that communities, groups and, in some cases, individuals recognize as part of their Cultural Heritage" (UNESCO 2003). Kiang and James, in this scheme, are for now "living human treasures," which are "persons who possess to

9   http://www.guitar77.com/. Accessed 23 February 2014.

a very high degree the knowledge and skills required for performing or recreating specific elements of the intangible Cultural Heritage." (UNESCO 2003). These elements include, as cited by UNESCO (2003), oral traditions, performing arts, local knowledge, and traditional skills.

In 2014 I was declared the newest member of The Straydogs. My addition to the original lineup was as a guitarist and lead singer. To some degree, my membership in the band, proposed by Kiang and accepted by the others, was motivated by a concert. The Straydogs were booked to perform with two of Singapore's most famous 1960s singers: Veronica Young, known as the "Connie Francis of Singapore," and Vernon Cornelius, also known as the "Cliff Richard of Singapore." The concert was part of a series of shows booked to celebrate the Singaporean state's 50th anniversary as a nation-state with some "heritage." The concert series was held in Singapore's "Esplanade," one of Asia's finest concert halls, and a crown jewel often used officially to represent Singapore as a creative, modern city.

The concert series was dubbed "A Date with Friends" (figure 5.7) and continues as a series today. Lectures on 1960s Singapore accompanied the performances; in fact, Joe was a featured speaker (figure 5.8). Like the Retrospin exhibition Kong (1999) examined, this management of heritage as an intellectual exploration of the past is of course the manner in which a controversial past is cleaned up and made presentable in the present. A "A Date with Friends" concert attempts to obscure "different constructions of heritage" in both expected and unexpected ways. Before we could perform, Singapore's Media Development Authority (MDA) reviewed the lyrics of the songs on our setlist for content that may be offensive to particular "racial" religious groups, as a preventive method for avoiding conflict and disharmony.[10] The producer of the show was worried about our performance but also our presence both backstage and onstage. The producer was suspicious that we were drinking alcohol, which we were—the bottles of whiskey were concealed in our guitar cases. We hid our bottles and cups whenever the producer checked up on us in our dressing room. Here the rocker meets the state as different constructions of heritage converge/diverge—the rebellious vernacular and the official cleansed version of the 1960s popular music scene in Singapore.

10   Censorship of music based on lyrical content by the Singaporean government continues today: See Crystal Tai, "Derision on social media as Singapore's list of 'offensive' songs by Lady Gaga, Ariana Grande hits the wrong notes," *South China Morning Post*, 2 April 2019, https:// www.scmp.com/news/asia/southeast-asia/article/3004352/derision-social-media-singapore-ministers-list-offensive. Accessed 5 May 2019.

Figure 5.7. Concert poster for the "A Date with Friends" concert series, 2015 (photo by Steve Ferzacca)

The producer and his assistants were also worried about whether or not we could actually perform our set list: eleven songs in forty-five minutes. And they were worried about our "professionalism" or lack thereof. The doubts and concerns about professionalism led the producer's assistants to suggest to us we amend our setlist to include fewer songs, which of course we refused. The fact that the original Checkmates, considered a thoroughly professional band, were backing both Veronica and Vernon also fueled the concerns.

We were bookended by Veronica and Vernon: Veronica opened with her setlist of 1960s English language cover tunes she sang as a 1960s pop singer. We followed Veronica (figure 5.9). The contrast could not have been starker. The blues rock of The Straydogs playing a set of original tunes recorded for EMI records in the 1960s and 1970s, compared to the sweetness of Veronica's music, was actually a quite remarkable sonic representation of differences

Figure 5.8. Lectures accompanying the concert series (photo by Steve Ferzacca)

in the music community at the time. For The Straydogs, the original music written and performed combined tangible and intangible heritage, making either indistinguishable from the other. The volume and intensity of The Straydogs' music energized the audience. An elderly Singaporean man turned to a colleague of mine and said, "these guys were the alternative."

Figure 5.9. The Straydogs performing at The Esplanade, 2015 (photo by Jamie Gillen)

Unexpectedly, the spirited response to our set upset Vernon as he took the stage. So much so that, instead of performing his set of cover tunes, he decided to tell stories about the 1960s and his accomplishments as a musician. However, he did so by belittling the accomplishments of other bands at the time, taking aim at The Straydogs. It was Vernon and the Checkmates that The Straydogs replaced as the house band at the Golden Venus Club. Some of his story telling referred to the social relations at that time among these young Singaporean singers and musicians who were once again, after many decades, together on stage. Vernon spoke of class differences between different neighborhoods that produced and allowed for certain kinds of bands—in this case cover bands versus bands playing original music. The Golden Venus was located on swanky Orchard Road. Vernon suggested that the location of the club precluded the possibility of upstart rockers from mixed neighborhoods having the opportunity to play for such an audience. A jealous spat anchored in the past was breaking out before the audience in the present.

The MC of the show, the producer, and his assistants became increasingly nervous about the direction Vernon's set was heading, and backstage began strategies to end his set. Vernon continued with his stories while the Checkmates played the same song (The Rolling Stones "I Can't get No Satisfaction") over and over as sonic background to the rant onstage. Finally, the MC saw an opportunity to return to the stage, thank Vernon, and announce the end of the concert. Vernon was furious, swore at the producer, which produced a couple of Singaporean police officers to record complaints from the producer and his assistants. Vernon was apparently banned from future performances at the Esplanade. Again, disentangling the official and vernacular here generated in a mode of cultural production/consumption in which the past serves the present (Kirshenblatt-Gimblett 1995: 369) seems futile. The vernacular can only exist in the relationality among these distinctions and constructions of heritage that are experienced in intersecting and dissolving networks formed in relations of gender, class, the state, urban residency, guitar gear, international popular music, and mall basements. This is the source of vernacular resilience.

Acting/Method: The Symposium as Heritage

Our intention motivating our participation in the symposium—a social event—was to examine vernacular heritage in the emergent and reassembled associations in various milieux—including the symposium itself. We were interested in observing and participating in classic Latourian notions of actor-networks—"associations of heterogeneous elements" of human and nonhuman "mediators and intermediaries" that entangle the connections of which Latour (2005) terms the social. All of this made sense to us; our acoustemologies emerge from and within such networks of persons, gear, icons, histories, sonographies, and more. We wanted others to have an opportunity to be "experienced." For without the social, vernacular heritage ceases to exist.

Figure 5.10. ARI symposium with some Straydogs (photo by Steve Ferzacca)

During the presentation, Kiang reads the lyrics of his original composition *Katong* (2005). The song tells the story of teenage life in one of Singapore's mixed neighborhoods. Record shops, the beach, bakeries, coffee shops, teen pranks, food, and, of course, various characters from that time and place all appear in the song. Kiang elaborates on the content for the audience and, while doing so, he smiles and says, "Katong was a great place for a young boy to grow up because of the close proximity of all girls' high schools." He laughs—the audience melts.

After the presentation, many from the audience made up of institute fellows, NUS academics and students, and some from our music community came up to Joe and Kiang, commenting on the presentation, but also life in Singapore back then (figure 5.10). The song about a place where he and The Straydogs were formed and grew up animates the potential for vernacular heritage. All that is required is the social. A month later,

Kiang was invited to participate in a writers' festival held by Singapore's Management University. He had learned something from his participation in the symposium and decided to repeat that performance. Once again the audience melted.

The presentation was performed in reflexive terms in order to discover the "extent to which different constructions of heritage converge or diverge" that interests Kong (1999: 1) in her examination of the invention of popular music heritage in Singapore in the 1990s. In the past, present, and in the here and now of the presentation, the social reflexivity involved allowed us to see for ourselves what E. P. Thompson (1993) refers to as the *evolution* of a customary consciousness he sees emerging in the nineteenth century. He, too, notes the conspiracy among elite and working class notions of custom. He notes the differing yet intersecting social and political agendas of elite and working classes for identifying and evoking custom. In the case of vernacular heritage, in its movement from basements and guitar shops, to bars and military bases, to research institutes and conference events, we can see, perhaps, a kind of vernacular heritage consciousness appear not unlike the customary consciousness that E. P. Thompson explores in England in the eighteenth and nineteenth centuries. Right before our eyes, we witnessed the effervescence of a way of life and knowing the world that, as heritage, "becomes a right protected" (Thompson 1993: 104). Right before our eyes, then, the social of vernacular heritage appears.

It is at a crossroads where this project began, and of course it is at a crossroads where this project remains. The local sites in Singapore made to do something as crossroads are the places where the vital energies of heritage potential are assembled and reassembled by the small community of musicians, friends, and fans I worked with, performed with, and learned from.

References

Appadurai, Arjun. 1986. "Introduction: Commodities and the Politics of Value." In *The Social Life of Things: Commodities in Cultural Perspective*, edited by Arjun Appadurai, 3–63. Cambridge: Cambridge University Press.

Barendregt. Bart. 2014. *Sonic Modernities in the Malay World: A History of Popular Music, Social Distinction and Novel Lifestyles 1930s – 2000's.* Leiden: Brill.

Connolly, William E. 2013. "The 'New Materialism' and the Fragility of Things." *Millennium: Journal of International Studies* 4 (3): 399–412.

Evans, David. 1971. *Tommy Johnson*. London: Studio Vista.

Feld, Steven. 2012. *Jazz Cosmopolitanism in Accra: Five Musical Years in Ghana.* Durham: Duke University Press.

Ferzacca, Steve. 2006. "Learning to Listen: Kroncong Music in a Javanese Neighborhood." *The Senses and Society* 1 (3): 331–58.

Ferzacca, Steve. 2012. *Deep Sound: Kroncong Music in a Javanese Neighborhood. Asia Research Institute.* National University of Singapore. Working Papers Series.

Geertz, Clifford. 1995. *Two Countries, Four Decades, One Anthropologist.* Cambridge, MA: Harvard University Press.

Hooykaas, Jacoba. 1955. "The Gateway on the Crossroads?" *Bijdragen tot de Taal-, Land- en Volkenkunde* 111 (4): 413–5.

Huizinga, Johan. 1950. *Homo Ludens: A Study of the Play-Element in Culture.* Boston: Beacon Press.

Kirshenblatt-Gimblett, Barbara. 1995. "Theorizing Heritage." *Ethnomusicology* 39 (3) (Autumn): 367–80.

Kong, Lily. 1999. "The Invention of Heritage: Popular Music in Singapore." *Asian Studies Review* 23 (1): 1–25.

Kosambi, Damodar Dharmanand. 1962. *Myth and Reality.* Mumbai: Popular Prakashan.

Latour, Bruno. 2005. *Reassembling the Social: An Introduction to Actor-Network-Theory.* Oxford: Oxford University Press.

Mignolo, Walter D. 2000. "The Many Faces of Cosmo-polis: Border Thinking and Critical Cosmopolitanism." *Public Culture* 12 (3) (Fall): 721–48.

Ong, Aihwa, 2011. Introduction Worlding Cities, or the Art of Being Global. In Worlding Cities: Asian Experiments and the Art of Being Global, edited by Ananya Roy and Aihwa Ong, 1–26. Oxford: Blackwell Publishing.

Pereira, Joseph. 1999. *Legends of the Golden Venus.* Singapore: Times Publishing.

Pereira, Joseph. 2011. *Apache Over Singapore: The Story of Singapore Sixties Music,* vol. 1. Bournemouth: Select Publishing.

Pickering, Michael, and Tony Green. 1987. "Towards a Cartography of the Vernacular Milieu." In *Everyday Culture: Popular Song and the Vernacular Milieu,* edited by Michael Pickering and Tony Green, 1–38. Milton Keynes: Open University Press.

Schneider, Jane, and Rayna Rapp, eds. 1995. *Articulating Hidden Histories: Exploring the Influence of Eric R. Wolf.* Berkeley: University of California Press.

Smith, Laurajane, Paul A. Shackle, and Gary Campbell. 2011. "Introduction: Class Still Matters." In *Heritage, Labour and the Working Classes*, edited by Laurajane Smith, Paul A. Shackle, and Gary Campbell, 1–16. London: Routledge.

Taussig, Michael. 1993. *Mimesis and Alterity: A Particular History of the Senses.* London and New York: Routledge.

Thompson, E. P. 1993. *Customs in Common: Studies in Traditional Popular Culture.* New York: New Press.

UNESCO. 2003. "Text of the Convention for the Safeguarding of the Intangible Cultural Heritage – intangible heritage – Culture Sector – UNESCO." https://ich.unesco.org/en/convention. Accessed 20 March 2024.

Wallach, Jeremy. 2008. *Modern Noise, Fluid Genres: Popular Music in Indonesia 1997-2001*. Madison: University of Wisconsin Press.

Yao, Souchou. 2007. *Singapore: The State and the Culture of Excess*. London: Routledge.

Social Media Resources

"The Crossroads in Hoodoo Magic and the Ritual of Selling Yourself to the Devil." http://www.luckymojo.com/crossroads.html. Accessed 15 October 2014.

"Kayagata-sati Sutta: Mindfulness Immersed in the Body" [Pali]. Translated by Thanissaro Bhikkhu (1997). http://www.accesstoinsight.org/tipitaka/mn/mn.119.than.html. Accessed 15 October 2014.

About the Author

Steve Ferzacca conducts ethnographic research in medical anthropology and popular culture. Steve's recent book, *Sonic City: Making Rock Music and Urban Life in Singapore* (2020) is based on ethnographic research in a community of amateur and semi-pro musicians in Singapore who congregate around several Singaporean 1960s rock music "legends."

6. The Liberation of Individual Cultural Vernacularity: Emancipating Citizens' Subjectivity through Art

Motohiro Koizumi

Abstract: I address the recent socially engaged art (SEA) movement in Japan, not only as art history, but also from citizen and community-based perspectives, focusing on its strengthening of vernacular heritage resilience. First appearing in Japan in the 1950s through the 1970s, and developed during the 1990s, after 2000 SEA particularly flourished in community-based art projects. Utilizing local vernacular architecture, they engaged with central and local administrations, nonprofit organizations, participants, residents, and volunteers. SEA, now considered a method of local revitalization, however, has been criticized for ignoring art's capacity to liberate diverse subjectivities. Using participant observation and interviews, I show how new SEA actively emancipates those subjectivities. Against the stereotype of Japanese homogeneity, SEA encourages the resilience of individual cultural vernacularity.

Keywords: socially engaged art, art project, community revitalization, participation, Japan

We live in an era of cultural consumption. Market fundamentalism and a consumerism based on cultural difference has created an accelerating race for survival among nations, cities, and local communities. In order to win a short-term competition, those who pursue such goals exhibit ignorance of minority peoples' vernacularity and do not accept that even within a single culture individual viewpoints vary significantly.

Since the 1990s, the dynamics of art have been increasingly focused on social transformation by collaboration among various kinds of people. This

Herzfeld, M., and R. Padawangi, eds. *Resilience as Heritage in Asia*. Amsterdam: Amsterdam University Press, 2025.
DOI: 10.5117/9789463728560_CH06

art form is described in various ways, such as social practice art, dialogue art, collaborative art, or relational art; here I will use the term *socially engaged art* (SEA). SEA is an art creation process that aims to transform society from human relationships to the prevailing social system through the practice of participation and dialogue. This art focuses on the significance of artists' unique ideas and concepts, since they can develop different points of view that do not necessarily depend on the interests of particular organizations or actors. Though SEA is not new—its origins being found in previous art practices such as the traditions of community-based art of the late nineteenth century or the historic avant-garde and the "neo" avant-garde in the 1910s and 1960s (Kester 2013: xvi; Bishop 2012: 3)—there is a marked tendency among artists to direct their interest toward the reconstruction of social systems and intersubjective relations among individuals, with the aim of breaking away from the confines of the established art world and bringing about some changes in the so-called real world (Bourriaud 2002; Bishop 2006; Foster 2007; Kester 2013).

In this chapter, I examine how SEA could assist in strengthening the resilience of vernacular heritage. In particular, I will explore the possibilities and challenges of SEA in today's world, where individual or small-scale cultural differences are often overlooked in favor of national and social actors' specific interests. The catalyst for awareness of this problematic larger context is the recent restriction of cultural frameworks by social actors such as national and local governments. According to Raymond Williams (2015: 52), in the modern era "culture" is defined in the following three categories:

i.   the independent and abstract noun which describes a general process of intellectual, spiritual and aesthetic development, from C18.

ii. the independent noun, whether used generally or specifically, which indicates a particular way of life, whether of a people, a period, a group, or humanity in general, from Herder and Klemm.

iii. the independent and abstract noun which describes the works and practices of intellectual and especially artistic activity.

Williams points out that the third usage is often now the most widespread in daily use: culture as music, literature, painting, sculpture, theater, and film. The important issue here, however, is that the meaning of culture has recently been strongly geared towards the second usage. Specifically, the sense of cultures conceived as particular *national* cultures, or as those of a particular city, is becoming a more significant influence.

Culture is today regarded as one of the ultimate resources for driving an economy (Hartley 2005). On a national level, for example, the British government's global economic strategy since the late 1990s has enfolded Britpop, fashion, art, and tourism in the so-called Cool Britannia policy. This strategy was strongly pursued, while, in the background, existing industries declined, and is a particularly representative example of the focus on cultural (or creative) industry by a nation-state. The same is true of the Korean wave policy, which started in the first decade of this century and was driven by the Korean government as a means of recovering from the Asian financial crisis through the promotion of exports of K-pop, TV dramas, and cosmetics. In yet another example, since the 2010s the Japanese government has pursued the Cool Japan policy, which aims to promote cultural tourism, animation, manga, games, fashion, food, and local products. Taiwan and China have similarly been focusing on cultural and creative industrial policies. Under these policies, national culture is represented by promoting the appeal of particular elements and characteristics, all deployed in the national interest as a form of soft power (Iwabuchi 2002, 2007).

Furthermore, economic revitalization using culture is not limited to nation-states. Culture is now also employed for similar purposes by a wide range of social actors, their expedient tendencies often driven by various social, political, and economic ends (Yúdice 2003). It appears in urban and regional policies, such as the Creative City Policy that includes industrial revitalization and tourism promotion as part of its objectives. This policy often encourages cultural projects such as regional art festivals and events, but along with the purpose of revitalization of cities by strengthening cultural industries, another important factor of the Creative Cities idea as an understanding that cultural diversity has tended to be overlooked and ignored (Inazu 2020; Koizumi 2020). As a result, some culture may be overlooked or even excluded even though it may be the source of future vernacular culture.

Among the many such examples, the momentum to promote certain cultures has been accelerating remarkably in Japan in view of the Olympics that were planned for Tokyo in 2020. For example, the government planned to promote the country's culture and economy with "200,000 events, 50,000 artists, and 50 million participants in cultural programs" from 2016 to 2020 (Agency for Cultural Affairs 2016: 5). This has driven a rising interest in the art festivals held in cities and local communities or in the art activities conducted by local artists. Among such notable developments, I single out for discussion those activities that focus on SEA from the perspective of the deconstruction of the centralized and homogenized power of the state to define culture. The examples presented in this chapter may provide valuable lessons for other Asian countries and regions with similar social backgrounds and policy issues.

How are various people's perspectives excluded? How is it possible to revitalize people's diverse subjectivities through art? On the basis of participant observation of, and interviews about, Japanese art projects, I aim to approach these questions using contemporary art projects in civil society as examples.

I intend this discussion to demonstrate that SEA can become a platform to recover individual cultural vernacularity by emancipating citizens' varying cultural and social subjectivities. As I discuss in the later sections, SEA in Japan has been criticized by the art community, since SEA's efforts to differentiate local communities have actually created a situation that has paradoxically caused SEA to become more homogenous. In fact, with the background of economic competitiveness in Japan's cities and localities, and a heightened focus on the rapidly aging society with a falling birth rate, Japanese SEA is consumed as a specialty product, that is, as a consumer product or service with unique cultural characteristics. Simultaneously, however, we can also see artists who have been attempting to expand people's subjectivities through SEA.

As Harumi Befu correctly pointed out, Japanese national character (*Nihonjinron*) has been described as homogeneous (Befu 1990, 2001). As a concept, *Nihonjinron* has been significant in Japanese studies ever since the Tokugawa period (seventeenth–nineteenth centuries), when scholars started asking, "Who are we Japanese?" Befu says, "belief in the uniqueness of the Japanese people is a salient and pervasive feature of 'Japanese mentality' and is the foundation of *Nihonjinron*" (Befu 2001: 66). Yet, the premise of such cultural theories—which are not limited to scholarship on Japanese culture—are thought to be equally applicable to all members of the culture, which is understood in terms of comparisons with other similarly reified cultures. Such views easily generate ethnocentrism, especially as, in Befu's (2001: 67) words, "this comparison is not objective, as one can surmise from the value judgment, either explicit or implicit, accompanying *Nihonjinron* propositions." Certainly, it is true that every culture has, in some sense, unique points, while at the same time social and political systems and consumerism have a tendency to promote uniformity; we cannot, and should not, ignore that fact. Nevertheless, among individuals there are indisputable social and cultural differences that are derived from their cultural, societal, and historical specificities. Also, people have always moved from one country or locality to another, not only since the recent upsurge in globalization, but even in the most ancient times (Clifford 1997). These various factors compose people's own personalities and cultural subjectivities. SEA can contribute to the resilience of individual cultural vernacularity despite the myths of national character and regional idiosyncrasies, and the approach may sometimes help to deconstruct the power that promotes claims to uniformity.

This chapter is divided into five sections. The next section highlights the flourishing trend of SEA in Japan. I will argue that, since around the 2000s, SEAs known as "Art Projects," which are cultural events in local communities, have been booming in Japan. The section after that examines the characteristics and social background of this development. The discussion highlights how SEA is used by the government as a symbol to differentiate certain areas in its advocacy of the regional revitalization policy. In the third section, I describe the issues raised by SEA projects in Japan. Art as a method of reinvigorating local areas (in which a region's fate is at stake) has come to be regarded as a formula for local revitalization in Japan since the 2010s. As a result of this tendency, SEA projects have been criticized by the art community for becoming more homogenous. Here, therefore, I will discuss the problems SEA projects may face when aiming at local invigoration. The fourth section covers new developments in SEA in Japan. In particular, while examining the works of Takayuki Yamamoto and Kimura Toshiro Jinjin as examples of new participatory art that challenge the structure of the homogenized art projects through people's participation, I focus on techniques for challenging the homogenization of art projects as well as the firmly secured social system by revitalizing people's diverse subjectivities. Moreover, I will point out that this kind of art can encourage the resilience of individual cultural vernacularity, which otherwise tends to go unnoticed in current dialogues about culture.

In addition to reviewing the literature on this topic, this study uses as primary sources the results of a field survey of the Echigo-Tsumari Art Triennale conducted in Tokamachi City and Tsunan Town between August 2006 and September 2024, the HOSPITALE project, and the Cotomeya project conducted in Tottori City between September 2011 and August 2024, as well as those of an interview survey of a total of thirty-one artists, curators, participants, viewers, and community residents. These interviews were carried out on 2 September 2012 and 15–16 August 2015 at Art Center Ongoing in Musashino City, Tokyo, HOSPITALE, and Cotomeya in Tottori City, Tottori.

The Flourishing of Socially Engaged Art as Art Projects in Japan

My concern in this chapter is to analyze the role of art in society, especially as a way of reinforcing the resilience of vernacular heritage, taking SEA in

Japan as an example. First of all, I introduce the discussion regarding the recent global flourishing of SEA operations, and then highlight their growth in Japanese contexts, using a key example to illustrate my main points.

The kind of art characterized by social participation that originally emerged in the 1910s and 1960s, and has had an even higher profile since the 1990s, is inseparably and more intimately connected to the social context than was the case previously (Bourriaud 2002; Kester 2013). Nicolas Bourriaud, who advocates for this recent SEA trend, argues that, given the advancement of urbanization in modern society and the tendency for individualization brought on by better electronics technology, interest is increasing in art that pays attention to "possible relations with our neighbors in the present [rather] than to bet on happier tomorrows" (Bourriaud 2002: 45), and especially in art that is formed by the mutual relationships among people. Bourriaud cites various examples such as the art of Rirkrit Tiravanija (1961–) in which Tiravanija treats visitors to the gallery with pad Thai or Thai curry.

Claire Bishop has pointed out that Bourriaud's discussion focuses only on artists who promote community formation and assumes the prior existence of social harmony and homogeneous relationships, and that he loses sight of the political aspects of the community such as a lack of consideration towards people who are excluded from it. Bishop (2004: 72) remarks, "it is precisely this act of exclusion that is disavowed in relational art's preference for 'open-endedness.'" Also, she indicates that SEA flourished under New Labour's policy in the United Kingdom: "The UK context under New Labour (1997–2010) in particular embraced this type of art as a form of soft social engineering" (Bishop 2012: 5). She objects to the evaluation of these practices according to an ethical sense of the good and without regard to its humanistic quality (Bishop 2006, 2012). Bishop's argument provides an important perspective on the conditions that allow SEA to exist not only as social projects but also as, more specifically, art projects as well.

Nevertheless, her discussion remains inadequate for several reasons. She states that she has been strict about the scope of her book, choosing to focus on countries in which art receives public funding and those with historical avant-garde traditions, "hence the decision to include Eastern Europe and South America, but not Asia" (Bishop 2012: 5). Here, Bishop overlooks the fact that, since the 1990s, Japan has experienced growth in publicly funded SEA of the order of similar developments seen in Western Europe. The avant-garde arts have also had a considerable influence on the country since the 20th century, and numerous Japanese artists have even taken their place in the "art worlds" (Becker 1982) emerging onto the global

Figure 6.1. Echigo-Tsumari Art Triennale (photo by Motohiro Koizumi)

stage (Thornton 2008). Precisely because of the ongoing global expansion of SEA, it is necessary to examine these developments through both the common global features of individual locations and in the context of their vernacular social backgrounds.

SEA in Japan also appeared gradually from the 1950s through the 1970s, and has flourished since the 1990s (Kajiya 2016). Especially since the 2000s, SEAs in Japan are strongly associated with art events and festivals such as Bienniales and Trienniales, and have close connections with vernacular architecture in local communities such as old houses (*kominka*) and abandoned schools (*haikō*). They have been collaborating with various social agencies such as central and local governments, nonprofit organizations, participants in the art projects, local residents, and volunteers (Kumakura, Kikuchi, and Nagatsu 2014; Koizumi 2019). These SEAs in Japan have continued to grow in recent years, with budgets ranging up to several billion yen despite the more general slashing of public funding for culture that has taken place in Japan.

These SEAs are often known as "art projects" (*Āto Purojekuto*). Art projects in Japan sometimes include activities covering a range of art trends (such as renovation projects, installations, dance, and video). It is common for many artists to participate in Japanese SEA projects; in general, however, the projects engage in realizing social changes (under themes such as "aging population," "community revitalization," and "establishment of city identity"), in dialogue and collaboration with local communities. As a result, we can say that in Japan large-scale art projects in general are SEA projects.

A prime example of a SEA project in Japan is the Echigo-Tsumari Art Triennale, which is aimed at community development through collaboration in local society and began across the entire Tsumari area (Tokamachi City and Tsunan Town) of 760 km² in Niigata Prefecture (figure 6.1).

The project transformed a small provincial city steeped in nature two hours by train from Tokyo into an enormous art field. Since its first year in 2000, the festival has been directed by the art director Fram Kitagawa. This art project created a new art trend in Japan based on the utilization of open-air spaces (Favell 2011; Kumakura, Kikuchi, and Nagatsu 2014). The art project commenced as a public project mainly featuring open-air sculptures, but the art that developed through the Echigo-Tsumari Art Triennale gradually changed each time the event was held. In comparison with open-air art, there was a relative increase in the presence of participatory art, where local residents and volunteers created works with artists using vacant properties that had proliferated because of depopulation (Kuresawa 2008). To promote local revitalization in the social sense, the theme of "collaboration," which had existed from the early years, gradually began to assume greater importance. As a result, in addition to sculptures and architectural pieces, a large number of closed school and folk house projects, totaling more than three hundred projects, developed through collaborations among diverse groups, including artists from Japan and overseas, and comprising both volunteers and local residents.

Many administrative agencies regard the ongoing Echigo-Tsumari Art Trienniale, which uses vernacular cultural heritage and citizen participation, as a new method of saving local societies currently reeling from the aging of their population and a falling birth rate (Kumakura, Kikuchi, and Nagatsu 2014). It appears that for this reason the project has received awards for its contribution to local revitalization from such prominent officials as the Minister for Internal Affairs and Communications (2004), the Minister for Land, Infrastructure, Transport and Tourism (2010), and the Commissioner for Cultural Affairs (2011). The project, which was developed using budgets for building roads and public facilities in addition to the reduced cultural budget, brought new scenery to the towns and caused the number of tourists to increase. The number of visitors to the Echigo-Trumari project reached 548,380 in 2018 (Echigo-Tsumari Art Triennale Executive Committee 2019). The number of tourists visiting the Echigo-Tsumari region, including foreign visitors, is also on the rise, with 2,196,963 in 2013, 2,284,794 in 2014, and 2,986,955 in 2015 (Ministry of Economy Trade and Industry 2019).

Besides the Echigo-Tsumari project, multiple art projects were also developed under the direction of Kitagawa. One of these was Art Setouchi, held on the islands in the Seto Inland Sea, in cooperation with private companies and foundations; another is the Oku-Noto Triennale, which incorporates the traditional culture and landscape of Noto Peninsula; and another is the Japan Alps Art Festival, which uses local resources such as the natural environment, history, and culture at the foot of the Northern Japan Alps. Also, aside from the Kitagawa-directed art projects, more than a hundred SEA projects have been initiated since the beginning of the century as SEA projects for local revitalization. These include the BEPPU PROJECT, the Aichi Triennale (Chojamachi area), and the Saitama Triennale.

Generally speaking, Japanese SEAs tend to be large-scale art projects with dozens of artists, and are intended to appeal to local cultural characteristics with the aim of addressing local issues such as the decline of industrialization and the depopulation of the communities. Kenji Kajiya has discussed the characteristics of SEA in Japan, along with the historical background of the practice, through a comparison with overseas discussions of SEA. He refers to SEA in Japan using the general term "art project" and shows that Japanese art projects were characterized by site specificity, collaborative work, process disclosure, and weak social critique. Next, he identifies three major historical factors behind these characteristics, namely, (1) open-air art exhibitions, (2) public art, and (3) the effects of the work of Jan Hoet, which are influenced by an approach centered on spatial positioning, operational structures, and distance from the social context (Kajiya 2016: 123–4).

From the perspective of the position of art projects in Japanese art history, Kajiya's findings hit the mark. On the other hand, his discussions on the sociopolitical conditions that form the background against which participatory art projects have flourished are limited. Also, he does not mention the relationship between art projects and the resilience of vernacular heritage. As Kumakura, Kikuchi, and Nagatsu (2014: 9) and Kajiya (2016: 123) himself indicate, however, Japanese art projects are characteristically site-specific and tend to emphasize public participation and collaboration. According to Kitagawa, these projects are realized through "complicity" and "collaboration" involving various people (Kitagawa 2014: 227). The words "complicity" and "collaboration" in this statement mean the cooperation among artists and local residents, as well as artists and participants as viewers. In other words, SEA in Japan goes beyond temporary participation, instead developing within the framework of intimate relations between artists and local society with public life and local culture. Therefore, we should contemplate the social as well as the historical aspects of art projects. This is why I am focusing here on the relationship between the SEA project and its participating citizens.

Characteristics of Japanese Socially Engaged Art: Socially Engaged Art as a "Specialty Product"

While considering the characteristics of SEA in Japan, we should investigate the social backgrounds and issues. In this section, I examine the social background to the florescence of SEAs in Japan and identify the problems associated with them.

First, their social background consists of (1) neoliberal policies promoting the strengthening of Japanese cities' and localities' economic competitiveness; (2) a heightened focus on such policies brought about by a sense of crisis generated by the rapidly aging society combined with its falling birthrate; and, as a result of these factors, (3) approaches to local revitalization that seek to employ art and local cultural resources as products designed to accelerate consumption.

Since the 1980s, Japan has taken a systematic path to "small government" and "neo-liberalism," which has entailed the increased privatization of public services abandoning earlier welfarist policies (Yoshimi 2009: 170–1). The Liberal Democratic administrations of Nakasone (1982–1987), Hashimoto (1996–1998), and Koizumi (2001–2006) advanced privatization policies that reached the domains of welfare, education, and culture and adopted neoliberal policies to encourage industrial enterprise (Yoshimi 2009). Also, in the first decade of this century, the Japanese government introduced a cultural project titled "Cool Japan," which was inspired by "Cool Britannia" (a policy promoted by British Prime Minister Tony Blair's administration); this initiative was intended to promote creative industries and to lead to the repackaging of Japan's popular culture as an export-oriented industry (Mōri 2014). Thus, in Japan, the trend of perceiving regional culture from the perspective of economic development has become stronger (Yamashita and Kanai 2015). Shigeru Ishiba (2015), a former minister in charge of regional revitalization, commented:

> The philosophy behind policies so far has been to "ensure that there are no regional disparities." But now we are demonstrating each region's individuality to the maximum extent possible, and the products that are unique to each of these regions are being established as the independent core of these policies.

His comment reflects the logic of using interregional competition to encourage economic independence. This approach represents a change of focus, in which culture is emphasized as a wellspring that generates individuality. The approach also leads to increased interest in cultural tourism as well as to competitions between mascots like yuru-chara (*yuru kyara*), which are clad in attire symbolizing each area's regional character. Cultural events in Japan today, including the art projects, often seem to exhibit the individuality of local areas, while echoing the intentions of the national government and emulating the precedents of other municipalities' cultural policies. In other words, the artists of these projects have become an instrument of consumption as a way of surviving competition at the municipal and regional levels (Sadakane 2016; Koizumi 2020).

Local governments have been facing an additional problem. In the 1980s, and before recession hit in the 1990s, they encouraged the industrialization of culture through the development of resorts, cultural tourism, and specialty products. In the regional social policy pursued by the Abe administration, the strengthening of regional competitiveness, referred to as "regional revitalization" (*chihou sousei*), has acquired great significance (Yamashita and Kanai 2015; Kaneko 2016). The tide of regional revitalization was spurred by the twin phenomena of a falling birthrate and an aging population, a double burden that emerged at the beginning of the century at a pace unseen in other countries. These issues created worrisome prospects at the local level as communities staked their survival on programs of local revitalization. Consequently, to contribute to regional revitalization and avoid becoming each a "city at the risk of disappearing" (*shoumetsu kanousei toshi*) (Masuda and Japan Policy Council 2014: 18), municipalities have been forced to focus on securing independence, most notably in terms of their economies. Consequently, local governments have laid emphasis on promoting cultural tourism projects to increase the number of visitors to the regions; while not only do their budgets come from the original Agency for Cultural Affairs, and local governments, and are explicitly earmarked for cultural purposes, they also draw on the central government's allocations for regional revitalization. Kumakura, Kikuchi, and Nagatsu (2014: 27) point out that "all over Japan, society has begun to request the hosting of art projects for economic reasons, such as the promotion of tourism."

In other words, within the framework of neoliberal competition in a socio-economic structure that is based on the post-Fordist mode of production, and in the context of anxiety about a demographically declining society, SEA projects in Japan have functioned as a product that drives consumption and gathers people. Through these projects, certain cities and areas are differentiated from others by means of cultural and artistic symbols. This recalls Baudrillard's (1998) prediction of a society in which consumption would be driven by the need for difference. Furthermore, Takao Mamada stated that the consumption of cultural values in Japan has consistently continued to increase even during the period of stagnation. Thus, art is consumed as a specialty product against a background of cultural consumption needs and of a government policy designed to encourage those needs. The food and traditional houses of each area, photographs of the attractive scenery, and the explicitly distinctive collaborative art in which people can participate have become devices for drawing in outsiders and satisfying local residents at the same time.

Of paramount importance is the citizens' own desire to take part in and enjoy such cultural events as special products. Authority, in this modern society, does not seek to subjugate people by overemphasizing discipline. Our energies are unconsciously directed toward a specific purpose—capitalistic interest that commercializes human emotion. When citizens choose to join in local art projects—as volunteers or through a citizens' program—their emotions can be manipulated so as to lead in a specific direction.

Thus, the various efforts to differentiate local areas have actually created a situation that has caused SEA projects—framed as specialty products—to become more alike despite their superficial differences. This makes them suitable for post-Fordist cultural consumption. Moreover, the latest trend in local revitalization (*chihou sousei*) endorsed by the government and intellectuals of Japan has turned art projects into a model that theoretically could be applied anywhere. In other words, as in the case of UNESCO's Creative Cities network, which originally sought to understand cultural diversity as an important philosophy, now local governments tend to focus on the revitalization of cities by strengthening the cultural industries. The philosophy of urban and regional resilience and the coexistence of multiculturalism (that is, the challenge of achieving conviviality) have been transformed to revitalize industry and tourism driven by the logic of competition among cities. As a result, policies are competitively focused on a certain culture, and overlook or even exclude living heritages that otherwise might have been able to lead toward greater cultural diversity in future generations.

Critiques of Socially Engaged Art in Japan

Naoya Fujita (2016) is one of the voices raising questions about Japanese art projects, and he comments that the political diversity that projects should include has given way to a unidirectional approach. Fujita (2016) indicates that Japanese art projects are losing their critical perspective since their emphasis on regional revitalization follows an agenda imposed by the government. He discusses how the focus of art differed from the government agenda, and argues that "when principles such as theory, philosophy, or ideology are more influential than aesthetics, the art genre will lose the specific meaning of its existence" (Fujita 2016: 41).

Certainly, this argument reflects the voices of artists who have participated in SEA projects as well as those of nonparticipants. For instance, artist Yoshio Shirakawa (2014) made this statement:

> Because we cannot see the immediate results of our thinking, the whole plan doesn't come out in advance. Also, it takes a long time, doesn't it? It's not easy to progress with my work [when it is held in conjunction] with the usual type of [art] project.

At the normative art projects, artists are required to follow the plan originally submitted to the selection committee, while emphasizing the substance and process of collaboration. The scheduling of their participation is especially constrained by their originally submitted proposals. These constraints represent a trend in SEA in which the practice has thoroughly lost its flexibility as local governments use art as a resource tailored to the purpose of regional revitalization and adapted to conform with the precedents of the art project.

In the context of globalization, cultural spheres, as well as social, economic, and political spheres, are becoming ever more closely intertwined (Morris-Suzuki 2004). The cultural sphere that includes the arts has come to be used for the benefit of such agencies as nation-states, local governments, and NGOs (Yúdice 2003; Iwabuchi 2007). Thus, culture and arts are being put into society as a resource for creating something different from the fruits of other social actors. Against this background and structure, it is necessary to pay close attention to maintaining diverse viewpoints among art projects, and not to allow them to become oriented toward the single, fixed purpose or direction (such as local revitalization) of governments or other institutional agencies. As I have already mentioned, Japanese art projects have close relationships with their local municipalities and communities (Kumakura, Kikuchi, and Nagatsu 2014; Kajiya 2016). Therefore, there is the danger that art activities in one area might become homogenized as a result of being oriented too strongly to a single channel. For instance, if art is forced to function by central or local government as a means of creating profits—a goal that might not favor the uniqueness of some regions—the diversity of artistic expression of art projects could easily succumb to homogenization.

Socially Engaged Art for Emancipating Citizens' Subjectivities

The logical next question regards identifying art that can expand people's subjective differences. Is it impossible to emancipate people's subjectivity through art itself without depending on these predefined specific directions?

I focus on the work of Takayuki Yamamoto and Kimura Toshiro Jinjin because they are rare among socially engaged artists; their activities are centered on SEA projects and are attempts to expand people's subjectivities. Although, like other artists, they also encounter difficulties in creating their works freely under the rules laid down for art projects for community revitalization, they use mechanisms and strategies from original concepts and thereby try to enable participants and viewers to expand their subjectivities.

Yamamoto's expressions consist of participatory workshops and video works made of these workshops for art projects, which are designed to provoke citizens into making explicit their hitherto implicit critiques of society. Children of approximately primary school age often participate in his workshops. Of course, initiatives had already been developed that focused on children and attempted to expand their creativities. In Japan, there have also been recent attempts to diversify children's expressive styles through art in fields such as education and welfare. These efforts, however, are education systems devised mainly for the purpose of cultivating the sensitivities of children exclusively and were not designed for adults, and in Japan it is only fair to say that art education in particular has tended to conform to the curriculum guidelines prescribed by the national government. Yamamoto, however, has adopted a different approach in which he seeks to induce situations that would encourage children's individual subjectivities, and he also tries to emancipate the subjectivities of the audience. This audience includes both the various people visiting the workshop and the viewers visiting the exhibition of the art projects.

For example, in "Telling Your Future," Yamamoto first has children devise their own new fortune-telling systems (figure 6.2). Next, he encourages the children to create their own fortune-telling methods and to perform them for visiting adult participants (figure 6.3). Thereafter, he creates video works in which the children themselves explain their fortune-telling systems for the spectators of the art projects.

The spectators who visit the performances and exhibitions laugh at the fanciful fortune-telling devices invented by the children which include, for instance, fortune telling based on shoes, stones, and other objects. The results of this fortune telling, however, with results that sometimes seem cruel or mere bluffs, have come to make the adult spectators rethink their

Figure 6.2. "Telling Your Future" by Takayuki Yamamoto, workshop (photo by Motohiro Koizumi)

Figure 6.3. "Telling Your Future" by Takayuki Yamamoto (photo by Motohiro Koizumi)

own subjectivities. Yamamoto (2012) notes: "To tell someone something that is based on a certain value system is actually a very risky thing to do." By this he means the precarious state of the children and adults who are being taught the value systems of society through uniform systems of formal enlightenment.

Yamamoto's gesture, I should note, is very different from the conventional art-education attitude of praising whatever the child expresses. Yamamoto often mimics the behavior of powerful actors intentionally. By doing this, he attempts to disinter their (or the spectators') awareness, frustration, or doubts about this system. Therefore, there is a great deal of humor and charm in his SEA, which seems to laugh away contemporary society's stubborn belief in uniform thinking.

The motivation for this idea came from Yamamoto's own experience as an educator, and also from the Fukushima Daiichi nuclear disaster in 2011. First, Yamamoto, who once served as an art teacher in an elementary school, saw the children being organized into a single hegemonic system even when the teachers claimed they were respecting the children's intellectual freedom. At the same time, he noticed that children exhibited more diverse subjectivity than adults, who may lose individual subjectivity in today's society. Through his workshops and artworks, Yamamoto therefore promotes activities that symbolize the importance of exhibiting the individual subjectivity of each child. In addition, the Fukushima Daiichi nuclear accident, triggered by the Great East Japan Earthquake in 2011, gave Yamamoto a clear and shocking example of the danger of blindly believing one value. Nuclear technology has been promoted as a Japanese government-private joint national policy since post World War II. Its safety and certainty have long been upheld as true through national and local policies and education. As a result of these experiences, Yamamoto thinks that modern society is a world of "bright dystopia," (Koizumi 2023) where people are persuaded to believe blindly in one system. Yamamoto, through videos and workshops with children, aims to challenge stereotypical official values and to create art that encourages the resilience of each person's individual subjectivity.

In this regard, interviews that I conducted show that the children and parents who participated in Yamamoto's activities were able to notice the importance of having different values from each other. From the late nineteenth century to World War II, the Japanese education system was geared towards gaining military power, and from the nineteenth century to the present day toward establishing a strong labor force in industrial society. It has remained essentially unchanged in more than a century, functioning well as a training stage for people to become a homogeneous power for the benefit of the nation, even though people have different characters and

Figure 6.4. "Tottori-style stall" (photo by Motohiro Koizumi)

points of view. Participants sometimes say that "it is difficult to realize individual subjectivity in a school," an established education system. In this regard, Yamamoto's challenge is significant.

The other example is the work of Kimura Toshiro Jinjin. Kimura originally operated a mobile café called Nodate (*no-dah-tay*), where he dressed like a drag queen and fired teacups that the participants painted on the spot so that they could enjoy Japanese tea in their own teacups. The mobile café traveled to places such as Kyoto, Otsuchi, and Tottori.

His activities at the Yatai Rakuen Project and HOSPETALE art project in Tottori have inspired projects, called "Tottori-style stalls" (figure 6.4), among citizens. The "Tottori-style street stall," which began with the name "Illusion Stall," is a project in which residents open their own street stalls in town. People inspired by Kimura, usually previous participants and viewers, eventually worked together with him to deploy street stalls (which are forbidden in principle in Japan) in various forms and at various places such as parks, bridges, and stations. For example, hometown cooking stalls, fortune-telling stalls, hand-warmer stalls, love-letter stalls, and stalls selling *hanko* (a personal name seal used as identification in Japanese society)—all temporarily occupied spaces and lent a new kind of scenery to the town (figure 6.5). Those who have participated in this project so far encompass a

Figure 6.5. "Tottori-style stall" at the Yayoi Park, Tottori (photo by Rieko Onishi)

wide age range, from college students to people in their fifties. In this way, they have sought to deconstruct the sense of value with regard to cultural production held by both the participants and the viewers who then manage the street stalls. Azumi Akai (2017), who is the director and curator of both projects, stated their aims as follows: "The artist gives us the [unspoken] message 'you can stay here.' They try to create spaces for us, and validate our presence through the arts they create."

The activities of Kimura in Tottori have been linked to the openness of people, not only as participants but also as viewers. Kimura's art allows people to act more imaginatively, and the participants and observers of his stall can emancipate their subjectivities. This is demonstrated in the "Tottori-style stalls" run by various citizens. The attitudes of the people who frequent these activities, as indicated by such comments as "we want to continue this project and hold it regularly," show that this site is taking on irreplaceable significance for its participants. Importantly, these activities are a place where participants can display their own powers of imagination to others. It is possible to spread illusions and wild ideas there, through mediation by artists and others. Additionally, visitors to the project have an opportunity to change their subjectivities, a process mediated by the other participants.

Yamamoto and Kimura's works are primarily arts designed to emancipate "active participants." Writing of theatre, Jacques Rancière (2009) has discussed how "active spectators" can exist in contrast to what happens with art designed for "enlightenment," which places the spectators in passive positions. If we use his term, it can be said that Yamamoto and Kimura try to transform the "active spectators" into "active participants." They examine ways in which retaining participants' unique activity and agency are possible in contrast to what happens with art that claims to enlightens its viewers through works while in reality rendering them passive participants. Yamamoto and Kimura's artworks can be seen to emancipate the subjectivities of its participants, who have been homogenized in typical Japanese art projects.

Furthermore, Yamamoto and Kimura also aim to emancipate the various active spectators through the already emancipated active participants by developing their works through participatory platforms of art projects involving various participants. Even though Yamamoto and Kimura occasionally undertake exhibitions at art museums, they develop many activities through art projects at the initial stage of these works. As I noted earlier, one characteristic of SEA projects in Japan is the involvement of local vernacular communities through their cultural lives. This means that, unlike works displayed in art galleries in Japan, diverse and sometimes unexpected spectators as well as regular participants can become involved in the projects by chance. Gallery exhibitions, to be sure, should not be regarded simply as places that reinforce elite cultural hierarchies (Bishop 2012: 37–9). Works of art displayed in gallery spaces, however, especially in Japan, although open to everybody, attract limited numbers. In contrast, SEA projects are visited by people from outside the art worlds; these include people of various social positionalities. Some are local residents, some parents uninterested in art, others are farmers, and yet others are students. The artists can therefore attempt to emancipate various active participants, and, what is more telling, they can emancipate a range of active spectators as well. That is the strategy of Yamamoto and Kimura's artworks. Here is Yamamoto (2012) again: "After all, the ultimate goal was to 'tell the fortunes' of adults [spectators]."

In other words, SEAs like those of Yamamoto and Kimura can give a greater voice to vernacular culture instead of emphasizing only elite values. This development can in turn help vernacular culture become more resilient by enhancing its value in the eyes of the general public. The activities of Yamamoto and Kimura are made up of small cultural units that could become a kind of meme for people to form a vernacular culture. They are anonymous but important, since they include each person's different points of view, or what I call cultural vernacularity—and they can lead to the future development of this cultural vernacularity. Moreover, SEA enables art-as elite-culture and art-as-citizen-culture to blend. At the same time, it maintains a distance from the expanding hegemony of the nationalist version of culture, which was established during Japan's emergence as a nation-state in the nineteenth century and was reinforced by economical industrialization movements as exemplified by the Cool Japan project. In this respect, such SEA can surely lead to the resilience of vernacular cultural heritage.

These activities still constitute only a minority of practices in the field of SEA. Also, these SEA practices cannot completely transform the current trend toward the reinforcement of so-called national and city cultures in the short term. SEAs such as those of Yamamoto and Kimura are neverthe-less all the more significant precisely because of the platform of people's diverse subjectivities. Their works offer a glimpse of the possibilities of the emergence of a new form of art in a society where individual cultural vernacularity tends to be overlooked.

Conclusion

In this chapter, I initially discussed the flourishing trend of SEAs in Japan and its characteristics not only from an art historical viewpoint but also from a social perspective. First, I underlined how SEA projects in Japan were flourishing and indicated that these art projects have come to be regarded as a breakthrough solution for local revitalization. In the process, however, as a result of its focus on regional revitalization, SEA in Japan has been increasingly criticized, as the diverse political arenas that projects should include have given way to government-imposed agendas. I do not deny the validity of this criticism, but consider it possible to encourage new SEA developments that assist in emancipating people's diverse subjectivities. In particular, I have pointed out the possibility of new SEAs, while citing the works of Takayuki Yamamoto and Kimura Toshiro Jinjin as examples of new participatory art.

When we observe SEA activities, it is important to note that this kind of art can bolster the resilience of individual cultural vernacularity. As I have mentioned above in discussing Befu and the "Creative City," the idea of a single national culture tends to emerge from a too exclusive emphasis on the characteristics of only one group or on a presumed commonality shared by the national majority. In addition, some are motivated by ethnocentrism, the view that one ethnic group is superior to all others. Another factor is the desire for economic industrialization in the context of intensifying competition between contemporary cities; its effect is exemplified by the push to create a Cool Japan and to revitalize local communities. I want to argue that, in the process, individual cultural vernacularity based on different cultural and social backgrounds can be too easily ignored. Against this background, the activities of Yamamoto's and Kimura's socially engaged projects show how art can play a role in releasing individual cultural vernacularity.

Finding the way to regain cultural vernacularity in the sense of the organic and diverse lives of nature and people—the original meaning of culture—should be a significant issue for all of us. SEAs, which try to emancipate citizen's subjectivities, show new potential paths to recovering cultural vernacular diversity.

References

Agency for Cultural Affairs. 2016. "Bunka puroguramu no jisshi ni muketa bunkachou no torikumi nitsuite" [Actions for cultural programs by the Agency for Cultural Affairs]. Accessed 29 January 2020. https://www.bunka.go.jp/seisaku/bunkashingikai/seisaku/14/02/pdf/shiryo1_1.pdf.

Akai, Azumi. 2017. Interview by author. Cotome-ya, Tottori, 11 August 2017.

Baudrillard, Jean. [1970] 1998. *The Consumer Society: Myth and Structures*. Translated by Chris Turner. London: Sage.

Becker, Howard S. 1982. *Art Worlds*. Berkeley: University of California Press.

Befu, Harumi. [1987] 1990. *Ideologi to shite no nihon bunkaron* [The theory of Japanese culture as an ideology]. Tokyo: Shiso no kagakusha.

Befu, Harumi. 2001. *Hegemony of Homogeneity: An Anthropological Analysis of "Nihonjinron."* Melborne: Trans Pacific Press.

Bishop, Claire. 2004. "Antagonism and Relational Aesthetics." *October* 110 (Fall 2004): 51–79.

Bishop, Claire. 2006. "The Social Turn: Collaboration and Its Discontents." *Artforum International* 44 (6): 179–85.

Bishop, Claire. 2012. *Artificial Hells: Participatory Art and the Politics of Spectatorship.* London: Verso.

Bourriaud, Nicolas. [1998] 2002. *Relational Aesthetics.* Translated by Simon Pleasance, Fronza Woods, and Mathieu Copeland. Dijon: Les presses du reel.

Clifford, James. 1997. *Routes.* Cambridge, MA: Harvard University Press.

Echigo-Tsumari Art Triennale Executive Committee. 2019. "Daichi no geijyutsu sai soukatsu houkokusho" [General report for the Echigo-Tsumari Art Triennial 2018]. Accessed 24 January 2020. http://www.city.tokamachi.lg.jp/ikkrweb-Browse/material/files/group/4/soukatsuhoukokusyo2018_honpen190507.pdf.

Favell, Adrian. 2011. *Before and After Superflat: A Short History of Japanese Contemporary Art, 1990–2011.* Hong Kong: Blue Kingfisher.

Foster, Hal. 2007. "(Dis)engaged Art." In *Right About Now: Art and Theory Since the 1990s*, edited by Margriet Schavemaker and Mischa Rakier, 73–85. Amsterdam: Valiz.

Fujita, Naoya. 2016. "Zenei no zombi tachi: Chiiki āto no shomondai" [Zombies of the avant-garde: The problems of local art]. In *Chiiki āto: Bigaku, seido, Nihon* [Local art: Aesthetics, institutions, Japan], edited by Naoya Fujita, 95–134. Hachiōji: Horinouchi Shuppan.

Hartley, John, ed. 2005. *Creative Industries.* Oxford: Wiley-Blackwell.

Inazu, Hideki. 2020. "Souzou no jikkenjyou toshiteno hisaichi" [The disaster area as an experimental field of creativity]. In *Āto ga Hiraku Chiiki no Korekara* [Arts for conviviality: To rediscover our creativities], edited by Kunihiro Noda, Motohiro Koizumi, Kiyoshi Takeuchi, and Shigeru Yanaka, 159-178. Kyoto: Minerva Shobo.

Ishiba, Shigeru. 2015. "Chiiki no kosei wo kaku ni jiritsu e" [Towards independence by focusing on the unique personality of regions]. Project Design Online, April 2015. http://www.projectdesign.jp/201504/challenge-vitalizinglocal/002015.php.

Iwabuchi, Koichi. 2002. *Recentering Globalization: Popular Culture and Japanese Transnationalism.* Durham: Duke University Press.

Iwabuchi, Koichi. 2007. *Bunka no Taiwaryoku* [The communication power of culture: Beyond soft power and brand nationalism]. Tokyo: Nihon Keizai Shimbunsha.

Kajiya, Kenji. 2016. "Chīki ni tenkaisuru nihon no Āto purojekuto" [Japanese art projects that take place in local regions]. In *Chiiki āto: Bigaku, seido, Nihon* [Local art: Aesthetics, institution, Japan], edited by Naoya Fujita, 95–134. Hachiōji: Horinouchi Shuppan.

Kaneko, Isamu. 2016. *"Chihou Sousei to Shoumetsu" no Shakaigaku: Nihon no komyunitei no yukue* [Sociology of regional revitalization and disappearing: The future of Japanese communities]. Kyoto: Minerva Shobo.

Kester, Grant H. 2013. *Conversation Pieces: Community and Communication in Modern Art*, updated edition with a new preface. Berkeley: University of California Press.

Kitagawa, Fram. 2014. *Bijutsu wa chiiki o hiraku: Daichi no Geijutsusai 10 no shisō* [Echigo-Tsumari Art Triennale concept book]. Tokyo: Gendaikikakushitsu Publishers.

Koizumi, Motohiro. 2019. "Governance with a Creative Citizenry: Art Projects for Convivial Society in Japanese Cities." In *The Rise of Progressive Cities East and West*, edited by Mike Douglass, Romain Garbaye, and Kong-Chong Ho, 185-202. Singapore: Springer.

Koizumi, Motohiro. 2020. "Watashitachi no Kurieithibithi" [Our creativities]. In *Āto ga Hiraku Chiiki no Korekara* [Arts for conviviality: To rediscover our creativities], edited by Kunihiro Noda, Motohiro Koizumi, Kiyoshi Takeuchi and Shigeru Yanaka, 3-19. Kyoto: Minerva Shobo.

Koizumi, Motohiro. 2023. "In the era of bright dystopia — for the future we can choose" In *The Future We Dreamt About Beyond 20XX*, edited by Arts Maebashi. Maebashi: Arts Maebashi.

Kumakura, Sumiko, Takuji Kikuchi, and Yūichirō Nagatsu, eds. 2014. *Āto purojekuto: Geijutsu to kyōsō suru shakai* [Art projects: A society that cocreates with art]. Tokyo: Suiyōsha.

Kuresawa, Takemi. 2008. "Public art o koete" [Beyond public art]. In *Biennāre no genzai: bijutsu o meguru komyuniti no kanōsei* [The present biennial: The possibilities of communities around the arts], edited by Takemi Kuresawa and Sachiko Namba, 45–74. Tokyo: Seikyusha.

Mamada, Takao. 2016. *21seiki no Shouhi* [The consumption of the 21st century]. Tokyo: Minerva Shobo.

Masuda, Hiroya, and Japan Policy Council. 2014. "Sutoppu 'jinkō kyūgen shakai'" [Stop "Society population reduction"]. *Chuo Koron* 129 (6) (June 2014): 18-31.

Ministry of Economy Trade and Industry. 2019. "Dōi kihon keikaku: Nīgataken Tōkamachi Shi" [Agreed basic plan: Tokamachi, Niigata]. Accessed 24 January 2020. https://www.meti.go.jp/policy/sme_chiiki/miraitoushi/kihonkeikaku/niigataken-tokamachishi.pdf.

Morris-Suzuki, Tessa. 2004 "Gurōbarizēshon no bunka seiji" [Globalization and the new cultural economy]. In *Gurobarizēshon no bunka seiji* [The cultural politics of globalization], edited by Tessa Morris-Suzuki and Shunya Yoshimi, 86–117. Tokyo: Heibonsha.

Mōri, Yoshitaka. 2014. "Hihyouteki kurieithibu sutadhīzu e" [For critical creative studies]. In *Afutā terebijyon sutadhīzu* [After television studies], edited by Mamoru Ito and Yoshitaka Mōri, 42–70. Tokyo: Serica Syobo.

Rancière, Jacques. 2009. *The Emancipated Spectator*. London: Verso.

Sadakane, Hideyuki. 2016. "Āto to chihou no kiken na kankei: āto fesu wa itsumade tsuzukunoka" [The dangerous relationship between art and regional cities: How long will "Art Fes" last?]. Accessed 24 January 2020. https://gendai.ismedia.jp/articles/-/49691.

Shirakawa, Yoshio. 2014. Interview by author. HOSPITALE, Tottori, 24 January 2014.

Thornton, Sarah. 2008. *Seven Days in Art World*. London: Granta Books.

Williams, Raymond. [1976] 2015. *Keywords: A Vocabulary of Culture and Society*, revised edition. New York: Oxford University Press.

Yamamoto, Takayuki. 2012. Interview by author. Art Center Ongoing, Musashino, 2 September 2012.

Yamashita, Yusuke and Toshiyuki Kanai. 2015. *Chihou sousei no shoutai* [The true regional revitalization]. Tokyo: Chikuma Shobo.

Yoshimi, Shunya. 2009. *Post Sengo Shakai* [Post post-war society]. Tokyo: Iwanami Shoten.

Yúdice, George. 2003. *The Expediency of Culture: Uses of Culture in the Global Era*. Durham: Duke University Press.

About the Author

Motohiro Koizumi is Associate Professor of art and sociology at Rikkyo University, Tokyo, Japan. He received his Ph.D. in sociology from Tokyo University of the Arts in 2009, and is also actively engaged in teaching courses at the International Christian University, Waseda University and Nihon University College of Art.

7. Making it Back Home: Displacement and Strategies of Resilience through Art

Tessa Maria Guazon

Abstract: Vernacular resilience is articulated as cultural enactments of local values in this chapter. Art projects, which are considered provocative and pragmatic resources for survival and transformation for communities facing disasters and natural hazards, are the vehicles for this exploration. Art is proposed as a tool for rebuilding and recollection, with creativity and aesthetic imagination as essential to a shared cultural heritage that is vital to collective resilience.

Keywords: creativity, aesthetic imagination, survival and transformation, contemporary art, Philippine communities

Filipinos are known as a resilient people rising above disasters and national tragedies. Photographs and news coverage depicting us in the aftermath of a crisis or natural disaster are most likely to include people smiling amidst catastrophic settings, whether rubble from earthquakes or typhoons or the sodden remains of floods. However, the attribute of resilience is not confined to or solely defined by national identity. Rather than regard resilience as an innate quality, we can try to understand the circumstances that bring people together in situations that demand resilience. In turn, we can consider the modalities and strategies through which localized notions of resilience are conveyed and enacted. What motivations and conditions propel us towards continuity and transformation?

A great number of natural hazards besets the Philippine Archipelago. The most common are tropical cyclones, typhoons, earthquakes, and volcanic eruptions. Data from the Manila Observatory between 1888 and 1897 recorded 5,050 storms that passed the archipelago, with an annual average of about fifty storms (Bankoff 2007: 34). Storms and typhoons from this

Herzfeld, M., and R. Padawangi, eds. *Resilience as Heritage in Asia*. Amsterdam: Amsterdam University Press, 2025.
DOI: 10.5117/9789463728560_CH07

period were assiduously recorded, but data for floods and storm surges were surprisingly scant. Town chronicles recorded significant floods between 1691 and 1900, describing their causes, marking locations where they were likely to occur, and noting their frequency in specific localities (Bankoff 2007). These few records of flooding chronicled uncommon devastation and great upheaval to community life—the disruption of a fireworks display meant for the beatification of San Ignacio in Cebu in 1811, the tremendous damage caused by a big flood in Ilocos Norte in October 1871, and the deaths and destruction from a surge in Central Luzon in October 1873 (Bankoff 2007). Flooding in metropolitan areas has become increasingly common and unusually harrowing. I recall wading through thigh-deep murky waters in one of Manila's main thoroughfares in the early 2000s, holding hands with strangers to form a human chain to avoid open sewers. Metro Manila residents have long regarded traffic and floods as banes of daily existence. To a great extent, they have come to shape the attitudes and behavior for survival, especially among the working class who routinely brave the hazards of the city.

Behaviors that arise from difficult and challenging situations can be considered responses to threats that are constantly present. This "normalisation of threat," as Bankoff (2004: 102) calls it, may have significantly shaped cultures across the Philippine Archipelago. The attitudes and perceptions that arise from experiences of natural hazards include "coping practices that have evolved to allow communities to come to terms with the constancy of hazard and to mitigate the worst effects of disaster" (Bankoff 2004,102). Similar practices deal with the "emotional and psychological requirements of living with uncertainty" (Bankoff 2004: 102). Bankoff, thus points our attention to how disasters are not entirely natural events but are also perceptual phenomena that occur and shape people's thoughts and actions (Bankoff 2004). The coping practices and attitudes towards uncertainty are salient elements of a cultural heritage "shaped by the threat of hazard" (Bankoff 2004: 99). These perceptual attitudes acknowledge the likelihood that disasters experienced in the past are likely to recur. Bankoff further cites devices that maintain cultural resilience in Philippine cultures. These include "anthropomorphising the event or investing hazard with personality," and "religious mysticism" (Bankoff 2004: 96–97). These are attempts to situate the incomprehensible into an everyday understanding of reality. Specific coping strategies and behavior inform the art practices that will be cited in the following sections. I will explore how art practices grounded in and shaped by interactions with communities contribute to a sense of collective resilience.

Art practices and expressions are elements of a cultural heritage founded on a collective resilience. Contemporary art projects from the Philippines explore in a performative manner the changing relationships of communities to the environment in the aftermath of disaster. They are provocative means to articulate and mobilize resilience towards transformative action. Through shared narratives, crafted images, and embodied affect, these projects are tools for recollection (a coming to terms), and reimagining (continuity and survival). The art projects that will be cited are Roberto Villanueva's *Panhumuko* ([Surrender to nature] 1991), a performance and ritual in a relocation area in Paulig Town, Pampanga, Central Luzon; Alma Quinto's *House of Comfort* (from 2007 onward), a workshop series for communities affected by disasters across the Philippine Archipelago; Francis 'Panx' Solajes's video project *Himurasak* ([A harvest of souls] 2016) on the devastation of his hometown Tacloban, Leyte Province, in the Visayas Islands; and Nathalie Dagmang's *Dito sa Barangay Tumana* ([Here in Barangay Tumana] 2015), an immersive and collaborative piece exploring a neighborhood's relationship to a river in Marikina City, Metro Manila. Altogether, they represent Philippine contemporary art's entanglements with social movements and its long-standing associations with citizen groups, grassroots initiatives, and people's organizations. I will ask whether contemporary art practices can become vehicles for vernacular articulations of resilience as framed by the local values of *talinhaga* or transformative capacity, *kapwa* or the self in other, and *sampalataya* or faith in mystery. How do these shared values mobilize people during a crisis and in its aftermath? How does Philippine contemporary art that is grounded in a long history of activism mediate and articulate forms of local knowledge that are core elements of a shared heritage? I will explore the means and strategies deriving from art and creativity in repairing communal bonds that have been rendered fragile or sundered by experiences of disaster. This framing simultaneously situates art across the imagination and the material world—intertwined realms where possibilities are considered and eventually realized.

Five calamitous typhoons passed the Philippine Islands in succession between October and December 1934. In early November, a letter from an old man in Mexico, Pampanga (a Central Luzon province), reached Fr. Miguel Selga, the first director of the Manila Observatory. It predicted an even stronger typhoon than the one that arrived in October. Mass hysteria followed, and there were reports of farmers abandoning fields, parents not sending their children to school, and a debilitating fear that the end of the world was coming. The rumor of "two powerful typhoons from two opposing paths striking one another over the bay [and] bringing big storm surges" began to spread, and fear spread rapidly among those living in Manila's coastal areas (Bankoff 2004: 179). Fr. Selga called this state of fear and mass hysteria "tifonitis," a condition he described as "a pathological state owing to nervous over-stimulation produced by the frequency or extraordinary intensity of typhoons" (Selga 1935). There was a shared sense of dread in the aftermath of Typhoon Ketsana in 2009. Typhoon Ondoy, as it was locally known, unleashed 341 mm of rain over seven hours and submerged large areas of the cities of Marikina, Pasig, and Cainta in ten-foot deep floodwaters. Metro Manila became a hulking river of roiling water that destroyed residential villages in its path. The apartment I lived in during this time was knee-deep in sludge. In the weeks that followed, a collective anxiety gripped residents and the mere sight of dark clouds would have people rushing to get home, as the rains could become a lashing thunderstorm.

Destructive typhoons are typical events in the Philippines. Typhoon Haiyan or "Super Typhoon Yolanda" struck the Philippines in November 2013. Leyte province was again ravaged by Typhoon Odette in December 2021. The hardest hit were towns on Leyte Island in Eastern Visayas. The port city of Tacloban was destroyed. There were six thousand confirmed deaths with eighteen hundred missing, over a million wrecked homes, and hundreds of destroyed ships and boats. Ships ran aground in residential areas and agricultural land, with upturned vehicles caught in tree branches. Felled trees in coconut plantations appeared like scattered match sticks among the rubble of buildings and houses. An estimated thirty-three million coconut trees were destroyed, leading to an estimated loss of sixty-nine million USD (Ottenhoff 2014). The Comprehensive Rehabilitation and Recovery Plan for areas walloped by Typhoon Yolanda was approved in August 2014 by then President Benigno Aquino III. It had a budget of 170.7 billion pesos or 3.93 billion USD (NEDA 2020). Then rehabilitation secretary and former Senator Panfilo Lacson presented the eight-volume plan and claimed that its implementation would employ a "bottom up, consultative and participatory" approach that closely adheres to the international principle of "build-back better" for disaster hit areas (Paterno 2014).

News coverage of Typhoon Haiyan celebrated Filipinos for their "innate" resilience. Many of them noted our ability to return to normal or to daily life routines (Clarke 2013). Several articles described volunteerism in Tacloban City—a Coca-Cola truck driver who brought ice to people who lost their homes, an open-air market that offered goods rescued from destroyed grocery stores, and a barber who readily offered his services. These anecdotes abounded, and many more acts of resilience were cited long after the passing of Typhoon Ondoy. It is assumed that Filipinos are naturally resilient, but reports overlook the structural conditions that made us this way. Disasters allow us to question institutional authority as they place the inadequacies of the state in a glaring light. Rebecca Solnit (2009) was right to cite people's ability "to govern themselves well in crises and in the absence of institutional authority."

A Place of Peril and Beauty

The Jesuit priest Fr. Miguel Selga, through the Manila Observatory, recorded the disastrous aftermaths of typhoons in the colonial Philippines, citing the Batanes Islands and Northern Luzon as the most exposed regions of the archipelago. The first systematic reports of earthquakes and seismic activity were from the Manila Observatory, which Fr. Selga oversaw. Given the archipelago's frequent experience of natural hazards, Greg Bankoff (2016: 335) proposes "transnational environmental history" as a historiographic frame that situates the Philippines in the context of the daily threats faced by its people. The historiography of the Filipino past is often focused on the archipelagic nature of the country, while this transnational approach situates the history of the islands within a wider orbit of geographic links and relations. Hazardousness of place is simultaneously relational (peoples' relationships to their surroundings), comparative (linking the Philippines to a broader world through shared experiences of risk), and geographically analytical (plotting the islands within a global map of risk and threats). Hazardousness becomes a function of an event, the resilience, and the vulnerability of affected populations. It is shaped by the "risk or exposure of people to the hazards in their environment and how they have adapted to them over time" (Bankoff 2016: 335). The Philippines share a common hazardousness of place with other cultures and societies located in the western North Pacific, where strong cyclones form, and the Alpine-Himalayan Orogenic Belt and the Pacific Ring of Fire, where seismic tremors originate (Bankoff 2016: 335). Bankoff's proposal for an "environmental transnational approach" to the Filipino past begins with recording shared risks, and providing new ways of looking at historical development (Bankoff 2016). This approach also underscores a view of the future within a more encompassing world, akin to how the pandemic showed the indelible links between geographic locations. This historical understanding emphasizes that Filipinos commonly face risks, and that these hazards are not exceptional but rather common events of daily life.

Responses to risks, threats, and vulnerabilities are understood as forms of resilience. The observations of "persistence to function in a world subjected to ongoing change" of ecological systems led to early studies of social resilience (Bankoff 2016: 351). Resilience has evolved to consider the social transformation demanded by global change. Keck and Sakdapolrak (2013: 8) proposed that these studies should be prefaced with the questions of becoming resilient to which force or circumstance, or the threat or risk that is being examined. Both noted a "persistent ability, adaptability, and transformability" as the core principles of social resilience (Keck and Sakdapolrak 2013: 8). "A system's capacity to persist in its current state of functioning while facing disturbance and change, and to adapt to future challenges and to transform in ways that enhance its functioning" defines social resilience. The operative phrases in this definition are "to persist," "to adapt," and "to transform." The central concerns of social resilience are the elements and forces that "enhance the capacities of individuals, groups, and organizations to deal with threats more competently." (Keck and Sakdapolrak, 2013: 14). Resilience should then be considered in terms of its relationality, dynamism, and reliance on "social learning, participative decision-making, and collective transformation" (Keck and Sakdapolrak 2013: 14).

Present-day community movements are increasingly heterogeneous and multilayered, with members brought together by interactions from events rather than filiation or collective identity (Tanabe 2016: 3). The shared experience of hazards and disasters can organize people into movements that weigh and put into practice notions and concepts of resilience and transformation. Tanabe (2016: 12) describes these community movements as marginal (forming in the edges or interstices, often "anti-structure," and allowing for the feeling of "*communitas*" as a binding force). They are open (allowing for wider linkages to other people, organizations, and institutions), and reflexive (allowing creation and reinvention that can lead to imagining alternative communities). It is worth emphasizing that "cultural pragmatics and personal experiences," (Tanabe 2016: 12) rather than collective identity, frame a more nuanced understanding of community movements. Supposing that relations between members of communities are shaped by a common desire towards transformation and change, we can begin to inquire about the scale and the settings where these happen. The notion of "translocality" becomes a suitable frame to analyze social resilience (Keck and Sakdapolrak 2013). Religious fraternities, unions, clubs, and associations before the twentieth century highlight the long history of informal networks in the Philippines, as Bankoff (2016) notes. Kinship and one's immediate community are the cornerstones of mutual dependence between members of these social groups. A more recent example would be the numerous initiatives and informal structures of support mobilized on social media during the early days of the Metro Manila lockdown following the declaration of the global pandemic. These efforts were well ahead of programs initiated by the state and its agencies.

Communities and "Being-in-Common"

Filipino poet Ninotchka Rosca (2013) offered a radical view of resilience in a bristling article with the subtitle "Why calling Filipinos resilient is an insult":

> We break when the world is just too much and in the process of breaking are transformed into something difficult to understand. Or we take [the] full measure of misfortune, wrestle with it, and emerge transformed into something equally terrifying. It is what is and what isn't.

The transformation she describes as "something difficult to understand" aptly captures a metamorphosis that displaces the widely accepted understanding of resilience as a "manner of bouncing back." She argues that we do not merely bounce back, rather, we are transformed into another state, one not easily recognized or deciphered. The imagination allows this alterity to take form. Appadurai (2000: 6) recuperates the role of the imagination in social life as a "faculty that informs the daily lives of ordinary people," through which "collective patterns of dissent and new designs for collective life emerge" or "creative forms of social life" are constructed. Imagination as such is revived and rendered expansive, as it veers away from its normative associations with individual genius and the reified realm of aesthetic experience.

Transformation and change are propelled by the imagination, a means by which collective experience encompassing political and sensuous aspects are articulated and understood. A changed state of being can be rendered comprehensible through "communities of sense," which "recognises the contingent and non-essential manner of being together," one that "acknowledges politics to contain a sensuous or aesthetic aspect" (Hinderliter et al. 2009: 2). The community of sense does not translate into a collectivity shaped by a common feeling. Rancière (2009: 31) understands it as a "frame of visibility and intelligibility" that "puts together things or practices under the same meaning, [shaping] a certain sense of community." An event frames a "being-in-common," and through this mode of togetherness, a form of collectivity, at once political and sensuous, arises. Communities can be imagined as a "contingent being together," as they are "temporary solidarities that are constantly negotiated through disagreement" (Hinderliter et al. 2009:2).

"Spacing" frames this relational aspect. Spacing proposes that "being is constituted only in relation to others," a "distribution and organization of sense," not only with regard to others but also one's relation to the self (Ranciére 2009:14). A disjuncture and interruption happens through spacing where "collectivity [is posited] as internally multiple and dynamic" (Ranciére 2009:14). To echo Tanabe's discussion, communities are inherently divided, and it is only through events that members of a community come together. This notion of collectivity as contingent and inherently dynamic may well bring us to the idea that communities are formed through a collective manner, or of being-in-common. Collectivities or the state of being-in-common are also rendered possible through art, specifically when they frame "practices, forms of visibility, and patterns of intelligibility" (Ranciére 2009: 13). Collective experience requires that art or aesthetics need not be confined to a specific regime or category, but would have it move towards a "sensible mode of being," a modality that recognizes that aesthetics is inherently a stage for politics, one that determines what appears, and what is spoken (Ranciére 2009: 5).

Coalitions, Collectivities, and Cooperation through Art

Transformation is at the core of artistic practices, which may be evident in the forms produced from various materials, and through practices that place emphasis on processes and relationships. These expressions and their accompanying methods likewise facilitate social relationships that often spill beyond the immediate circle of the artist or maker. Contemporary art then can be considered a "culture that matters to itself, its subcultures, to the local cultural transformations [where it is embedded], to the complex exchanges between proximate cultures, a trendsetting force within [an] international high culture" (Smith 2009: 242). Consequentially, contemporary art has a globalizing attribute, and can mobilize nationalities and localisms in complex ways (Smith 2009: 243). Artists explore indigeneity and various localisms to articulate notions of the vernacular. The enduring and persistent elements of a shared culture, whether as components of the past or a shared memory, or as hybrid expressions resulting from globalization, can represent the vernacular. These may also significantly figure in contemporary art that deals with questions of identity and the structure of communities within modern societies.

Judith Rodenbeck (2011) identifies a relatively new phenomenon in contemporary art, a collectivist practice that is greatly discursive and produces a form of sociability simultaneously theorized and enacted. These art initiatives may refer to themselves as "spaces," "collectives," or "coalitions." These art practices can be a "project," a "laboratory or experimental space," a "center," a "hub," a "network," an "art house," or a "foundation," as I found from fieldwork carried out in Thailand and Indonesia in 2014.[1] Members of these platforms or collectives gather through informal associations or adhere to an organizational structure. They can belong to different groups but may work together for specific projects, or they can be a team pursuing a goal. They often occupy spaces that serve a variety of uses, either as workspaces, libraries, cafés, video and lecture rooms, exhibition spaces, and shops. These varied configurations eventually shape the conduct and outcome of their exchanges and interactions with communities. A range of art historical terms are used for these artistic endeavors and practices. They are alternatively called "participatory, interactive, collaborative or relational" (Finkelpearl 2013: 4). Claire Bishop (2006) likewise uses the terms "socially engaged, community-based, experimental communities, dialogic, littoral [art], interventionist, research based or collaborative" (quoted in Finkelpearl: 6). While collectives or artist organizations are not new, Rodenbeck (2011: 161) identifies three qualities that mark their more recent formations—they "enter the exhibitionary economy residually with productions that are often than not textual and discursive," they are shaped by an extraordinary degree of interlinkage aided and enhanced by current and emergent communication technologies, and produces a "dialogical network" that becomes "a form of sociability both theorized and enacted." These distinct qualities might help us understand how contemporary art projects, like those that will be cited in later sections deploy aspects of a cultural heritage that define and shape a collective form of resilience.

A long history of activism shapes Philippine art. Many Filipino artists advocate human rights and social justice. Over the decades, artist organizations have answered to overtly political calls, including toppling the Marcos dictatorship, unseating Joseph Estrada from presidential power, fighting

---

1   My fieldwork in Thailand (Bangkok and Chiang Mai) and Indonesia (Jakarta, Jogjakarta, and Bandung) was conducted through the Asian Public Intellectuals grant from the Nippon Foundation in 2014.

the gross violations of human rights during the Arroyo administration, exposing graft and corruption during Benigno Aquino III's term in office, and protesting the extrajudicial killings from Rodrigo Duterte's war on drugs. While artist organizations and collectives from the 1960s to the 1980s were organized along ideological lines, recent collectives and alliances from the 1990s onward were consolidated as responses to specific issues and advocacies. Alice Guillermo (2017: 3) described the collective practice of artists in the late 1970s as Social Realism, which is "a movement in art which exposes the true conditions of society as based on the artist's keen observation of reality and proffers alternatives for human development." Artists' organizations like the Center for Advancement of Young Artists established in 1976, together with *Lingkod Sining* and *Buklod Sining*, were part of a more significant resistance movement against martial law under the Marcos regime. This continued well into the 1980s, which saw the consolidation of artists into organizations including *Tambisan ng Sining* (1980), *Alyansa ng Artistang Bayan* (1981), *Binhi, MASKARA*, Concerned Artists of the Philippines (CAP) (1983), *Artista ng Bayan* (ABAY), and *Salingpusa* (1985). Several of these groups collaborated with community theatre groups and made props for mass rallies and similar campaigns against the Marcos dictatorship.[2]

Post-1986 EDSA Revolution (Epifanio de los Santos Avenue was the site of the protests) saw the founding of bigger organizations of artists, several of which were based outside the capital Metro Manila. These were the *Artista at Manunulat ng Sambayanan* founded in 1987, and the feminist group *Kababaihan sa Sining at Bagong Sibol na Kamalayan* (KASIBULAN) founded in 1989. Some of those based outside the capital were *Pamilya Pintura* established in 1980, Black Artists of Asia founded in 1986, and *Hubon Madia-as* organized in 1983. Artist collectives were established in the 1990s and 2000s, including the *Ugnayan at Galian ng mga Tanod ng Lahi* (UGATLahi) Artist Collective, *Alay Sining, Sanggawa and Tumbang Preso,* founded sometime in the mid-1990s. UGATLahi is known for presidential effigies paraded at mass protests during the annual State of the Nation Address (SONA), which is a mandatory report from the country's chief executive. These elaborate and satirical effigies are set on fire during protests. A more pronounced turn in the early to mid-2000s was the emergence of artists' alliances that addressed specific issues and advocacies. Groups that were subsequently

2   The timeline of art and activism is from Lisa Ito, "Visual Arts & Activism in the Philippines: Notes on a New Season of Discontent," in *Art Archive 01*, edited by Patricia Tumang, Mariko Okeda, Marc J. Ocampo, and Karen Batino (Manila: The Japan Foundation), 20–33.

organized were broader in reach and addressed specific issues of national and global relevance. *Tutok Karapatan* (2005) and Artists for Peace (2001) protested the Arroyo administration's support of the US war in Afghanistan and the national human rights situation. Artists and cultural workers gathered to protest the corruption that beset the Aquino administration in 2013 through the *Artista Kontra Korapsyon* or Artists Against Corruption (AKKSYON). Duterte's drug war let loose a spate of extrajudicial killings that prompted artists, cultural workers, and media to gather and convene Respond and Break the Silence Against the Killings (RESBAK) in January 2017.

Other artists banded in smaller groups, sharing a form of collectivism that allowed explorations of art forms and practices across different sites for art production. These include the Neo-Angono Artist Collective (2004), Pilipinas Street Plan (2006), *Ang Gerilya* (2008), *Windang* Army Labor Aesthetics (WALA) (2014), and TALA Photo Collective (2015). These later smaller-scale groups may well have responded to a need for shifting forms of collectivity. Two recent protests happened at the University of the Philippines Diliman campus grounds, where police and military have no jurisdiction. These were against the pending Anti-Terrorism Act of 2020 that the Philippine Congress and the Senate passed and was awaiting the signature of President Rodrigo Duterte. The act would significantly curtail civil liberties, and allow surveillance, warrantless arrests, and detentions by the police and the state. The cultural sector spearheaded the #ArtistsFightBack campaign. These protests happened even with enforced restrictions against mass gatherings during the pandemic. This clearly illustrates that artists respond to the world around them, keenly observing and offering alternatives to situations of strife. Artist activist organizations abound in the Philippines, with varying aims and structures, across different scales and reach.

Participatory, collaborative, or socially engaged art typically questions the authorship attributed to the artist who, in most cases, would be the initiator of the art project. Finkelpearl (2013) proposed a term that redefines the relationship between an artist and her community—cooperation or cooperative art. Collaboration implies the ownership of a project for all participants from conception to conclusion, which does not always happen, as many art projects are "authored" by an artist, overtly or implicitly. Participants and artists are very rarely on equal terms as collaborators. Cooperation, on the other hand, implies that "people have worked together on a project" on the grounds of "reciprocity, altruism and interconnection" (Finkelpearl 2013: 6). This form of collaboration will guide the discussion of the four contemporary art projects realized with members of Philippine communities. These concerns, whether about contentious authorship, the nature of collaboration, or social relationships, can lead us to art's use within settings of crisis and strife. Jacques Ranciére (2009: 38) argues that the equality and freedom afforded by the aesthetic experience can be translated into "communities of sense" where the aesthetic becomes a "form of collective existence... embodied in living attitudes" through which "the common of the community will thus be woven into the fabric of the lived world." This view is emphasized in the art projects *Panhumuko* (Surrender to nature), House of Comfort, *Himurasak* (A harvest of souls), and *Dito sa Barangay Tumana* (Here in Barangay Tumana). These art projects restructure everyday life through aesthetic reworking of vernacular understandings of transformation and survival.

Rituals, Conversations, and Interventions: Cooperative Art Projects in Philippine Communities

Transformation and survival are salient to the definition of resilience offered by Rosca (2013), which is an indeterminate state. She claims it to be rooted in the indigenous concept of *talinhaga* or mystery. *Talinhaga* is "communication through approximation and metaphors," and a way of "talking through symbols" (De Guia 2005: 19). Ileto's (1979: 30) writings on popular movements in the nineteenth-century Philippines define these associations as "mysteries and metaphors," those that can only be grasped and understood through "a life of prayer and devotion." Conjuring compelling metaphors, however, is not mere divination—it is a disruption of the "total orientation of one's being toward an order of reality in which the disruption of one's 'normal' role in society, including death itself, was a distinct possibility," a "conscious act of realizing certain possibilities of existence" (De Guia 2005: 19). Therein emerges an understanding of the Filipino self or personhood that is one's *kapwa*. In the Tagalog language, *pakikipagkapwa* means an intention to connect and recognize the humanity in everyone. *Kapwa* or personhood speaks to human interaction, which unfolds in "mutual openness, participation, and sharing" (De Guia 2005: 19). *Kapwa* and *talinhaga* are complemented by *sampalataya*. According to Ileto (quoted in De Guia: 50), it is a "strong belief, a personal conviction which is spiritual in nature." Actions based on *sampalataya* are driven by deep feelings (De Guia 2005: 20). These cultural values will frame the discussion of the art projects mentioned, conceived, and realized by Filipino artists of different generations as a response to and a form of intervention on the world around them. Cooperation with different communities intimately shapes the relationships initiated and forged by these artists. Their projects can probably shed light on how people enact and mobilize attitudes and actions toward resilience.

Resilience is a salient aspect of our cultural heritage. As mentioned in the introduction, coping practices and related behaviors and attitudes are expressions of resilience. Many Filipinos attribute a human persona to the forces of nature. Nature, for example, is often feminized; sudden changes in the weather are likened to a woman's fickle character or even childish behavior. A widely shared belief is that disasters and calamities are means by which the forces of nature restore harmony or balance between human activity and the environment (Bankoff 2004: 95). These forces are also imagined to serve and fulfil the commands of a divine entity, often represented as generous, and bestowing gifts (*grasya*) or "the grace of the supernatural that abound in the gifts of Nature" (Bankoff 2004: 100). Yet, this divine persona is likewise capable of anger (*tampo*), and can exact punishment or retribution (*gaba*) for wrongdoings and ill behavior (Bankoff 2004: 100). F. Landa Jocano refers to the traits of resilience previously mentioned, *kapwa, talinhaga, sampalataya* and related attitudes as "cultural coping practices" (Bankoff 2004: 104). *Pakikipagkapwa*, or "being one with the other or with others," or "being part of the group," informs the other traits. It is commonly understood as being with others, becoming empathetic to the situation of others, and, more importantly, being willing to partake of and share their burdens. The traits of *talinhaga* and *sampalataya* are further given depth by the Tagalog expression *bahala na*. Often misconstrued as a fatalistic attitude, Jocano insists that *bahala* na is instead about "courage, daring, and a sense of finely calculated assessment of the odds" (Bankoff 2004: 103). All three (*talinhaga, sampalataya*, and *bahala na*) are founded on an "element of faith … faith in the efficacy of prayer, and in the intercession of divine protection" (Bankoff 2004: 103). Efforts given to aid and mutual support in the Philippines are often in step with calls for prayer and rituals of healing. When asked how we are after suffering an illness, a loss, the death of a loved one, or a particularly difficult phase of life, many Filipinos would often reply with "*nakakaraos naman*," which means we are surviving with formidable faith, and are hopeful that situations will improve and become better. A related behavioral concept is *pagdadala*, which literally means to carry one's burden (Bankoff 2004: 106). The ability to bear the weight of our burdens lightly (*magaang magdala*) is greatly admired. These coping practices are honed and practiced in a communal context, often reinforced and validated by members of a community. Altogether, they "express a sense of shared community" (Bankoff 2004), whereby support is guaranteed among its members during hardships. This was expressed in various ways in the interactions spurred by the art projects that will be later discussed.

Two natural disasters devastated Luzon Island in the Philippines in the 1990s, the earthquake in Baguio City in July 1990, and the eruption of Mt. Pinatubo in Zambales the following year. The quake destroyed about two thousand homes and caused the death of four hundred residents. One of several organizations and citizen groups that mobilized to provide immediate aid was the Baguio Arts Guild. Members readily set up a soup kitchen and provided two thousand meals a day for displaced residents. The Baguio Arts Guild (BAG) was established in 1987, the year after the People Power Revolution (EDSA 1 of 1986) that toppled the Marcos dictatorship. Their 1992 statement "The Artist and Nation Building" stated that art was considered a part of the lives of Filipinos in the past, and that precolonial Filipinos were "skilled craftsmen, artisans, boat builders and weavers" (Yamamura 2019: 105). Art is likewise manifest in rituals "equipped with a wealth of materials used as symbols of communication" (Yamamura 2019: 105). These realizations come from deep reflection imbued with mysticism or spirituality as they consider the place of artists in society. Artists from the Baguio Arts Guild also organized art classes for children of affected families at an evacuation camp at Burnham Park. These classes called "Art Aid" "helped families come to terms with the physical and emotional trauma" from the earthquake (Yamamura 2019:122).

Artist Roberto Villanueva (1947–1995) was among the most active members of the Baguio Arts Guild. In 1989, he restaged his Baguio Art Festival piece *Atang ti Kararua* (Offering for the soul) to make space for communal healing. Spirit boats ferried food and paper money alongside photographs of those who perished from the quake. Villanueva is known for ephemeral art informed by indigenous aesthetics. Yamamura (2019: 105) cites his "sustainability aesthetics" as a significant force that shaped his practice, focusing on indigenous values and collaborative participation. *Archetypes: Cordillera Labyrinth* (1989) is one of his more well-known works. The mazelike structure of *runo* reeds, stone, and wood echoing a mandala was installed at the lawn of the Cultural Center of the Philippines on 22 April 1989. It is a 150-foot-wide centripetal spiral of two thousand feet that terminates in a *dap-ay,* a round spot constructed of stones that is a sacred meeting area for the Ifugaos. His 1992 artist statement described the process of creating artworks as "collaborating with nature… borrowing [materials] from the natural environment—earth, wind, fire and other elements having organic cycles" (Villanueva 1992 cited in Yamamura). His art is often marked by rituals at their beginning and end, culminating with a return to the earth.

When Mt. Pinatubo erupted in 1991, Villanueva visited the evacuation camp for the Aeta, an Indigenous tribe in Zambales. He had no preconceived plan for the artwork he had in mind. Journalist Howie Severino, who accompanied Villanueva on that trip, wrote that the artist opted to "surrender [to nature rather than resist it] … and to make an offering to appease Apo Namalyari (the supreme god of the Aetas)," thus the title *Panhumuko* for the work, which meant surrender (Yamamura 2019: 123). The Aetas worried that the drilling being done by the Philippine National Oil Corporation would disturb the goddess sleeping in the mountain. The artist "quietly chose the poorest part of the tent city, [and] approached the Aeta elders" (Yamamura 2019: 123). When the Aetas heard his intention, they joined the ritual of making Panhumuko without specific instructions from the artist. He started building Panhumuko with bamboo poles in an ash-covered area by an open well. The Aetas joined by scattering coal around it, installing broken mirrors, and placing black and red candles often used for lowland folk rituals. Vegetables and similar offerings were hung from the bamboo, and ritualistic dances were performed initially by Villanueva and the community shaman, and later by the Aetas themselves who performed a healing ritual for the artist. The artist later complained of body pains during the ritual, which may have been early signs of leukemia from which he died in 1995 (Yamamura 2019).

Roberto Villanueva used a mystical language to communicate not only with his audiences but also with his collaborators, many of whom were not entirely familiar with the categories and structures of Western art. Among such artworks were his installation and performance *Ego's Grave* (1993) for The First Asia Pacific Triennial in Brisbane, Australia, and the *Burning Man's Ego* (1991) in Staten Island for a New York City residency. Both were markedly imbued with a ritualistic element that symbolized oneness between the material and spirit worlds, and both enacted a return to nature. The artworks were dismantled and eventually disappeared, signifying the intention to move away from capitalist profit and the art market, and focus on healing people's relationship with the earth. Roberto Villanueva's sustainability aesthetics can perhaps steer us towards a new direction, one that augurs a new way of thinking and doing that redefines our relationship with the environment, and for us to draw from our vernacular practices in making sense of our connection to nature and to others.

Alma Quinto's socially engaged practice stemmed from her early interest in volunteerism. She initially worked with marginalized communities through student organizations at the University of the Philippines, and with a non-government organization after her graduation. She became actively involved with the Philippine Art Educators Association (PAEA), which organized art workshops for communities and cultural institutions. This community-oriented practice became pronounced through her House of Comfort project and numerous others for the Artists for Crisis program of the National Commission for Culture and the Arts (NCCA) and various nongovernment organizations in the Philippines and other countries in Asia. As an artist, Alma regards herself as "a facilitator …[working] with participants in [such a] way that they can express themselves freely and are involved in the creative process" (Earth Manual Project 2013:6). She enables workshop participants to create new meanings so "they can organize similar workshops on their own after you leave the community" (Earth Manual Project 2013: 6).

The idea for House of Comfort came from Alma's numerous visits to communities of survivors. One of her more remarkable visits was to Mapaniqui, Pampanga, on Luzon Island where the *Malaya Lolas* (Free Grandmothers) lived. They survived the horrors of the Japanese Occupation, which saw the massacre of the men from their village by Japanese soldiers. They were later brought to the *Bahay na Pula* (Red House), which was a ride away from the village, where they were raped by soldiers, like many other comfort women in Asia during the Japanese Occupation.

The first art healing workshop Alma organized was for survivors of Typhoon Reming in Barangay Binitayan, Albay, in Southeast Luzon in 2006. They suffered vast devastation when heavy rains caused mudslides from Mt. Mayon, an active volcano. The workshop focused on three themes that participants interpreted through drawings that represented their perceptions of natural disaster, their daily life at the evacuation center, and their dreams for the future. They were encouraged to share stories about their pictures. These images and the stories that accompanied them were meant to "liberate survivors from negative experiences of the disaster" and "enable them to feel connected [to others]" (Earth Manual Project 2013). The artist calls these "relationships promoting liberation" (Earth Manual Project 2013) allowing freedom and building solidarity among disaster survivors. These workshops combined a variety of creative activities.

Another workshop she organized and facilitated in Barangay Puntod, Cagayan de Oro City, on Mindanao Island, included drawing, theatre, dance, storytelling, creative writing, and cooking. It was at a public school repurposed as an evacuation area for survivors of Typhoon Sendong in 2012. As with the workshop in Bicol, the one in Cagayan de Oro promoted a sense of liberation and offered connection, which became pronounced when the participants cooked for each other and shared meals. The House of Comfort art workshops culminated in a cloth house simultaneously tactile

Figure 7.1. Workshop with communities in Cagayan de Oro City facilitated by artist Alma Quinto (courtesy of the artist)

and eloquent, the outcome of a dynamic and polyvalent process. The artist envisioned the house "to empower marginalized communities" through art's creative sharing of a vision of a life that was rebuilt. The House of Comfort allowed "release and participation, creation and storytelling, [establishing] a sense of community; collaboration and [fostering] resilience and network building" (Earth Manual Project 2013). It was held together by stories and dreams, not just the artist's but, more importantly, those of her workshop partners. It was a house built from the foundations of hope that allowed dreams to persist and made room for thriving.

Many of the participants in Alma Quinto's workshops were survivors who lost much. Through shared narratives, and as channeled through drawing, sewing, pasting, quilting, and storytelling, they enacted a rebuilding not only of their lost homes but also of their lives that disasters had deeply changed. Alma's workshops with vulnerable communities allow partnerships between local governments, private foundations, and nongovernment organizations. It is a practice that articulates a resonance through recovery and reclamation. The House of Comfort travelled in several exhibition spaces, mainly museum exhibitions where the artist installed it like various forms of shelter.

Residents of Southern Leyte witnessed sea waters receding in October 2013. Fish jumped out of the water, and a plentiful catch suddenly appeared. They said that thousands of fish filled the shore, and people only needed to pick them up. It worried people, as this was an omen of a forthcoming disaster. This phenomenon is called *himurasak* in the local language. Townsfolk believed that the fish generously offered by the sea would be the same number of lives it would take back. Typhoon Haiyan (Yolanda) arrived in November 2013. The vision was prescient of the thousands of lives lost from the destruction it wrought on Tacloban City and other towns in Leyte province. *Himurasak* (A harvest of souls) is the title of the video work by artist Francis "Panx" Solajes, which debuted in 2016. We screened the work in an exhibition on regionality and placemaking in 2017. The artist described the work as "[forging] collaboration between video art and oral tradition" (Solajes 2017). In the poignant and quietly powerful video work, Himurasak interspersed scenes of the night sky, a dusky moon, and lone figures by the sea—a man towing his boat to shore and a lone figure strolling the seaside, with the waves lapping at her feet. Three different voices narrate the story, sharing recollections of events that were signs of the disaster that was to arrive in 2013. The first is a woman's voice narrating a pilgrimage of the sect The Sanctuary of the Holy Spirit to Calvary Hill on 8 November 2012. Their spirit medium shared a vision that in the coming year, 2013, surges would bring sea vessels inland, and those who did not believe the warning would die. The hypnotic cadence of the soundtrack floats the following story—that of a man who dreamt about a warning he received a year before the destruction of Tacloban City by Typhoon Haiyan. He was told to go and bring his family to the next town and hike to Mt. Purisima, where they would be saved. He thought of the dream while struggling for his life during the flood and realized God must have visited him. People also shared visions of the Virgin Mary—a year before the typhoon, she was seen walking the shore but with her clothes wet and full of thorns. Those who saw this vision were left wondering. During the onslaught of the typhoon in Tacloban, survivors claimed to have seen the Virgin Mary gesturing at the waves to change direction so people could be saved from drowning.

Artist Panx Solajes documented these memories in the aftermath of Typhoon Haiyan. These omens were the sudden drying up of the sea (*himurasak*) in warnings shared by spirit mediums, in dreams where messages were relayed, and through visions of the Virgin Mary. The narratives in the video piece befuddled time's structure by merging stories thought to be omens and that later functioned as memory prompts in the aftermath of the typhoon. These recollections are as vital as the visions themselves, as they weave a thread between memories of life before and after the typhoon.

Figure 7.2. Still from video work Himurasak by Francis 'Panx' Solajes, 2017 (courtesy of the artist)

The mystery that cloaks them is how the spirit world spoke to them through omens and warnings. This video piece was presented alongside another work that documented mass graves in Tacloban City. Solajes tinted the piece orange, like burning coals, to transport viewers back to when the omens of the typhoon appeared and its aftermath. The final scenes are without sound, like an invitation to prayer. The stories the artist gathered are ingrained in the collective psyche of Tacloban City residents. She notes that these stories have been passed from one generation to another: "[serving] as a way of purging the trauma ... and a warning to people inheriting them" (Solajes 2017).

One of artist Nathalie Dagmang's striking photographs shows objects placed under the sun to dry: a mattress, toys, dolls, and a school textbook, among others. Rain and floodwaters drenched these objects, which were remnants rescued from a flood by residents and now laid out like votive offerings on an altar outside their homes in Barangay Tumana. Nathalie brought me to her grandmother's home on our last visit to Tumana—the house was one of a few with three stories in the neighborhood. When Typhoon Ketsana (Ondoy) unleashed waters from the nearby river, the house became a refuge for over fifty people who squeezed themselves into the third floor's modest space. Records from the Marikina City Health Office noted fifty-three dead found in the city after the typhoon; thirty-five were Marikina residents with thirteen from Barangay Tumana. Many were affected by flood-related diseases such as diarrhea and leptospirosis; others had typhoon related injuries. Data on casualties from Typhoon Ketsana were lost, as government buildings in the city were inundated by floodwaters in recent years.

The Marikina River was the gem of what was an agricultural plain—fertile plains bound its 220 hectares of land. Up to this day, residents cultivate plants for harvest in designated areas near the river. The river was choked by sewage and trash and drained by erosion and quarrying in the 1970s and 80s. Chemical waste had muddied its waters, making it unsuitable for domestic use. The river returned to the spotlight in 1993, when it became the center of a city rehabilitation plan. Bayani Fernando, the mayor at the time, had a vision of people "touching and feeling the waters" once more (Marikina City Government). Houses around the 96-meter easement were demolished, and jogging lanes, a skating rink, and an amphitheater were built near the river. The Marikina River rehabilitation became the flagship project of the local government under Fernando. Swarms of janitor fish were let loose to get rid of garbage particles, which led to dwindling numbers of edible fish in the river.

Nathalie Dagmang's solo exhibition, *Turbulent Waters* (2019), was about Barangay Tumana, which used to be a prized farming estate in the nineteenth century. Its fertile plains attracted farmers and settlers. Tumana's streets were named after local produce (*talong* [eggplant], and *mais* [corn], among others). Over the years, residential and commercial development took over the paddy fields. Maps showed marshlands in Marikina in the 1940s and 50s, which later became residential areas, factories, mills, and industrial plants. Floodwater from Typhoon Ondoy submerged many of these residential subdivisions in 2009. Dagmang's photographs document various aspects of life in Barangay Tumana—they show people at work or leisure (farmers herding carabaos in the fields, children frolicking on the river's floodwalls, people strolling on the bridge). Quite striking is the sludge in the river and objects or portions thereof floating in its murky waters. These can be agglomerations of trash and waste, stray verdant greens that thrive in the river, or remains of fast-food packaging and fractured plastic toys. These images are awash with a stark luminosity, like the light that bathes the earth after a downpour. We are made aware that the river becomes the receptacle for refuse from our modern lives.

Over the years, residents of Barangay Tumana learned to adapt to the rising river during typhoons. During our visit, Nathalie pointed my attention to a make-shift boat of recycled soda bottles to be used in case the waters from the river reach alarming levels. Some of the residents also raised their houses with another floor, others built make-shift bridges and dug gravel for rip rap. The local government also installed an instrument that monitors the river's rising waters that serves as a warning system for residents to vacate homes and move to evacuation centers. The city also established the Marikina City

Figure 7.3. A view of Barangay Tumana of children frolicking on the river's floodwalls (photograph by Nathalie Dagmang)

Disaster Risk Reduction and Management Office (MCDRRMO) to oversee and implement a comprehensive disaster risk management program. Barangay Tumana itself had received awards for best practice during a disaster and zero casualties during floods after Ondoy. Dagmang's ethnographic and documentary practice is shaped by listening, giving, and partaking, a cycle that defines her relationships with those who live in Barangay Tumana. Her artistic practice evokes a coherence, one where the self and the collective meld. They are regarded as unitary and not separate. It is a manner of placing herself within a wider communal sphere of action.

These four art projects were realized in the aftermath of natural disasters— a volcanic eruption in 1991, and the strongest typhoons that hit the Philippine Archipelago from around 2009 to more recent years. The tools and approaches used by artists are relational, and processual, and rely greatly on expressions that are conversational, collectively authored, and that incorporate aspects that are ritualistic. They range from healing dances and prayers, shared images and narratives, and reconstructed structures for dwelling. They explore memories of past events to imagine how the future can be. The interactions that these projects birthed were shaped to a great extent by a shared need to come to terms with a collective experience of disaster and loss. Yet they were founded on vernacular understandings of survival, recuperation, and transformation that were buoyed by the cultural values of resilience. Faith in mystery (*sampalataya, talinhaga*), being with others (*pakikipagkapwa*), and sharing the burden with others (*pakikiramay*) are shared values that allow survival (*nakakaraos, magaan ang pagdadala*) and continuous transformation.

"A Cue from Life Itself"

Artist-educator Brenda Fajardo, through her pioneering work for the Philippine Educational Theatre Association (PETA), proposed that "a sensitivity to the world emerges as an expression," one arising from a "culture of material poverty" (Fajardo 2010: 193). In the 1970s, artists from PETA established the beginnings of a people's theatre. Several of them traveled to communities to give workshops that became instrumental in building a national theatre movement. The workshops culminated in two theatre festivals called MAKI-ISA, with theatre becoming a potent political expression during the martial law years (Fajardo 2010). PETA productions were guided by their commitment to a Philippine theatre that mirrors social realities: "a people's theatre for empowerment, a potent agent toward personal and societal transformation" (Fajardo 2010: 181). The designs for many of PETA's productions, Fajardo notes, were instances when artists deliberately chose to express what they perceive, conditions of "economic deprivation, cultural pollution, and senseless violence" (Fajardo 2010: 194). She describes an "aesthetics of poverty" that arises from these conditions of privation and lack. In perceiving the conditions surrounding them, artists take a "cue from life itself" (Fajardo 2010: 189).

The arts are effective tools for advocating social change. Artistic practices rely on collaboration, whereby exchanges happen between an artist and her collaborators, as it was for the art projects discussed above. As artists and members of collectivities engage as cocreators in artistic production, their exchanges undergo a cycle of art activist intervention—a "repeating spiral of dialogue, collaboration (including action and creation) with reflection, [and] revision" (German 2017: 10) Berman further highlights the relevance of the arts to resilience because of their quality and inclusive nature. These make room for the powerful evocation of imagination and the creation of alternative visions. This was evident in the shared ritual that Roberto Villanueva initiated for *Panhumuko*, where he and the Aetas realized the work without specific instructions or detailed discussion between them. The imagination empowered the survivors of disaster and abuse in Alma Quinto's House of Comfort workshops. Sewing and telling stories helped them articulate and visualize their dreams while coming to terms with loss and despair. The imagination mobilized in these art projects discussed above is not confined to individuals but is rendered collectively, as was the case when recollections of omens and visions that presaged the disaster from Typhoon Haiyan were narrated in Panx Solajes's *Himurasak* video work. More so, the imagination allows for adaptation and transformation, in much the same way that residents of Barangay Tumana found ways to live with the Marikina River.

These illustrations show that creativity is central to resilience through the practice of "reciprocal generosity to create a mutual relationship" (Finkelpearl 2013: 47). Our experiences of disasters and displacement underline the notion that the self and others are inseparable on so many registers. Art may well be the beacon along the path to reclamation and reform as it was in the collectivities generated by Roberto Villanueva, Alma Quinto, Francis 'Panx' Solajes, and Nathalie Dagmang through their art. Transformation was both articulated and explored through Villanueva's sustainability aesthetics that enact a ritualistic cycle of returning to earth, in the conversations allowed by Quinto's workshop as gradual recuperation of liberation, through the recollections of visions and messages from other spheres mediated through a contemporary video by Panx Solajes, and by way of Nathalie Dagmang's immersive method and empathetic approach to art.

References

Appadurai, Arjun. 2000. "Grassroots Globalization and the Research Imagination." *Public Culture* 12 (1): 1–19.

Artforum. 2020. "Filipino Artists Unite to Fight the New Anti-Terror Bill." *Artforum.* 12 June 2020. https://www.artforum.com/ news/filipino-artists-unite-to-fight-new-anti-terror-bill-83228? Accessed 14 June 2020.

Bankoff, Greg. 2004. "In the Eye of the Storm: The Social Construction of the Forces of Nature and the Climatic and Seismic Construction of God in the Philippines." *Journal of Southeast Asian Studies* 35 (1): 91–111.

Bankoff, Greg. 2007. "Storms of History: Water, Hazard and Society in the Philippines, 1565-1930." In *A World of Water: Rains, rivers, and seas in Southeast Asian histories*, edited by Peter Boomgaard, 153–86. Singapore: National University of Singapore Press.

Bankoff, Greg . 2016. "Hazardousness of Place: A New Comparative Approach to the Filipino Past." *Philippine Studies: Historical Ethnographic Viewpoints* 64 (3–4): 335–58.

Berman, Kim. 2017. *Finding Voice: A Visual Arts Approach to Engaging Social Change.* Ann Arbor: University of Michigan Press.

Chak, Ashlyn. 2020. "Philippines #ArtistsFightBack Against Anti-Terror Bill." *Art Asia Pacific.* 11 June 2020. https://artasiapacific.com/news/philippines-artistsfightback-against-anti-terror-bill.

Clarke, Paul. 2013. "Case Study: Resiliency after Typhoon Haiyan." *WaldenLabs.* 15 December 2013. https://waldenlabs.com/case-study-resilience-after-typhoon-haiyan/.

Dagmang, Nathalie. 2015. "Dito sa Barangay Tumana" [Here in Barangay Tumana]. Unpublished thesis, College of Fine Arts, University of the Philippines Diliman, Quezon City.

De Guia, Katrin. 2005. *Kapwa: The Self in Other.* Pasig City: Anvil Publishing.

Earth Manual Project. n.d. "Alma Quinto: Floating Wombs." http://www.earth-manual.org/p20en/. Accessed 23 June 2020.

Fajardo, Brenda V. 2010. "The Aesthetics of Poverty: A Rationale in Designing for Philippine People's Theater 1973-1986." *Kritika Kultura* 15: 179–94.

Finkelpearl, Tom. 2013. *What We Made: Conversations on Art and Social Cooperation.* Durham and London: Duke University Press.

Guazon, Tessa Maria. 2019. "A Restless and Raging River." http://tin-aw.com/uploads/exhibitions/publications

Guillermo, Alice G. 1987. *Social Realism in the Philippines.* Manila: Asphodel.

Guillermo, Alice G. 2001. *Protest/Revolutionary Art in the Philippines, 1970-1990.* Quezon City: University of the Philippines Press.

Hinderliter, Beth, Vered Maimon, Jaleh Mansoor, Seth McCormick, eds. 2009. *Communities of Sense: Rethinking Aesthetics and Politics*. Durham and London: Duke University Press.

Ileto, Reynaldo. 1979. *Pasyon and Revolution: Popular Movements in the Philippines 1840-1910*. Quezon City: Ateneo de Manila University Press.

Ito, Lisa. 2017. "Visual Arts & Activism in the Philippines: Notes on a New Season of Discontent." In *Art Archive 01*, edited by Patricia Tumang, Mariko Okeda, Marc J. Ocampo, and Karen Batino, 20–33. Manila: The Japan Foundation.

Keck, Markus, and Benjamin Etzold. 2013. "Risk and Resilience in Asian Megacities." *Erdkunde* 67 (1): 1–3.

Keck, Markus, and Patrick Sakdapolrak. 2013. "What is Social Resilience? Lessons Learned and Ways Forward." *Erdkunde* 67 (1): 5–19.

Kester, Grant. 2013. "Temporary Coalitions, Mobilized Communities and Dialogue as Art." In *What We Made: Conversations on Art and Social Cooperation,* edited by Tom Finkelpearl, 115–31. Durham and London: Duke University Press.

Lee, De-nin D. 2019. *Eco-Art History in East and Southeast Asia.* Newcastle upon Tyne: Cambridge Scholars Publishing.

Lopez, Patricia Marion. 2006. "From Red House to Dream House: Alma Quinto's House of Comfort." *Crtl+P* 1: 2–5. https://www.ctrlp-artjournal.org/pdfs/CtrlP_Issue1.pdf. Accessed 23 June 2020.

Marikina City Government. n.d. "A River Reborn: Marikina's Gift of Life." Marikina City, Metro Manila.

Murcia, Alvin. 2020. "Man Walks 5km Carrying Son's Body." *Philippine Tribune*. 15 April 2020. https://www.pressreader.com/search?query=Man%20walks%20 5km%20carrying%20sons%20body&in=ALL&orderBy=Relevance&searchFor =Articles. Accessed 28 June 2020.

NEDA (National Economic and Development Authority). 2020. *Disaster Rehabilitation and Recovery Planning Guide*. Pasig City: NEDA.

Ottenhoff, Robert G. 2014. "Life after a Super Typhoon." *Disaster Philanthropy* (blog). 7 March 2014. https://disasterphilanthropy.org/blog/life-after-a-super-typhoon/. Accessed 12 September 2021.

Pandey, Vikas. 2020. "Coronavirus Lockdown: The Indian Workers Dying to Get Home." *BBC News*. 19 May 2020. https://www.bbc.com/news/world-asia-india-52672764. Accessed 28 June 2020.

Paterno, Esmaquel II. 2014. "Before SONA, Aquino OKs Yolanda Rehab Plans for Tacloban, 5 Others." *Philippine News*. 28 July 2014. https://www.rappler.com/ philippines/64584-aquino-approves-yolanda-rehabilitation-plans/.

Quinto, Alma. 2006. House of Comfort project concept. *Trauma Interrupted* exhibition brief. Quezon City.

Quinto, Alma. 2013. "Floating Wombs: A Healing Project through the Arts." https://www.earthmanual.org/p2oen/. Accessed 7 August 2021.

Ramzy, Austin. 2013. "For Young Typhoon Survivors, Return of Play is a Sign of Hope." *New York Times.* 19 November 2013. http://www.nytimes.com/2013/11/20/world/asia/children-philippines-typhoon-haiyan.html? src=twr&_r=1&. Accessed 31 October 2014.

Ranciére, Jacques. 2009. "Contemporary Art and the Politics of Aesthetics." In *Communities of Sense: Rethinking Aesthetics and Politics,* edited by Hinderliter, Beth, Vered Maimon, Jaleh Mansoor, and Seth McCormick, 31–50. Durham: Duke University Press.

Rodenbeck, Judith. 2011. "Working to Learn Together: Failure as Tactic." In *Globalization and Contemporary Art,* edited by Jonathan Harris, 161–72. Oxford and Cambridge, MA: Wiley Blackwell.

Rosca, Ninotchka. 2013. "Commentary: Calling Filipinos Resilient is an Insult." *Yahoo Southeast Asia Newsroom.* 18 November 2013. https://web.archive.org/web/20131121174425/https://ph.news.yahoo.com/commentary--calling-filipinos-resilient-is-an-insult-011053161.html Accessed 31 October 2014.

Selga, Miguel. 1935. *Charts of Remarkable Typhoons in the Philippines, 1920-1934.* Manila: Bureau of Printing.

Smith, Terry. 2009. *What is Contemporary Art?* Chicago: The University of Chicago Press.

Solajes, Francis. 2017. Unpublished Artist statement for Himurasak for the exhibition *Traversal/Trajectories: Expansive Localities,* University of the Philippines Jorge Vargas Museum and Filipiniana Research Center.

Solnit, Rebecca. 2009. *A Paradise Built in Hell: The Extraordinary Communities That Arise in Disaster.* New York: Viking.

Tanabe, Shihegaru, ed. 2016. Introduction to *Communities of Potential: Social Assemblages in Thailand and Beyond,* 1–17. Chiang Mai: Silkworm Books.

Villanueva, Roberto G. 1992. "Artist Statement." In *New Art from Southeast Asia,* edited by Yasuko Furuichi. Tokyo: Japan Foundation ASEAN Cultural Center.

Yamamura, Midori. 2019. "Making the Art Object Disappear: Roberto Villanueva's Response to the Anthropocene." In *Eco-Art History in East and Southeast Asia,* edited by Din-dee Lee, 87–111. Newcastle upon Tyne: Cambridge Scholars Publishing.

About the Author

Tessa Maria Guazon is curator of the University of the Philippines Jorge B. Vargas Museum and Filipiniana Research Center. She teaches courses in art criticism, curatorship and contemporary art at the Department of Art Studies, University of the Philippines Diliman.

8. Muddied Memories as Vernacular Heritage of an Unnatural Disaster

Anton Novenanto and I Wayan Suyadnya

Abstract: The 2006 birth of a mud volcano in Porong, East Java, became a politically enthralling catastrophe contested by two discourses. Public perception treats the mudflow as human generated, the result of negligent exploratory drilling, whereas the company operating the well (Lapindo Brantas) and the government treat it as a natural disaster by blaming an earthquake. The mud volcano submerged fifteen villages and subdistricts in three districts. We discuss the interrelation of monuments, human actors, and social time in preserving memories of lost space and supporting broader circulation of these memories. Commemorative practices record collective memories of this unnatural event. We focus on collective memory as vernacular heritage—local people's sole inheritance being memories of homes and houses and associated commemorative practices.

Keywords: heritage making, collective memory, environmental disaster, Lapindo mudflow

In memory of Abdul Rokhim (1968–2025), a Lapindo mudflow victor

A Scene from Fieldwork

How to study heritage from a people who have nothing to bequeath? Let's begin with a scene from fieldwork that one of us conducted:

> One afternoon of mid-June 2012, I was heading to the Besuki Timur hamlet through the dysfunctional toll road of Gempol-Porong. When I crossed

Herzfeld, M., and R. Padawangi, eds. *Resilience as Heritage in Asia*. Amsterdam: Amsterdam University Press, 2025.
DOI: 10.5117/9789463728560_CH08

over the bridge of the Porong River, I saw beautiful scenery, that is, a
sunset, and one thing that came into my mind at the time was that I had
to capture that rare moment from the top of the mud embankment. In
Sanggar Alfaz there was a seventeen-year-old, Hisyam, and I asked him
to bring me on his motorcycle to *Titik 25* (Point 25) on the embankments.
There we met some local tourists who were escorted by some *ojek tanggul*
(motorcycle-taxi drivers). While the local tourists took pictures of the
twilight and some other things, I overheard one *ojek tanggul*, who was
acting as a professional tour guide, explaining to them the mudflow
disaster that has been occurring since 29 May 2006. In so doing, he
pointed to some areas where he claimed his former village was located.
"Now all has gone" (*semua sudah hilang*), one *ojek tanggul* said to their
guests. Shortly after taking some pictures and as the day was getting
dark, Hisyam and I headed back to the Besuki village. This time he took a
different path, to the northeast (we had entered from the south), but still
across the embankment east of the main eruption. I could see more areas
covered by mud. Hisyam recalled that the embankment we passed over
was new. It had been built in 2008 or 2009 as a secondary layer after the
construction of the inner embankment ring. The rationale was to hold the
mud from flowing to his village if the inner embankment collapsed. While
driving the motorcycle, he told me some memories about his childhood,
playing around that area with friends. "There were houses, buildings and
schools, playgrounds," he said, "but everything is no more" (*semuanya
sudah tidak ada lagi*).[1]

In this chapter, we address the interrelations among human actors, physical
monuments, and social time in preserving (and contesting) memories of a
lost space and how these memories are circulated to broader publics and
through generations through a series of commemorative practices/routines.
It is not our intention to examine the accuracy of what people remember.
What matters is how certain collective memories about the catastrophe are
organized in accordance with preexisting structures of cultural narrative
and how commemorative performances contribute significantly to the
reproduction of a specific identity. Such a focus continues previous studies
on the politics of narratives, which argue that the recollection of mudflow
victims' memories has been shaped by individual motives, political interests,
and social intentions (Drake 2017; Novenanto 2015b). We argue here that
the effort to recollect certain memories happens, not only in "monumental

---

1   Anton Novenanto's fieldnote, Saturday, 16 June 2012, originally written in Bahasa Indonesia.

time" (disaster commemoration in this case), but also in "social time" (as manifested in daily routines) (Herzfeld 1991: 6–10).

The scene at the outset represents how some people's memory has played a key role in others' knowledge production about nothingness. Indeed, the concept of *collective memory* has been a key concept in the sociology of knowledge (Brian, Jaisson, and Mukherjee 2012) and is therefore essential, as we propose here, in a study of heritage (McDowell 2008; Marschall 2013; Harvey 2008). World War II was a key event for the burgeoning study of collective memory as the survivors and witnesses of the war were obliged to recollect and share their memories of the crisis for the purpose of historical writing about the event/process from various angles. While scholars began to construct historical narratives about that fraught yet pervasive sequence of events in world history, the media industry also started to produce images, fiction, and documentaries about its horror and heroism (Olick, Vinitzky-Seroussi, and Levy 2011). The reconstruction of the past, especially of a catastrophic event or process, has never been a neutral process; intersubjective conflicts subsist among individuals, and these conflicts may have influenced the recollection and reconstruction of certain memories of the past (Forrest 1993).

In the following, we begin with a theoretical discussion connecting the concept of vernacular heritage with collective memory. Subsequently, we present a brief account of the social, political, and cultural context of the Lapindo mudflow before discussing vernacular monuments, commemorative practices, and commemorative routines in greater detail. We conclude the chapter by discussing the importance of memory studies in the heritage-making process, especially with respect to the so-called vernacular heritage of a lost space.

Vernacular Heritage and Collective Memory

UNESCO accepts two kinds of heritage: tangible and intangible. For some, the former is easier to identify as it can be observed with our senses—although the heritage-making process of certain objects (natural and built environment) is not merely a matter of sensory apperception. Intangible heritage, which we take to include memory, remains a problematic term ideationally and practically. As such, we prefer to focus more on the outcome(s) or projection of a heritage-making process and less on the inherited objects themselves.

The Cartesian nature of the distinction used by UNESCO has been widely criticized in the field of heritage studies. Anthropologist Michael

Herzfeld (2014), for instance, criticizes it for the neglect of daily practices and categories of various cultural contexts. In that sense, the tangible-intangible categorization has been used as an instrument to select which cultural features would be included or excluded as heritage. Every heritage, according to British geographer David Harvey (2008: 21), has *a* historical narrative and should be understood as relating to "a *prospective memory*, as tokens that represent a desired future—reflecting both future pasts and past futures." Heritage making is a process that materializes the identity of a group of people into certain objects so that they can be sources of knowledge for the continuity of the group (or the memory of the group if it no longer exists), not only through commemoration events but also by its lived incarnation in daily routines. Within the context of these ideas, we turn back to French sociologist Maurice Halbwachs (1980: 52) who coined the concept *collective memory*. From Halbwachs we learn that historical recollection tends to establish and defend an objective truth about the past that is fabricated from historical records (documents, media, witnesses' testimonies). On the other hand, social remembrance aims to search for anything in the past that may be relevant for our present lives and futures with the help of both physical monuments and social time. It refers to the reconstruction of the past from our own experience of events (Truc 2011). Simply put, history is "the past that [is] no longer an important part of our lives," while collective memory is "the remembered past that actively shapes our identities" (Olick and Robbins 1998: 111).

In Halbwachsian sense, following Harvey, we can then define *heritage* as "a form of collective memory, a social construct shaped by the political, economic and social concerns of the present" (Graham and Howard 2008: 2). Heritage making is not only about a process of selecting, demolishing, or altering inheritable objects, but more about contests of power about what meanings to embed in those objects. Heritage is about making objects from the past matter and appear worthy of preservation for the creation of the future (Harvey 2008). To remember is therefore not merely a psychological, mental process, but also a social process, an exercise of power in the form of interactive, sometimes even conflicting relations between the relevant actors. People cannot pass on everything they have ever possessed; they would and could only be inheriting certain features with which to mark and strengthen the cultural identity of the social groups with which they are affiliated. In many cases, a group's identity not only differs from, but also competes with, official recognition (Stangl 2008; Marschall 2013). In the heritage-making process, different groups of people produce, shape, maintain, and negotiate various, conflicting collective memory through commemorative practices and routines they perform at specific social moments as well as the artifacts associated with those moments (Coser 1992; Marschall 2013). The most challenging competition over heritage making is seen in the economic, cultural, and architectural homogenization of certain objects, including the representation of collective memories as intangible objects. We then rely on urbanist Paul Stangl's idea of *vernacular* as "public spaces, buildings, and objects (inside and outside, public and private, state and non-state), which as their primary purpose, constitute the everyday city, the realm of routine activity" (Stangl 2008: 246). The vernacular links spatial features and day-to-day routines as "expressions of collective memory" (Stangl 2008: 246); in most cases, these are exclusively relevant to specific groups.

For many people, environmental disasters are episodic, monumental, catastrophic events (Bryant and Bailey 1997: 26–32; Forrest 1993). In the case of the Lapindo mudflow in Java, however, the disaster is still ongoing: the mud is still erupting and flowing and there is no sign that it will stop soon. We focus here on commemorative practices by categorizing them as *habit-memory*, a notion proposed by sociologist Paul Connerton (1989). This is the act, not only of recollecting autobiographical and historical memories of the past, but also of articulating those remembrances in specific performances and bodily practices.[2] The notion of habit-memory helps us to understand that such activities are not merely actions in which people share their personal experiences and historical records of the past, but are the basis on which we challenge others' experiences and historical records of the past through the production of vernacular monuments and the reproduction of commemorative practices and routines.

One Unnatural Mudflow, Two Competing Discourses

On 29 May 2006, a burst of gas and hot mud was detected in the middle of a paddy field adjacent to Lapindo Brantas's drilling well of Banjar Panji-1.[3]

2   Connerton's (1989: 22-24) other conceptualizations of memory are: *personal memory*, which refers to any acts of remembering of a subject's particular life history event: "I did such and such, at such and such a time, in such and such a place"; and, *cognitive memory*, in which "the person who remembers that thing must have met, experienced or learned of it in the past."

3   Lapindo Brantas is owned by Bakrie & Brothers. The family owned half of Lapindo's share, and the other half was shared between another Indonesian mining company, Medco (32%), and an Australian company, Santos (12%). At the time the incident occurred, a leading figure of the Bakrie, Aburizal, was the coordination minister of people's welfare. Until May 2016, Aburizal

Geologists name this phenomenon a *mud volcano*. It had the highest eruption rate ever recorded for such phenomena, up to 180,000 cubic meters per day, and has submerged an approximately eight hundred-hectare area in fifteen villages in three districts (Novenanto 2015a).[4] Despite the ongoing debate about the cause of the eruption, geologists agree on one fact: Porong is a perfect spot for the birth of a mud volcano (Batubara 2013). In the course of the mudflow, we can identify two competing discourses that people attribute to the Lapindo mudflow: the "man-made disaster" discourse and the "natural disaster" discourse (Batubara 2013). We should understand the context and formation of each discourse, as they play a crucial role in shaping how people organize themselves in responding to the hazard and to each discourse.

The formation of the "man-made disaster" discourse can be traced in early statements that appeared after the initial eruption. One important statement appeared on two columns on the front page of *Kompas* daily on 30 May 2006. It came from Syahdun, Lapindo's drilling foreman, who claimed, "the gas explosion was triggered by the fracture of the borehole formation" (Saputra 2006). This statement was repeatedly quoted in subsequent reports in *Kompas*. In addition, early public statements from Lapindo's representatives claimed that the situation was under control and promised that compensation for all the damage, if it turned out that any damage had indeed occurred, would be paid through the company's mining insurance scheme (Energi Mega Persada 2006a; 2006b). A week after the initial incident, one shareholder of the Banjar Panji-1 well, Medco Brantas (henceforth, "Medco"), issued a letter to Lapindo on 5 June 2006, stating that the eruption was triggered by the drilling activity in the well. Lapindo

was the chief of the largest political party in Indonesia, Golkar, and nurtured strong ambitions to run in the 2014 presidential elections. Former president Yudhoyono never had the courage to force Lapindo to take all the responsibility because Aburizal was one of the major donors of his 2004 and 2009 presidential campaigns (Schiller, Lucas, and Sulistiyanto 2008). We can therefore easily see why Lapindo and the family are trying hard to reduce their legal liability for the effects of the mudflow (Novenanto et al. 2013).

4   The mudflow is not a single, isolated problem. It generates other problems such as land subsidence, huge mud craters, dried mud, basin pollution in the Brantas River, riverine ecosystem damage, and human health problems (McMichael 2009). An Indonesian environmental NGO consortium, Walhi, claims that the mud contains hazardous, dangerous, and toxic waste material (Nusantara 2010). Ignoring this fact, the government has been redirecting the mud to the Madura Strait through the Porong River, thereby triggering more social and ecological issues in the river's catchment areas as well as in the strait. The Indonesian government is only concerned with how to pay the remaining compensation and with the physical management of the mudflow and its surroundings, leaving the people in Porong to deal with and survive these multidimensional impacts of the mudflow by themselves (Novenanto 2017).

had neglected the installation of a safety casing inside the borehole.[5] The incident, Medco claimed in its letter, was due to the "gross negligence" of Lapindo, which did not follow the drilling procedure according to the original plan.[6] These initial statements formed a public perception that the mudflow was caused by careless drilling.

The "man-made disaster" discourse has also dominated the scientific field. The first scientific paper on the event was published in the February 2007 edition of the Geological Society of America monthly magazine, *GSA Today* (Davies et al. 2007).[7] Four British earth scientists led by Richard Davies at Durham University proposed the argument that the event occurred owing to the absence of a safety casing, which had led to a fracture in the borehole. In July 2007, a response was published in *Earth and Planetary Science Letters*. Adriano Mazzini, a professor of geology at the University of Oslo, Norway, was the corresponding author and Lapindo's in-house geologist Bambang Istadi was a coauthor (Mazzini et al. 2007). It therefore seems likely that the argument proposed in the article was a strategy intended to contest the "drilling theory" proposed by Davies's camp. Mazzini's camp touted the theory that blamed the mud volcano on a major earthquake that occurred on 27 May 2006. In other words, it promoted a discourse based on the hypothesis of a natural disaster as the cause.

Scientists' debate concerning the cause of the mudflow took place not only on paper but also in other academic forums. Among these was the American Association of Petroleum Geologists (AAPG) conference in Cape Town, South Africa (26–28 October 2008), at which the issue was brought to a vote in a plenary session. Of seventy-four participants who had the right to vote, more than half (forty-two) voted in favor of the view that the mudflow was anthropogenic, triggered by Lapindo's drilling. Of the rest, three agreed that it was a naturally born mud volcano caused by an earthquake; thirteen voted for the hypothesis that the mudflow was a hybrid (the result of a combination of both drilling and the earthquake); and sixteen

5   The letter, entitled "The Banjar Panji-1 well drilling incident," was originally written in English.
6   In that same letter, Medco mentioned that a few days before the incident (on 18 May 2006), a meeting had taken place at which Medco's representatives had warned Lapindo of the need to install the casing to a certain depth, but that Lapindo intentionally neglected to do this. Additionally, Medco funded two independent consultants (e.g., TriTech Petroleum and Neal Adams Services) to conduct research on what caused the loss of the well (Wilson 2006; Adams 2006). After the Bakries bought Medco's well shares in March 2007, however, Medco was no longer involved in the production of knowledge over the incident.
7   The article adopts the name *"Lusi,"* abbreviated from *lumpur Sidoarjo* (Sidoarjo mudflow), a shorter name that became popular usage in scientific and other fields such as the media and formal politics.

voted for the need for further research on the matter before final conclusions could be drawn. Needless to say, those who voted for the earthquake were affiliated with Lapindo. The voting mechanism was already problematic for a scientific forum; instead of using scientific evidence to come to appropriate conclusions, the conference used a democracy-by-numbers mechanism. As a consequence, it has muddied the waters of debate and prompted unproductive counter discourses in subsequent forums.

Proponents of the "natural disaster" discourse have become more deliberate than other camps in insisting that their claim is the more valid of the two positions. One particularly influential work was a special edition on mud volcanism in the November 2009 edition of the *Marine and Petroleum Geology* journal. Mazzini edited the volume; it consisted of seventeen research papers on mud volcanoes all over the world and includes one on Mars. Five papers on the mudflow in Porong were grouped together in a special section of the volume; all these draw on the "earthquake theory." One paper, authored by Lapindo's drilling engineers, attempts specifically to refute the "drilling theory (Sawolo et al. 2009)."[8]

Efforts to refute the "man-made disaster" discourse have increased, generated mostly by actors affiliated with Lapindo and/or the Government. Among others, the organization of an international geology symposium hosted in late May 2011 in Surabaya by the Humanitus Sidoarjo Fund (HSF), a program of the Humanitus Foundation (an Australian NGO), does call for a critical response. The foundation received a one million US dollar grant from the Russian Institute of Geology to conduct research into the persistent Porong mud volcano. With the support of Russian scientists, the HSF planned a project to map the geodynamics of the mud volcano and its surrounding area, with the intention of fending off future impact. In the course of their program, the HSF has been coordinating with the government to support the "earthquake theory." Recently, the HSF funded a simulation research project conducted by a team of German geologists who published their findings in *Nature Geoscience* journal (Lupi et al. 2013). Relying on their simulation, the authors claim that the enormous amount of seismic energy released by the 27 May earthquake resulted in an increase in volcanic activity, including the Porong mud volcano in Porong, on Java, and claimed that "the borehole [of Banjar Panji-1] was a witness to, and not the perpetrator of, the initiation of Lusi" (Lupi et al. 2013: 642).

---

8   It received a long commentary from the proponents of the anthropogenic disaster camp (see Davies et al. 2010). It was followed a few months later by a response article from the authors of the original paper (Sawolo et al. 2010).

Highly energetic efforts to circulate the "natural disaster" discourse are occurring in the media. Lapindo is a subsidiary of an Indonesian conglomerate controlled by the Bakrie family. The conglomerate is the parent company of one media giant in Indonesia and some local media in East Java, which means that they can easily arrange for their representatives, family members, or other actors (geologists, lawyers, politicians, cultural/religious leaders, government officials, and even victims) to deliver opinion-shaping statements on the "natural disaster" discourse in the public sphere (Novenanto 2013; Tapsell 2010; Andriarti and Novenanto 2013). We can identify a strong effort on the part the company as well as the government to contest the "man-made disaster" discourse, which has already achieved a circulation similar to that of the "natural disaster" discourse.

At the present time, it is difficult to identify any systematic public effort to question the normalization openly. The scientific debate represents the ongoing struggle and contestation of truth about what caused the mudflow. The debate shows that different interests are engaged in the course of heritage making among the scientists, while other interests contest the cause of the Lapindo mudflow. We argue that whatever the conclusion of the debate, it will have strong implications for victims' memories. The government's and the company's claim that the mudflow is a natural disaster, however, should be seen as cultural politics, designed to intervene in victims' memories by obliterating other memories suggesting that the mudflow had been a disaster created by human beings and that the unsatisfactory governance of post-disaster management resulted in other forms of violence. We are dealing with the politics of recognition in heritage making (Harvey 2008). While international scientists might reach a decisive conclusion, we must be concerned about what would happen if the views of the government and of the company were to prevail.

The foregoing does not mean that there are no more popular forms of resistance to formal government statements. In what follows, we discuss some of the kinds of resistance that have continued in the hands of a group of mudflow survivors as they strive to maintain the "human-generated disaster" discourse through various deployments of habit-memory.

Vernacular Monument of a Tombstone

A monument does not only help people remember the past; it is also a tool to deliver—and often to force people to remember selectively—aspects of the past that can be fitted to the ideology of the present (Hui 2009). Monumentalization is a practice of articulating particular statements by freezing them and at the same time excluding those who are considered not

Figure 8.1. Monument of Lapindo mudflow tragedy (photo courtesy of Lutfi Amiruddin 2013)

to belong (Assmann 2009). At Porong there is a huge physical monument recalling the moment of destruction. It is an eight-hundred-hectare artificial mud lake. What matters for us is not only the mud lake, but also every single physical building (house, factory, store, office, school, health facility, mosque, and many more), and social life that is buried at the bottom of the lake. Those objects only exist now through the monumentalized memory of the people.

We discover one intriguing monument (figure 8.1) when we climb up the embankment's wall. It is more like a tombstone. It was built and erected at the seven-year commemoration in 2013 on the top of the embankment wall on the western side. The idea of making a monument was something new during the eruption's annual commemoration, every 29 May. Common practices at this event have included throwing objects into the mud (Drake 2012). On the tombstone, there is an inscription that reads as follows:

Lapindo Mudflow Tragedy Monument
Lapindo mudflow has buried our hamlets
Lapindo only sells out fake promises
The State fails to rehabilitate our life
We will never silence our voice for the nation shall not forget[9]

9   The original text reads: "Monumen Tragedi Lumpur Lapindo, Lumpur Lapindo telah mengubur kampung kami, Lapindo hanya mengobral janji palsu, Negara abai memulihkan kehidupan kami, Suara kami tak pernah padam agar bangsa ini tidak lupa."

From the text we can observe two major themes that the creator of the tombstone tries to convey. First, it tells us what happened, which the authors frame as a tragedy ("Lapindo mudflow has buried our hamlet"). The use of the word "hamlet" (*kampung*) means something deeper than mere physical houses. It refers to a sociocultural atmosphere, a homey space. If we look back to the scene at the outset of the chapter, the message is similar; the mudflow has not only destroyed the buildings and landscape but also every single social life-form that ever existed in relation to those objects and places. Second, it identifies the interrelated actors in the event for us and shows us how they are framed. The first two actors, Lapindo and the state, are framed as the unreliable parties: Lapindo for selling out fake promises and the state for failing to overcome the crisis of the people. The only actors people can rely on are those who continue to articulate their stories to sustain the memory of the nation about the tragedy. These people are guardians of the memory of the Lapindo mudflow. The making and erecting of a tombstone was one form of action they took.

The tombstone, built by a group of people living in Besuki village, has become a vernacular monument of the Lapindo mudflow. On several occasions, such as the commemoration of the start of the mudflow every 29 May, various groups of victims perform certain acts over the tombstone—acts that are more of a symbolic political performance than religious rituals.

Commemorative Practices

The emplacement of the tombstone was only one activity in the seven-year commemoration of the mudflow. Also of interest was an effigy (*ogoh-ogoh*) of a male figure wearing a yellow suit, carrying a briefcase full of money, and sitting on a mud volcano. The effigy was paraded along with the tombstone by hundreds of Lapindo mudflow survivors in a rally on the Porong highway. After they erected the tombstone, they focused on the escorting of the effigy to the edge of the embankment and throwing it into the mud lake. It was meant as a symbolic act of hope for the sinking of Aburizal's political career and, with it, of the representation of business as being as valuable as the people's lost livelihoods.

In Indonesia, there is a widely held view of disasters as anthropogenic features of the environment. That view interprets environmental disasters as stemming from both individual and collective misconduct (Lapian 1987). A recent anthropological study of cultural interpretations of volcanic eruptions in Central Java showed that many people consider natural hazards (volcanic eruptions) to be an outcome of the abuse of power by their rulers, whether at the local or the national level (Schlehe 2009). Such hazards are believed to balance disharmonious humans against human-nature relationships. More specifically in East Java, people view misfortunes, including natural hazards, as a result of evil spirits that have possessed local communities; that understanding relies on the Javanese principle of the porosity of human bodies (Wessing 2010). Human bodies, Wessing (2010: 53) notes, "are thought to be porous, allowing spirits and other influences to move in and out, and leaving the person involved open to a loss of personal spirit or to possession, the invasion of the body by an alien spirit." In accordance with this principle, some rituals aim to prevent the original spirits from coming out of the bodies and to allow alien spirits to enter them. If a misfortune has already happened, a different ritual, *ruwatan* (cleansing), casts out alien spirits from the bodies and restores the original spirits to their original bodies. This concept informed the structure of the Lapindo mudflow commemoration in 2013, showing that the victims—and the general public in Indonesia—basically accept the proposition that the mudflow was man made.

As we have noted above, Aburizal's role as a leading figure in both the company and the government was very problematic. He was certainly the main target of the victims' anger during the commemoration as they framed him not only as a wicked person but also, and even more significantly, as an evil spirit who had possessed the government and society. The effigy was understood to be that of Aburizal. According to Irsyad, the leader of the procession that led to the dissolving of the effigy in the mud, the idea of making an effigy was inspired by a Balinese ritual a few days before *Nyepi* (the first day of Balinese New Year). The ritual aims to cleanse villages of evil spirits entering a new year. Nowadays, beside making an effigy of mythological, demonic creatures, the Balinese also creatively make figures of real-life persons thought to have exercised a bad influence on the life of the community. In Bali, the climax of the procession is the burning of the effigy as a symbol of cleansing the village of evil spirits and bad luck.

The mudflow victims adopted this concept. They made an effigy of Aburizal and drowned it, instead of burning it as the Balinese do, as a way of cleansing society of this particular evil spirit.[10] The victims perceive Aburizal as an evil spirit who brought them nothing but misery and suffering. While dissolving the effigy in the mud lake, Irsyad yelled to the crowd:

---

10   The practice of throwing objects into the mud lake was not the first to be performed in Porong; it was a common mythically based practice for ending an eruption (Drake 2012).

> Dear friends, our intention is to remove destruction. This [throwing the *ogoh-ogoh* to the mud] is a sign of throwing out our misfortune made by [Aburizal] Bakrie. We dispose of misfortune.[11]

One person from the crowd replied out loud, "Goodbye, Aburizal Bakrie! Goodbye!"[12] Then Irsyad started to pelt the effigy with mud, and other victims followed suit.

We believe that the practice of dissolving Aburizal in effigy was influenced by a Javanese folktale, *Timun Mas*, to which the mudflow gives discursive immediacy. The main plot of the folktale is about the struggle of a peasant girl, *Timun Mas* (Golden Cucumber), against an ogre, *Buto Ijo* (Green Ogre), who wants to eat her. Before Timun Mas was born, so the story goes, her mother, Mbok Sirni, made a deal with Buto Ijo to deliver her to the ogre. Instead of obeying the deal, Timun Mas chose to fight the ogre. To face the ogre, Timun Mas used four essences that she received from a hermit: a) a cucumber seed that grows as a dense cucumber field; b) a needle that becomes a dense bamboo forest; c) salt that turns into a sea; and d) *terasi,* shrimp paste that becomes a mud lake. The story ends with Buto Ijo's death by drowning in the mud lake, after which Timun Mas returns home safely.[13]

The Javanese do not particularly perceive the folktale as a mudflow-related narrative. It represents the struggle of Javanese peasants against a profiteering *ijon* system, a traditional economy that provides peasants with high-interest loans that they repay with their subsequent harvest.[14] The system is believed to have a detrimental effect on poor peasants, as they are bonded to certain *pengijon* (moneylenders) by preexisting contracts requiring them to sell their crops exclusively to the moneylenders and therefore the peasants cannot sell elsewhere at a higher price (Partadireja 1974). The system is of long standing since many Javanese landless peasants do not have sufficient cash to finance unprecedented needs such as the education of their children and medical supplies. Thus, instead of serving the poor, the system appears to have played a crucial role in the impoverishment of many Javanese peasants. For many years, the government's efforts to stimulate

11   *Kawan-kawan semua, niat kita adalah membuang kehancuran. Ini tanda membuang kesialan yang dilakukan oleh Bakrie. Kita membuang sial.*

12   *Selamat tinggal Aburizal Bakrie! Selamat tinggal*!

13   This version of the folktale was first raised by a government geologist, Awang Harun Satyana (Satyana 2007).

14   The term *ijon* has its origin in the Javanese *ijo* (meaning green), referring to the still green, young crops. The name of the ogre in the Timun Mas folktale, *Buto Ijo*, is derived from this same word.

the creation of microcredit through its banking system do not seem to have succeeded in eliminating the system. The relationship of Timun Mas and Buto Ijo symbolizes the relationship of peasants with moneylenders in the system.[15] In the folktale, instead of obeying the contract, Timun Mas chooses to struggle against Buto Ijo. She does not wait for a savior to come and rescue her; rather, she searches for some means to fight the ogre. The story ends with Timun Mas's victory and the defeat of the ogre.

According to a local journalist-cum-environmentalist, Henri Nurcahyo (2014), there are many variants of the folktale. These mention other causes of the death of Buto Ijo, such as drowning in the sea, having been incapacitated by its saltiness, or tripping over a rock. The folktale delivers a message to the people to keep on struggling and not to succumb easily to present difficulties; it thereby offers hope to Lapindo mudflow victims as they face the collusive relationship between Lapindo and the government (Nurcahyo 2014). Moreover, it provides them with a concrete example to act when facing trouble instead of passively waiting for a *ratu adil* (messiah, savior) to come. This contradicts Benedict Anderson's (2007) theory that Javanese perceive power as something that can be possessed by—and is usually centralized in—several figures, mostly kings or governmental apparatuses, or sacred objects. In Anderson's interpretation, people's freedom is locally seen as derived not from their struggles, but rather from the goodwill of the rulers, the kings of the Javanese courts who are believed to be the messiahs of the Javanese (Ricklefs 2001; Priest 1995). This is clearly the opposite of what is happening in Porong. Instead of standing up for the mudflow victims, the state apparatuses have been shielding Lapindo and the Bakrie by gradually protecting them from the obligation to compensate the victims (Novenanto 2015a). Instead of punishing Lapindo and the Bakrie, the government has taken over their liability for any further damages resulting from the mudflow. Expecting the government to show willingness to solve the problems arising from the mudflow is nothing but a waste of time because an evil spirit has possessed it; it is therefore time for the people themselves to cast the spirit out from the government and from society. This idea perfectly matches the folktale's narrative structure. Focusing on the part of how the notorious ogre sank into a mud lake, victims are utilizing and reproducing the folktale in a series of theatrical commemorative practices. Aburizal's drowning in effigy parallels Buto Ijo's fate.

15   Operating from a slightly different perspective, anthropologist Azzah Nilawaty (2012) interprets the relationship between the two by analogy with the unequal power relation between the mudflow child victims and Lapindo.

Commemorative Routines

Even though the Lapindo mudflow has resulted in the demolition of land-marks and the disruption of the people's social life, various commemorative efforts are embodied in day-to-day activity. Among others, Abdul Rokhim, a villager from Besuki, frequently visits the location where his former house stood. This location is under five hundred meters from the embankment walls built by the government to restrain the mudflow. This routine of "just paying a visit" (*ndelok* [Javanese]) is less about curiosity about what is now happening there and more about a kind of habit-memory.

When he visits the area, Rokhim recalls some aspects of what had hap-pened or used to exist there. Driving along the dysfunctional toll road in our car, he pointed to an empty land lot which, he claimed, had been the location of his house. As one of us had never experienced living in the area, we did not all have the same image of what was there. All that was left was a single broken *mushalla*, a small Islamic prayerhouse. We found many handwritten inscriptions on its walls cursing Lapindo, along with other abusive, sexist phrases, such as: "Beware of wandering widows,"[16] "Widow doesn't matter, as long as her 'hole' is tight,"[17] and "Mbak Intan lovers" (figures 8.2 and 8.3). The asphalt road in front of his former house was already overgrown with adult-ankle-high weeds indicating that the road has not been used for quite some time. Besides showing us the former borders and boundaries of his house, he can still point clearly to the location of each of his neighbors' houses along the street from one end to the other. The location was now being used as a motor cross-training ground initiated by the local government.

We continued our journey to a mosque across the toll road. Rokhim and many other Besuki villagers are still using the mosque for their weekly Friday prayers. This religious routine usually begins with the communal prayer (*shalat*) and is followed by individuals praying in the graveyard next to the mosque. But there are some people who say their individual prayers in the graveyard on Thursday afternoons before joining the communal prayer on the following day. This was happening long before the mudflow and continues to this day. We were very intrigued when we found out that the two-floor mosque was still in good shape, in contrast to its surroundings. Rokhim explained that the villagers were still receiving "village funds" (*dana desa*) from the national government. The funds were being used to

---

16   *Hati-hati rawan janda berkeliaran.*
17   *Masi rondo gpp, sing penting bolongane cilik.*

Figure 8.2. A ruined prayer room exterior (photo by I Wayan Suyadnya 2019)

Figure 8.3. A ruined prayer room interior (photo by I Wayan Suyadnya 2019)

renovate the mosque and recondition the graveyard next to it. With the money, people could buy paint and fix the well; some was allocated for elevating the graveyard. We found this very fascinating. Although Besuki Village is no more, the government still recognizes it administratively, so that it is entitled to receive funding for certain development programs.

When we asked several people why, after living elsewhere, they still came to the mosque for Friday prayers, many replied that they had bonds with their predecessors and that many have family members buried next to the mosque. They perceived the mosque and the graveyard next to it as the only place representing their past social lives. Mosque and graveyard do not function only as cultural features for their religious activities but also as mnemonic and commemorative place and space (Cutcher et al. 2016), in which they spend social time as a form of what they called a "retreat to inner life" (*wisata bathin*). This practice allows them to preserve collective memories that would otherwise begin to fade as a result of aging as well as of the ignorance of the state and the general public.

The Besuki villagers' routine exhibits a fundamental aspect of the commemorative practices of one group of mudflow survivors—that physical features such as a mosque and a graveyard are physical monuments that shape mnemonic practices as people classify them as valuable, heritable objects from their past lives. Such meaning is produced and reproduced through the continuous organization of people's routines around what might superficially seem to be merely abandoned places that nevertheless remain memorable for them. These places are "hidden in plain sight" (Guthey and Jackson 2005: 1058). They have mnemonic power that derives from their capacity as structural features to generate social practices. We see that the resulting routines in both sites transform personal reminiscences into collective memory through such episodic but continually repeated social encounters. In other words, these sites, unlike the abandoned school building adjacent to the mosque, have the power to connect people's individual lifeworlds in a shared space. Although the school was an important place, not all villagers understood it as a monument since routine practices are no longer performed there.

To comprehend how the two sites could have such a capacity to organize and reorganize people's collective memories of the Lapindo mudflow disaster, we should consider the sociological notion of "social time" (Forrest 1993). The social time people spend on "just paying a visit" (*ndelok*) is a key component of the process whereby these physical monuments become a source of meaning making. People's daily, weekly, and yearly commemorative practices have created a social time related to these sites. The sites themselves have become heritable objects for Lapindo mudflow survivors. For the survivors, the social time at their disposal is a key to preserving memories of their families, neighborhoods, and communities, of their status as victims of an environmental and political disaster, and perhaps also of the inability of the state to protect their homes and livelihoods.

Another activity, motorcycle-taxi tourism (*ojek wisata*), offers a different type of social organization for distributing personal experiences and interpretations of the event to a broader public (Suyadnya and Fatanti 2017). The preservation of collective memory is maintained simultaneously through collecting and storing memories and through continual commemorative practices and routines as strategic mechanisms for sustaining the intergenerational inheritance of identity (see Olick and Robbins 1998). Thus, what is being inherited through such commemorative routines is not only merely a set of repetitive actions but a series of collective memories.

Conclusion: Space, Place, Commemoration, and Resilience

The concept of vernacular heritage centers on the link between the spatial form and the practice of everyday life. Recent literature has focused more on monumental buildings, memorial parks, and historic sites, and less on everyday practices. Tales, folklore, old stories, legends of places (rivers and lakes), traditions of urban planning, and architecture are no less expressive of a society's past. In this chapter we have tried to pay attention to monumental architecture (physical time) in relation to collective memory in which, however, we also describe routines or practices that constitute a kind of social time. In this sense, vernacular heritage coexists with places and spaces. Disaster destroyed buildings and disconnected them from the people. But, the loss of tangible objects, such as buildings, does not mean that the people are losing everything as they still have their memories of vernacular spaces (such as the mosque and the graveyard). That said, there is also a group of mudflow victims who are trying to monumentalize some memories by building a vernacular monument (a tombstone).

We have shown how victims of the Lapindo mudflow are utilizing tools of collective memory to contest the official claim of the mudflow proposed by the company and the government, and to promote their own version of truth through a series of commemorative practices. Disaster commemoration is more than a few acts of recollection and representation of catastrophic events. It also serves to give new meanings to such events for the future. It is a social time in which disaster victims have the opportunity to articulate and perform their own meanings and memories related to the event as well as the beloved ones they have lost. Commemoration has become a discursive field in the sense that it restores power to the victims through the recollection of particular memories related to the disaster and its subjective meanings. It is also a social time in which disaster victims have the opportunity to add or modify some of the meanings of the event and of the actors involved; those now remembering the event have a chance to select some of their memories and exclude some others. Collective memory functions not only as heritage making but also as a strategic means of empowering the victims so that they can play a part—representing the vernacular perspective—in the ongoing contestation of the right to interpret the significance of the mudflow.

References

Adams, Neal. 2006. "Causation Factors for the Banjar Panji No 1 Blowout." Jakarta: Unpublished Report.

Anderson, Benedict. 2007. "The Idea of Power in Javanese Culture." In *Culture and Politics in Indonesia*, edited by Claire Holt, 1–70. Singapore: Equinox Publishing (Asia).

Andriarti, Anastasya, and Anton Novenanto. 2013. "Kasus Lapindo Di Balik Layar 'Tivi Merah.'" In *Membingkai Lapindo: Pendekatan Konstruksi Sosial Atas Kasus Lapindo*, edited by Anton Novenanto, 67–91. Jakarta & Yogyakarta: MediaLink & Kanisius.

Assmann, Aleida. 2009. "'Plunging into Nothingness': The Politics of Cultural Memory." In *Moment to Monument: The Making and Unmaking of Cultural Significance*, edited by Ladina Bezzola Lambert and Andrea Ochsner, 35–49. Bielefeld: Transcript.

Batubara, Bosman. 2013. "Perdebatan Tentang Penyebab Lumpur Lapindo." In *Membingkai Lapindo: Pendekatan Konstruksi Sosial Atas Kasus Lapindo*, edited by Anton Novenanto, 1–16. Jakarta & Yogyakarta: MediaLink & Kanisius.

Brian, Éric, Marie Jaisson, and S. Romi Mukherjee. 2012. "Introduction: Social Memory and Hypermodernity." *International Social Science Journal* 62 (203–4): 7–18.

Bryant, Raymond L., and Sinéad Bailey. 1997. *Third World Political Ecology*. New York: Routledge.

Connerton, Paul. 1989. *How Societies Remember*. Cambridge: Cambridge University Press.

Coser, Lewis A. 1992. "Introduction: Maurice Halbwachs, 1877-1945." In *On Collective Memory*, edited by Lewis A. Coser, 1–34. Chicago: The University of Chicago Press.

Cutcher, Leanne, Karen Dale, Philip Hancock, and Melissa Tyler. 2016. "Spaces and Places of Remembering and Commemoration." Edited by Leanne Cutcher, Karen Dale, Philip Hancock, and Melissa Tyler. *Organization* 23 (1): 3–9. https://doi.org/10.1177/1350508415605111.

Davies, Richard J, Michael Manga, Mark Tingay, Susila Lusianga, and Richard E Swarbrick. 2010. "Discussion – Sawolo et Al. (2009) the Lusi Mud Volcano Controversy: Was It Caused by Drilling?" *Marine and Petroleum Geology* 27 (7): 1651–7.

Davies, Richard J, Richard E Swarbrick, Robert J Evans, and Mad Huuse. 2007. "Birth of a Mud Volcano: East Java, 29 May 2006." *GSA Today* 17 (2): 4–9.

Drake, Phillip. 2012. "The Goat That Couldn't Stop the Mud Volcano: Sacrifice, Subjectivity, and Indonesia's 'Lapindo Mudflow.'" *Humanimalia* 4 (1): 80–111.

Drake, Phillip. 2017. *Indonesia and the Politics of Disaster: Power and Representation in Indonesia's Mud Volcano.* Oxon: Routledge.

Energi Mega Persada. 2006a. "ENRG Reports Well Control Issues at Banjarpanji-1 Stabilizing, Losses Minimized." Jakarta: Energi Mega Persada.

Energi Mega Persada. 2006b. "The Company's Explanation in Response to Letter from PT Bursa Efek Jakarta." Translated by Uki Ukanto. Jakarta.

Forrest, Thomas R. 1993. "Disaster Anniversary: A Social Reconstruction of Time." *Sociological Inquiry* 63 (4): 444–56.

Graham, Brian, and Peter Howard. 2008. "Heritage and Identity." In *The Ashgate Research Companion to Heritage and Identity*, edited by Brian Graham and Peter Howard, 1–15. Farnham: Ashgate Publishing.

Guthey, Eric, and Brad Jackson. 2005. "CEO Portraits and the Authenticity Paradox." *Journal of Management Studies* 42 (5): 1057–82.

Halbwachs, Maurice. 1980. *The Collective Memory.* New York: Harper & Row.

Harvey, David C. 2008. "The History of Heritage." In *The Ashgate Research Companion to Heritage and Identity*, edited by Brian Graham and Peter Howard, 19–36. Farnham: Ashgate Publishing.

Herzfeld, Michael. 1991. *A Place in History: Social and Monumental Time in a Cretan Town.* Princeton: Princeton University Press.

Herzfeld, Michael. 2014. "Intangible Delicacies: Production and Embarrassment in International Settings." *Ethnologies* 36 (1–2): 47–62.

Hui, Andrew. 2009. "Texts, Monuments and the Desire for Immortality." In *Moment to Monument: The Making and Unmaking of Cultural Significance*, edited by Ladina Bezzola Lambert and Andrea Ochsner, 19–33. Bielefeld: Transcript.

Lapian, A. B. 1987. "Bencana Alam Dan Penulisan Sejarah (Krakatau 1883 Dan Cilegon 1888)." In *Dari Babad Dan Hikayat Sampai Sejarah Kritis*, edited by T. Ibrahim Alfian, H. J. Koesoemanto, Dharmono Hardjowidjono, and Djoko Suryo, 211–31. Yogyakarta: Gadjah Mada University Press.

Lupi, M., E. H. Saenger, F. Fuchs, and S. A. Miller. 2013. "Lusi Mud Eruption Triggered by Geometric Focusing of Seismic Waves." *Nature Geoscience* 6: 642–6.

Marschall, Sabine. 2013. "Collective Memory and Cultural Difference: Official vs. Vernacular Forms of Commemorating the Past." *Safundi: The Journal of South African and American Studies* 14 (1): 77–92.

Mazzini, Adriano, H Svensen, G G Akhmanov, G Aloisi, S Planke, A Malthe-Sorenssen, and Bambang P Istadi. 2007. "Triggering and Dynamic Evolution of the LUSI Mud Volcano, Indonesia." *Earth and Planetary Science Letters* 261 (May): 375–88.

McDowell, Sara. 2008. "Heritage, Memory and Identity." In *The Ashgate Research Companion to Heritage and Identity*, edited by Brian Graham and Peter Howard, 37–53. Farnham: Ashgate Publishing.

McMichael, Heath. 2009. "The Lapindo Mudflow Disaster: Environmental, Infrastructure and Economic Impact." *Bulletin of Indonesian Economic Studies* 45 (1): 73–83.

Nilawaty, Azzah. 2012. "Areke Nelongso, Pemerintah Karo Lapindo Ora Rumongso: Dinamika Dan Perjuangan Anak-Anak Korban Lapindo." In *Bencana Industri: Kekalahan Negara Dan Masyarakat Sipil Dalam Penanganan Lumpur Lapindo*, edited by Heru Prasetia, 149–82. Yogyakarta: Yayasan Desantara.

Novenanto, Anton. 2013. "Kasus Lapindo Oleh Media Arusutama." In *Membingkai Lapindo: Pendekatan Konstruksi Sosial Atas Kasus Lapindo*, edited by Anton Novenanto, 93–115. Jakarta & Yogyakarta: MediaLink & Kanisius.

Novenanto, Anton. 2015a. "Membangun Bencana: Tinjauan Kritis Atas Peran Negara Dalam Kasus Lapindo." *MASYARAKAT: Jurnal Sosiologi* 20 (2): 159–92.

Novenanto, Anton. 2015b. "Manusia Dan Tanah: Kehilangan Dan Kompensasi Dalam Kasus Lapindo." *Bhumi* 1 (1): 1–11.

Novenanto, Anton. 2017. "Multidimensionalitas Lumpur Lapindo." *Jawa Pos*, March 2017.

Novenanto, Anton, ed. 2013. *Membingkai Lapindo: Pendekatan Konstruksi Sosial Atas Kasus Lapindo*. Jakarta & Yogyakarta: MediaLink & Kanisius.

Nurcahyo, Henri. 2014. *Rekayasa Dongeng Dalam Bencana Lumpur Lapindo*. Surabaya: Asosiasi Tradisi Lisan.

Nusantara, Bambang Catur. 2010. "Empat Tahun Janji Tak Pasti." *Jurnal Dinamika HAM* 10 (2): 105–21.

Olick, Jeffrey K., and Joyce Robbins. 1998. "Social Memory Studies: From 'Collective Memory' to the Historical Sociology of Mnemonic Practices." *Annual Review of Sociology* 24: 105–40.

Olick, Jeffrey K., Vered Vinitzky-Seroussi, and Daniel Levy. 2011. Introduction to *The Collective Memory Reader*, edited by Jeffrey K. Olick, Vered Vinitzky-Seroussi, and Daniel Levy, 3–62. Oxford: Oxford University Press.

Partadireja, Ace. 1974. "Rural Credit: The Ijon System." *Bulletin of Indonesian Economic Studies* 10 (3): 54–71.

Priest, Doug. 1995. "Keys to Communication." In *Completing the Task: Reaching the World for Christ*, edited by Edgar J. Elliston and Stephen E. Burris, 229–42. Joplin: College Press Publishing Company.

Ricklefs, M. C. 2001. *A History of Modern Indonesia since c. 1200*, 3rd ed. London: Palgrave Macmillan.

Saputra, Laksana Agung. 2006. "Sumur Gas Bocor, Penduduk Diungsikan" [Gas well leaked, residents evacuated]. *Kompas*, May 2006.

Satyana, Awang Harun. 2007. "Bencana Geologi Dalam 'Sandhyâkâla' Jenggala Dan Majapahit: Hipotesis Erupsi Gununglumpur Historis Berdasarkan Kitab Pararaton, Serat Kanda, Babad Tanah Jawi; Folklor Timun Mas; Analogi Erupsi LUSI; Dan Analisis Geologi Depresi Kendeng, Delta Brantas." In *The 36th IAGI, The 32th HAGI, and the 29th IATMI Annual Convention and Exhibition*. Bali.

Sawolo, Nurrochmat, Edi Sutriono, Bambang P. Istadi, and Agung B. Darmoyo. 2009. "The LUSI Mud Volcano Triggering Controversy: Was It Caused by Drilling?" *Marine and Petroleum Geology* 26: 1766–84.

Sawolo, Nurrochmat, Edi Sutriono, Bambang P. Istadi, and Agung B. Darmoyo. 2010. "Was LUSI Caused by Drilling? – Authors' Reply to Discussion." *Marine and Petroleum Geology* 27: 1658–75.

Schiller, Jim, Anton Lucas, and Priyambudi Sulistiyanto. 2008. "Learning from the East Java Mudflow: Disaster Politics in Indonesia." *Indonesia* 85 (April): 51–77.

Schlehe, Judith. 2009. "Cultural Politics of Natural Disasters: Discourses on Volcanic Eruptions in Indonesia." In *Culture and the Changing Environment: Uncertainty, Cognition and Risk Management in Cross-Cultural Perspective*, edited by Michael J Casimir, 273–300. New York & London: Berghahn Books.

Stangl, Paul. 2008. "The Vernacular and the Monumental: Memory and Landscape in Post-War Berlin." *GeoJournal* 73 (September): 245–53.

Suyadnya, I Wayan, and Megasari N. Fatanti. 2017. "A Tale of Two Disasters: How Is Disaster Emerging as a Tourist Destination in Indonesia?" *Asian Journal of Tourism Research* 2 (2): 33–64. https://doi.org/10.12982/AJTR.2017.0009.

Tapsell, Ross. 2010. "Newspaper Ownership and Press Freedom in Indonesia." In *The 18th Biennial Conference of the Asian Studies Association of Australia*. Adelaide.

Truc, Gérôme. 2011. "Memory of Places and Places of Memory: For a Halbwachsian Socio-Ethnography of Collective Memory." *International Social Science Journal* 62 (203–4): 147–59.

Wessing, Robert. 2010. "Porous Boundaries: Addressing Calamities in East Java, Indonesia." *Bijdragen Tot de Taal-, Land- En Volkenkunde* 166 (1): 49–82.

Wilson, Simon. 2006. "Preliminary Report on the Factors and Causes in the Loss of Well Banjar Panji-1." Jakarta: Unpublished Report.

About the Authors

Anton Novenanto is a researcher with formal training in sociology and anthropology in Yogyakarta, Leiden, and Heidelberg. He is an assistant professor at the Department of Sociology and researcher at the Centre for Culture and Frontier Studies (CCFS), Universitas Brawijaya, Indonesia. He is the secretary general of Perkumpulan Peneliti Eutenika.

I Wayan Suyadnya is a lecturer of sociology and co-founder of the Centre for Culture and Frontier Studies (CCFS) at Universitas Brawijaya, Indonesia. His main fields of research are critical tourism, cultural properties, and frontier issues.

9. Threatened Flood-Prone Alleyway Neighborhoods of Ho Chi Minh City: What "Tactics" for Vernacular Heritage?

Marie Gibert-Flutre

Abstract: Ho Chi Minh City is especially challenged by flooding. Drawing on ethnographic data on resilience and social differentiation, and applying political ecology to flooding risk, I use de Certeau's concept of "tactics" to embrace quotidian actions and negotiations undertaken to address largely shared problems, thereby illuminating urban heritage as a source of resilience but also of local socioeconomic inequalities. Local communities' capacity for resilience largely depends on neighborhoods' specific historical trajectories; shared heritage is essential for increasing communal resilience. Vernacular flood management, with its improvisatory adaptations, indexes local inequalities, while growing individualism allows authorities to instrumentalize flooding risk as justification for eviction and radical redevelopment. The consequent clearing of vernacular neighborhoods for development thus also vests control in powerful forces.

Keywords: flood management, citizens practices, daily resilience, vernacular neighborhoods, Ho Chi Minh City

Introduction

Ho Chi Minh City is one of the most challenged metropolises in the world with regard to flooding. This is due to the cumulative impacts of heavy rainfall in a low-elevation tropical coastal area, direct subjection to tides, and an uncontrolled expansion of soil sealing, together with bad management of its canals and sewer networks. Years 2016 and 2017 have been

Herzfeld, M., and R. Padawangi, eds. *Resilience as Heritage in Asia*. Amsterdam: Amsterdam University Press, 2025.
DOI: 10.5117/9789463728560_CH09

particularly dramatic, with not only severe disturbances at the international airport Tân Sơn Nhất, but also repeated flash flooding in many low-lying neighborhoods of this metropolis of over ten million inhabitants.[1] Once an exceptional event, chronic flooding tends to become a constituent element of the ordinary way of life of many urban dwellers. The severity of this issue explains the recent increase in the publication of reports and studies dedicated to the understanding of this environmental hazard (Tran Thi and Ha 2007; Tấn Long 2011; Long Phi and Tan Sinh 2012; Lempert et al. 2013; Katzschner et al. 2016; Vachaud et al. 2019). In addition, the authorities of the city province of Ho Chi Minh widely advertise their engagement in different international cooperation projects focusing on financing and organizing the fight against floods (*Nhân Dân* 2016; Hau 2016; *Communist Party of Vietnam Online Newspaper* 2018). Nevertheless, most research and official programs remain mostly technically orientated and ignore the highly sociopolitical aspects of the issue. Moreover, by highlighting global climate change and the city-site condition, these discourses end up depoliticizing both the causes and the consequences of local flooding.

Seeking to move away from this truncated conception, I envision Ho Chi Minh City's flooding as a lived neighborhood experience within a political ecology framework. Thus, I focus on the individual and collective experiences of flooding at the neighborhood level, with the goal of investigating local community initiatives and their capacity for adaptation and resilience. The chapter is thus based on an empirically grounded discussion of the relationship between resilience and social differentiation at the neighborhood level. Indeed, faced with the inefficiency of the global fight against flooding at the metropolitan level—mainly owing to a problematic lack of coordinated management—local inhabitants improvise their own solutions through various initiatives to adapt their living conditions to this chronic threat. Tactics, such as regularly upgrading their ground floor in order to be above street level and efficiently fighting the flooding of their houses, and contracting informal loans between neighbors to deal with floods, have been progressively fully integrated into residents' way of life. I use the notion of a "tactic" in de Certeau's (1988) sense to embrace all the small day-to-day actions and negotiations, supported by official decision-making authority, that urban dwellers undertake to deal with an urban condition from which

---

1   The official census acknowledges only 8.4 million inhabitants in Ho Chi Minh City in 2017, because it does not include the "floating" population of unregistered city dwellers (General Statistics Office of Vietnam, 2020). Thus, the actual population of Ho Chi Minh City can be estimated at around eleven or twelve million inhabitants.

most of them suffer. "Tactics" are opposed to "strategies," a concept that contrastively implies the use of control and power. De Certeau, however, does not understand tactics as a simple subset of strategy, but as a true capacity of adaptation to the environment, a subset that has been framed by the strategies of the powerful. While strategies often tend to become exclusive and self-referential, tactics, by contrast, are actions in a constant state of reassessment, directly based on observations of the actual environment, which make them very reactive. Drawing theoretically on this distinction between tactics and strategies allows for a renewed understanding of both the causes and the consequences of Ho Chi Minh City's flooding at the local scale. This perspective relies on a political ecology framework to provide a more contrasted understanding of urban heritage and its capacity of resilience in a challenging context.

Primary data for this research comes from an in-depth ethnographic exploration of ward 22 in the inner district of Bình Thạnh, conducted from 2010 to 2017. This densely populated and low-lying area is located along the riverbank of the Sài Gòn River and includes many small canals and swamps. The local population is getting increasingly diverse, with both large numbers of long-term residents and rural migrants, the latter often settled along canals in ramshackle houses on piles or along narrow alleyways, as well as much wealthier newcomers who invest in brand-new apartment buildings along the Nguyễn Hữu Cảnh Boulevard. This ward exemplifies the massive metropolitan changes occurring in Ho Chi Minh City today. These changes have produced a complex juxtaposition of vernacular alleyway neighborhoods and new high-rise buildings and towers, directly overlooking popular residential areas. The ward particularly welcomes three striking high-rise buildings projects, representative of two distinct moments of the verticalization of the metropolis, as early as the end of years 2000, and again at the end of years 2010. They are The Manor I and II (completed in 2007 and 2010, respectively); Saigon Pearl I, II, and III (completed in 2009 and 2010); and Vinhomes Central Park (completed in 2018), the latter including the emblematic Landmark 81 tower, which is the highest building in Vietnam today. As a result, the countless vernacular alleyways of the ward are now directly connected with widened urban arteries and highways; individual shophouses, with an average of two to four floors apiece, are located right next to towers of between twenty and eighty floors.

But, despite its spectacular—as a redevelopment but also in the sense of "putting into spectacle" (Debord 1977)—the area has also become the symbol of flooding hazard in Ho Chi Minh City, with not less than thirty flooding episodes per year, some of them lasting for more than one or two days in a row (Nguyen Xuan, Kopec, and Netzband 2016: 165). The Nguyễn Hữu Cảnh 2x3 lanes,[2] in particular, are now inevitably flooded—with water depths between 0.20 and more than 0.60 m—after a heavy rain episode or a high tide event. As a consequence, the adjacent alleyway network is now famously known as the "flooded alleyways." The issue has become so crucial that, when the general secretary of the Communist party, Nguyễn Thiện Nhân, scheduled a local visit in damaged areas of Ho Chi Minh City after the great flood of May 2017, he chose ward 22 of Bình Thạnh District and, more especially, the alleyways located along the Manors towers and Nguyễn Hữu Cảnh road.

Taking an empirical and ethnographic approach based on a long-term engagement with ward 22 of Bình Thạnh District (between 2010 and 2019), I approach flooding risk in an integrative and comprehensive way. My analyses are based on repeated on-site observations, articulated with biographic interviews with thirty local inhabitants—mostly living on alleyways along Võ Duy Ninh street—in a diversity of social statuses (a snowball technique allowed access to various profiles of residents and interviews comprise both rural migrants and long-term residents). I also conducted four interviews with representatives of the local authorities at the People's Committee of the ward, and at the local urban management unit (ban quản lý khu đô thị). This long-term study allows for analyzing local changes across nine years of metropolitan transformations and for rethinking state-society relations at the prism of local flooding management.

In the first part of the chapter, I focus on the three main elements that contribute to produce the "catastrophe foretold" in alleyway neighborhoods in Ho Chi Minh City. While remembering the specific environmental conditions of the city, I insist on the role of an uncontrolled and expanding soil sealing, but also on short-term and highly problematic political decisions in the management of risk. The second part expands on the different tactics that local inhabitants are implementing to make their life sustainable in flood-prone areas. My main point is that, despite shared conditions of threatened livelihood in flooding areas, the resilience process is mainly effective at an individual level. This can be partly explained by the specific political regime that still prevails in Vietnam today, where each collective action has to be formalized and officialized with the "Vietnamese Fatherland Front" (Mặt Trận Tổ Quốc Việt Nam). The final part discusses the lack of acknowledgment

---

2   This main road was built and opened in 2009 to facilitate the connection between the central business district with the Sài Gòn bridge and the dynamic eastern districts (district 2, 9, Thủ Đức).

of local inhabitants' and communities' capacity for resilience in a context of growing land pressure. It also underlines how a so-called natural hazard can be instrumentalized for the purpose of metropolitan "modernization and civilization." It shows how "tactics" of local residents are more and more falling behind discriminating "strategies" in the metropolitan management. This discussion allows for a deeper understanding of the numerous and intertwined challenges faced by vernacular communities in contemporary Southeast Asian cities, their social and cultural heritage being threatened in many ways, both from outside forces and from within.

Flooded Neighborhoods in Ho Chi Minh City: "Chronicle of a Catastrophe Foretold"

Flooding in Ho Chi Minh City occurs in a more and more unequal city setting, where precarious populations are clearly those first threatened by the risk of flooding. This situation intensifies the articulation between urban poverty and environmental threats from a spatial and environmental justice perspective (Dufaux et al. 2010; Padawangi 2012; Padawangi and Douglass 2015; Batubara, Kooy, and Zwarteveen 2018). Indeed, so-called natural hazard management is more than ever impacted by political choices. In Ho Chi Minh City, massive flooding of the main metropolis arteries—leading to massive congestion in the city—has become commonplace during the rainy season, conveying a damaging image for a city that seeks to be known for global "modernity and civilization" (đô thị hiện đại, văn minh). In response, the city-province authorities have engaged in a vast program of major city-road elevation over the past several years. This initiative contributed directly to the creation of flooding basins in adjacent alleyway neighborhoods. Such a partial management of the flooding threat is therefore a dramatic indicator of the "selection of spaces" inherent to the metropolization process (Swyngedouw 2004; Douglas et al. 2008; Ranganathan 2015; Schramm 2016; Batubara, Kooy, and Zwarteveen 2018). Despite their vitality for their own sake, vernacular alleyway neighborhoods suffer from a growing lack of interest on the part of the metropolitan authorities. Local community members are rarely invited to participate in the decision-making process, despite their vernacular expertise. Moreover, authorities tend to blame them for clogging sewers and waterways with garbage and other waste. Flooding has thus become an argument for radical metropolitan redevelopments that compel the poorest inhabitants to relocate to more distant areas. Erecting high-rise buildings in notoriously flood-prone areas, however, contributes directly to an increase in soil subsidence and hence to a worsening of the overall situation.

Repeated flash flooding in Ho Chi Minh City is the result of combinations of different intertwined factors: the location of the city in a low-elevation tropical coastal area particularly subject to tides, an uncontrolled urban development and soil sealing, but also short-term, badly coordinated and highly selective political decisions in the overall context of metropolization.

A Low-Lying Metropolis in the Mekong Coastal Area

Ho Chi Minh City is located in the north of the Mekong Delta. This explains the dominance of swamp lands on its site. The altitude of the city is very low—between 0.5 and 3.4 meters above sea level—and 65 percent of the city-province area is located less than 1.5 meters above sea level. Moreover, the southern part of Ho Chi Minh City's province opens directly onto the South China Sea. As a consequence, the city is subject to tidal movements through its numerous canals, rivers, and wetlands. Despite the draining and embankment of many canals throughout history,[3] the urban districts of Ho Chi Minh City still contain more than 8,000 km of canals (Downes et al. 2016: 92). This topographical element is becoming critical today, under the joint effects of the rise in sea level and the progressive subsidence of the city ground (Lê and Ho 2009; Tong Minh Dinh, Van Trung Le, and Le Toan Thuy 2015). This is mainly due to the overexploitation of ground water resources.

Within a subtropical monsoon context, the rainy season extends locally from May to November—with heavy rainfall from September to October. In total, about 160 rain events occur yearly, with an average cumulated rainfall of roughly 2,000 mm (Vachaud et al. 2019). In this environmental context, flooding can be caused either by the overflowing of the Sài Gòn and Đồng Nai Rivers—or some of their upstream tributaries—especially during periods of high tides, or by surface flooding during the intense periods of rain and typhoon. In the lowest parts of the metropolis, such as ward 22 of Bình Thạnh District, high tide levels are now sufficient to flood entire zones of the city without any associated rain fall. In the worst cases, these different factors can be combined.

---

3   Most of the main city boulevards of Ho Chi Minh City today were designed through the filling of canals around the 1870s. For example, the route of the actual Lê Lợi Boulevard corresponds to the early colonial Coffyn Canal.

In the early colonial period, the French administrators established their administrative headquarters on an upper area called "the Plateau," where the ancient Vietnamese citadels also used to be located. This choice was guided by the risk of flooding that characterized the lower areas along the main rivers and canals. These low areas were then dedicated to commercial functions and to the resettlement of so called "indigenous populations" expelled from the Plateau. The colonial decision of 6 May 1862 conceded plots of land to displaced Vietnamese people along the Bến Nghé Canal between Sài Gòn and Chợ Lớn (Wright 1991: 171). Local communities of inhabitants adapted these low and wet areas to their needs. They built their dwellings—negatively called "straw huts" by the colonial regime—along the canal, mostly on piles. This use of piles shows an early form of urban adaptation in these vernacular neighborhoods. Some local urban communities even set up directly on the canals and rivers in their sampans (they were called the *lai dô* people). Teulières and Nguyen (1962: 167) estimate these poor sampan communities accounted for up to eighty thousand people in 1950. Since this early period, the canal banks have remained the main location of precarious settlements in Ho Chi Minh City. This is particularly the case of ward 22 of Bình Thạnh District, located between the left bank of the Sài Gòn River and the Văn Thánh Canal. The area still counts many dead-end small canals and swamps, completely enclosed in the local urban fabrics. They have progressively become spaces of relegation, filled with garbage at the back of poor settlements.

An Uncontrolled Urban Development and Soil Sealing

The history of Ho Chi Minh City has been characterized by the overlapping of planned and spontaneous developments (Gibert 2014). Thus, the development of soil sealing has always—at least partly—escaped from the authorities' control. This element has nevertheless become critical with the recent accelerated urban growth of the metropolis since the *Đổi Mới* reforms launched in 1986. Between 1989 and 2006, the built areas of the province have doubled (Tran Thi and Ha 2007), leading to an exponential increase in impervious sealed soils, leaving less and less area for infiltration. The highly sealed areas are located in the central part of the metropolis, where the majority of the urban population lives. Ward 22 of Bình Thạnh District, for instance, is now sealed at a rate above 80 percent (Nguyen Xuan, Kopec, and Netzband 2016: 155). As a result, a large proportion of precipitation is immediately converted into surface runoff. This accelerating land covering process often concerns low-lying urban areas and wetlands, which have remained free from constructions until recently. Yet, these open areas used to be natural zones for water evacuation during the period of rivers overflowing. Their sealing is therefore highly problematic for the whole metropolis.

Today, 60 percent of flood-prone plots of the city are located in the inner districts, where the density of population is at its highest rate (Tấn Long 2011). In this context, the few basins for water retention have become insufficient. The draining capacity of the metropolis has also deteriorated due to the importance of solid waste released in the canals. This also causes serious water pollution problems (Huynh et al. 2013: 14). In most streets of the inner districts, manholes are clogged by trash, which intensifies the weakness of the draining capacity. The increase of construction sites in the city also leads to a massive amount of sand and mud that degrades the sewer system.

Beyond its specific location and topographical pattern, Ho Chi Minh City is particularly flood prone because of its uncontrolled urban development and bad management of its canals and sewer networks. Often categorized as a "natural hazard," flood risk is actually a social and political product. Moreover, this risk does not concern the different neighborhoods equally and is often associated with the poorest areas of the metropolis. This is linked to the historical production of the city in a colonial context, but also to more recent urban management decisions that compromise the idea of spatial justice as far as environmental questions are concerned.

Flood Risk as a Sociopolitical Product

Facing recurrent flooding of the main arteries during the rainy season, the provincial authorities have engaged in a vast program of elevation of major streets, generally from 20 to 80 cm, in the past ten years (Nguyễn 2010). This decision is in complete opposition to most experts' recommendations, who call for an integrated management of risk at the metropolis level (Katzschner et al. 2016; Vachaud et al. 2019). Upgrading a few arteries is indeed a very local and incoherent way of managing the complex risk of flooding. While quite efficient on a few chosen arteries, this official initiative has contributed to the transformation of the adjacent alleyway neighborhoods into flooding basins.[4] As a result of the implementation of this public works program, the

---

4   The management of main roads of Ho Chi Minh City is under the responsibility of the provincial People Committee while the management of alleyways—every street under twelve meters in width—are locally managed by the ward authorities.

houses along the upgraded roads ended up around 20 to 80 cm below road level, and so too were the entrances to adjacent alleyway neighborhoods. This recent evolution has dramatically increased the vulnerability of many residential areas in the metropolis during heavy rains (Đông 2013).

Interviews with the inhabitants of ward 22 of Bình Thạnh District located along the recently upgraded Nguyễn Hữu Cảnh road reveal both the importance and the recurrence of damages due to flooding. They insist on the fact that they have to repaint their ground floor nearly every year at the end of the rainy season. The situation has become terrible for shopkeepers, whose shops and stocks are usually located on the ground floor, and who can lose everything at any time due to flooding. Their neighborhood has always been flood prone but the elevation of the adjacent street has brought this situation to a critical point: even a moderate shower can lead to a dramatic rise of water in their alleyway, which has become the natural spillway of the main road. During these episodes, people are then trapped inside houses and forced to wait until water withdraws and leaves a passage to circulate again. But water flows very slowly when trapped in low-lying alleyways of the area and can stay stuck for one or two days in a row. This phenomenon also increases bad hygiene condition in the neighborhood. The residents feel "sacrificed" by the public authorities. Some main arteries have even been upgraded several times. This is, for instance, the case for the Phạm Thế Hiển Street, along the Kênh Đôi Canal in district 8, which was upgraded by a meter for the first time in 2010–11 and for a second time by 40 cm in 2013 (Thanh Đông 2013). This example shows the use of emergency and short-term measures in the fight against flooding in the city province.

The partial management of the flooding threat reveals dramatically the selection of spaces in the course of the metropolization process in Ho Chi Minh City. In a more and more global and competitive context, the first purpose of the provincial authorities is to assure a good image of the most economically strategic areas of the city, such as main boulevards and arteries. The recurrent flooding of Hai Bà Trưng, or Nguyễn Hữu Cảnh and other main roads provokes serious traffic congestion between key economical centers, such as the international airport, the central business district, and the new development areas of districts 2 and 9, which sends a very bad sign to investors. The flooding of these arteries has become such a problem that the authorities have decided to elevate these streets without consulting the local authorities or with the dwellers of the adjacent neighborhoods. Moreover, the construction of Phạm Văn Đồng road (2x5 lanes, opened in 2016) at the north of Bình Thạnh District–in order to alleviate traffic between the international airport Tân Sơn Nhất and the north-eastern districts—also affected the sewage capacity of the area and contributes to increased chronic flooding in adjacent alleyways of ward 11 (Cường 2018). The urge to produce mega-infrastructures of transport outweighs the need for an integrated fight against flooding, especially when vernacular alleyway neighborhoods are in the balance. Bình Thạnh District is especially concerned by those unbalanced political choices, as it has been classified as a new "city gate" due to its strategic location at the interface of the historical city center and eastern economically dynamic districts. The district has thus seen the development of massive transport infrastructural nodes in the past years.[5]

The opposite of these upgraded metropolitan infrastructures and new vertical mega-projects, alleyway neighborhoods are representative of the inherited urban fabric of Ho Chi Minh City and consist of individual tube houses aligned along narrow alleyways. These house around 85 percent of the metropolis population and are one of Ho Chi Minh City's most defining features (Gibert 2018a). Even though they are very far from welcoming only poor residents and contribute greatly to the identity of the city, the vernacular nature of their production is today considered antagonistic to the "modernization" the authorities are calling for. This idea of urban "modernization"—although rarely defined and questioned in official documents—is indeed associated with the image of a vertical city organized along large-scale transport infrastructures. Thus, despite its vitality for its own sake, this vernacular urban heritage is suffering today from a growing lack of interest on the part of the metropolitan authorities. Moreover, despite being worried and angry at being potentially displaced by modernization projects, most of the alleyways' inhabitants generically express approval of modernization and its forms (wider streets, mega-infrastructures, and verticalization of the built environment). This paradox reveals the fierceness of the authority's propaganda in promoting a shared vision of the urban future, despite its very unequal character and its drastic changes to the urban and social life (Harms 2012). This also leads to the atomization of any potential dissent movement.

In the end, the neighborhood living arrangement and social relations within these alleyway neighborhoods represent a certain setting of everyday life, the vernacular, that has passed down through generations. However, the exacerbation of floods by new mega-developments challenges this setting and requires continuous adaptation.

---

5   Ward 22 will also welcome soon one of the first metro stations of the metropolis, at the edge of Văn Thánh Canal.

Flooding as a Residential Experience: Everyday Tactics of Local Inhabitants

Everyday Tactics in the Face of Risk

Faced with this growing and chronic threat, local inhabitants of alleyway neighborhoods improvise their own solutions through various initiatives to adapt their living conditions. The way inhabitants of alleyway neighborhoods manage flood risk today remains in line with the historical process of production of the city. Most vernacular neighborhoods of Ho Chi Minh City are the product of a spontaneous urbanization process outside of any planning programs (Gibert 2014). Long a swamp away from urban development, ward 22 of Bình Thạnh District was made viable and divided into plots in the late 1970s when the army sold the land to private individuals. From then, a dense, working-class neighborhood progressively emerged, and most original plots were divided again and again. Today, the ward is also known for fostering many workers' dormitories, in which local landlords invest whenever they have a courtyard or some available space on their plot. As in many wards of Ho Chi Minh City, alleyways are primarily made from the juxtaposition of individual shophouses built through an uncoordinated process over the past decades. In this urban context, dealing with flooding remains firstly a family and individual matter: common initiatives only come in second place. The different tactics used by each household are therefore revealing of socioeconomical inequalities at this very local scale. Households who can afford it are firstly upgrading their ground floor in order to be above street level and to fight efficiently the flooding of their house. When this type of work is too costly, families mainly use sand bags to barricade themselves during heavy showers.

The richest families often even proceed to a complete destruction of their house to rebuild an elevated one, more resilient to chronic flooding. This is also seen as an opportunity to modernize the house and sometimes to enlarge their land plot by negotiating the purchase of the neighboring plot from poorer neighbors who despair of recurrent flooding and simply leave the neighborhood. Thus, chronic flooding increases socioeconomic hierarchies and differentiation, which affect, in return, the capacity of a communal resilience.

In some local alleyways, the community is nevertheless trying to find a collective solution to this environmental hazard. The 51 Phú Mỹ alleyway has, for example, been elevated by the local inhabitants themselves. They collected money among local residents and hired a private company to elevate their alleyway. The representative of this neighborhood community—a retired civil servant who has been living there for more than forty years, and who is locally highly respected—insisted during his interview on the locally based initiative for this: they did not benefit from any official funding. He analyzed the success of the initiative as being due to the specific history of his alleyway, mainly inhabited by soldiers' families for several generations since the 1970s. This relatively long history explains, in particular, that most families were able to provide proper tenancy status and property titles, which helped to avoid issues during the upgrade. Also, this elevation project was not understood as a manifestation of top-down pressure, but rather as a means to swiftly improve urban conditions from the ground up. Residents stress in particular the favorable location of their alleyway, close to the city center and propitious for trading activities. Their sense of belonging to the place is very strong, despite the environmental insecurity. This element contributes greatly to explaining why they are absolutely reluctant to move to other places and, therefore, why they agreed to invest collectively in the alleyway upgrading.

In general, the local communities' capacity for resilience very much depends on the historical trajectory of the neighborhood. Their sharing of a specific culture or a common past is an essential element to increasing the resilience of the local community as a whole. In that way, we see how the notion of heritage can play a great role in the capacity of local resilience. In 51 Phú Mỹ alleyway, local inhabitants feel proud of their collective answer to the threat, while they also regret a greater and more sustainable intervention of the local authorities. The inhabitants are not fooled by the fact that the elevation of their alleyway will not be able to resist a new elevation of any adjacent roads by the metropolitan authorities, such as the main axe Nguyễn Hữu Cảnh. So, they always keep ready to deploy other small tactics, such as sandbag barricades, which remain stored in the back of their house. Shopkeepers have often reorganized their shophouse and stored their stocks upstairs instead of the back of the ground floor.

Thus, "tactics" to deal with flooding have been progressively fully integrated into residents' ordinary way of life. Drawing theoretically on the distinction of "tactics" and "strategy" (de Certeau, 1988) allows for a better understanding and assessment of the capacity of local inhabitants to constantly adjust to their worsening environment. Their local environment is more and more framed by the strategies of the powerful—namely the metropolitan authorities, hand in hand with private real estate groups, seeking available space to build high-rise construction projects, whatever the social and environmental costs are. While "strategy" tends to become exclusive and self-referential, "tactics," on the other hand, are indeed actions in a constant state of reassessment, directly based on observations of the actual environment, which make them very reactive. But, nowadays, the worsening environmental context is nevertheless threatening the unity of the neighborhood.

Threatened place-based communities

In many flood-prone vernacular neighborhoods, interviews with locals show what can be seen as a form of interdependence between neighbors (Gibert 2018b). In a context where borrowing money from official offices is highly complicated—especially for families who have migrated recently from the countryside—possibilities of loans are only conceivable informally, at the community level, between neighbors (Pannier and Pulliat 2016; Polese 2018). Often presented as a form of local mutual assistance, these practices also reveal important inequalities at the very local scale and the relationship of dependence between neighbors (Lange and Henaff 2010). The interest rate of these local community loans is fixed informally and can be quite usurious. A popular expression explains that borrowed money is like "a knife under the throat" (*cho vay tiền cắt cổ*). Interviews conducted in Bình Thạnh District reveal that house repairs after flooding constitute the first reason for informal loans between neighbors. This invites us to consider critically some of the community-based tactics to adapt to natural hazards. The vernacular management of flooding is then an interesting indicator of power relationships at the local urban scale. In addition, growing individualism in the management of natural hazards is often exploited by the authorities.

Ho Chi Minh City is now engaged in accelerated and globally-driven metropolitan transformations. The latter are not only architectural, but also economic and social: they lead to the reconfiguration of urban forms, to the reshaping of urban management, and to a renegotiation of daily urban practices (Gibert 2018a). In the context of what is presented as a process of "modernization," the urban authorities are also encouraging the atomization of any potential dissent movement (Harms 2012). This is the case in the management of flood-prone neighborhoods. The elevation of main roads has never been discussed with any representative of the local communities, and people do not get a chance to organize collectively to protest against such a project or even to raise their concerns. Repair and building permits for houses are, for instance, always negotiated individually with each household. This implies a different capacity for negotiation between neighbors, depending on their socioeconomic profiles, but also on their integration in the circles of power. In particular, personal links with local authorities play an important role in decision-making capacity. On the other side, collective initiatives are neither encouraged, nor even recognized by the urban authorities. This is partly explained by the specific political regime that still prevails in Vietnam today, where each collective action has to be formalized and officialized with the "Vietnamese Fatherland Front" (*Mặt Trận Tổ Quốc Việt Nam*) (Thayer 2010). Indeed, the regime maintains its power through a system of socialist political structures that covers the entire territory up to a very fine scale and offers the central power various relays at every level of the nation (Gibert and Segard 2015; Kerkvliet 2018). The sense of place in community building in Ho Chi Minh City alleyway neighborhoods is then doubly threatened today, both internally—with growing socioeconomic inequalities among local inhabitants and uneven power relationships that emerge from it—and externally, by the metropolitan authorities, who instrumentalize the flooding risk as a strong argument to justify people's eviction and radical redevelopment programs.

Concluding Remarks: Flood-Prone Neighborhoods Facing Urban "Modernization"

The increase of flooding risk in vernacular neighborhoods, especially after the implementation of the main roads elevation program, justifies many radical redevelopment programs today. Flood management plans tend to use technical arguments to justify the—yet deeply political—selection of particular urban spaces as critical to flood protection. The implementation of any new urban projects in the heart of a very dense city such as Ho Chi Minh City requires indeed the displacement of local residents. This task is both time consuming and costly for the authorities. So, the eviction of the poorest communities—especially those without official property rights—is seen as the easiest option and the argument of natural hazard management contributes to making these decisions more acceptable. This process is not specific to Ho Chi Minh City and, as in many other metropolises of Southeast Asia, the irony is that vernacular urban spaces earmarked for clearing are often redeveloped without any integrative plan against flooding (Batubara, Kooy, and Zwarteveen 2018). In a context of critical pressure on metropolitan land, every strategic location—meaning with a good accessibility—is coveted by investors for ambitious redevelopment projects and could be subjected to vernacular communities clearing.

    In Ho Chi Minh City, this has historically been the case of the Nhiêu Lộc—Thị Nghè Canal's banks—where there used to be thousands of precarious settlements on piles. All these poor residents were evicted in the beginning of years 2000 and displaced from the city center (Wust et al. 2004). The two combined arguments to develop this program were the fight against poverty and the control of flooding risk. The zone has now been redeveloped into an enlarged urban boulevard, together with green open spaces. In ward 11 of district 6, also, the presence of the Lò Gốm Canal—which also used to be a symbol of urban poverty—has recently been revalued for its strategic location in a fast-growing metropolis. Its proximity to the new main east-west boulevard—which connects the Mekong Delta provinces with the central business district of Ho Chi Minh City—explains the recent change in the conception that authorities and investors have of this ward. It welcomes today a mega-urban project with many high-rise buildings. Only a few alleyways with low-rise vernacular houses still remain along the canal. In many cases, official discourses on flooding risks for local people hide the plans for redevelopment projects—namely high-rise buildings—which represent a good return on the land for investors. Such programs are examples of joined "strategies" of both public authorities and private investors who manage the metropolitan "production" today (Lefebvre 1991; Harms 2016). In general, the new residents have a very different interest in the place and do not develop a deep sense of belonging. During my interviews in ward 22 of Bình Thạnh District, the new residents were always stressing the importance of the strategic location of the place instead of the sense of community in the neighborhood.

From another perspective, the clearing of vernacular neighborhoods for development is also an act of control by the powerful. Alleyways are seen as more difficult to control from the top. As highly appropriated spaces, alleyways are indeed contested spaces, where many "forces" and microlocal power networks interact and sometimes oppose each other. They are also privileged spaces of collective experience and places for encounters and social innovation. Both their spatial characteristics and relationships recall the traditional role of alleyways as a form of "urban commons." They correspond to an ordinary landscape providing the setting for everyday urban life and place-based identities being shaped by varied everyday practices, collective experiences, and forces. The alleyway marks the intersection between public and private forms of use and habitation, which can allow us to understand the socio-spatial, personal, and cultural dimensions of urban heritage. As such, they provide multiple narratives of urban change and the process of resilience.

In Ho Chi Minh City, despite its long-term capacity of resilience through various adaptive and dynamic tactics, the vernacular heritage of alleyway neighborhoods seems, nevertheless more than ever, threatened by the selection of places inherent to the metropolization process. This global process, and its local adaptation to the Vietnamese case, goes hand by hand with the triumph of "strategy" over "tactics." This calls into question the historical modes of "production of the city" in Vietnam and, thus, raises concerning questions about the sustainably of such a metropolitan management in the age of growing environmental risks.

References

Batubara, Bosman, Michelle Kooy, and Margreet Zwarteveen. 2018. "Uneven Urbanisation: Connecting Flows of Water to Flows of Labour and Capital Through Jakarta's Flood Infrastructure." *Antipode* 50 (5): 1186–205.

Certeau, Michel de. 1988. *The Practice of Everyday Life*. Berkeley: University of California Press.

Communist Party of Vietnam Online Newspaper. 2018. "Ho Chi Minh City Calls on Investment for Flood Prevention." *Communist Party of Vietnam Online Newspaper*. 30 May 2018.

Cường Kiên. 2018. "Đường Đẹp Nhất TP.HCM Ngập Do Đâu?" [Where is the most beautiful flooded street in Ho Chi Minh City?]. *Pháp Luật Việt Nam*. 9 November 2018.

Debord, Guy. 1977. *The Society of the Spectacle*. Detroit: Black & Red.

Đông, Thanh. 2013. "Nâng Đường, Dân Chạy Theo Nâng Nền Nhà Không Xuể" [With the elevation of streets, people cannot follow with their homes]. *Tin Nóng*. 25 April 2013.

Douglas, Ian, Kurshid Alam, Maryanne Maghenda, Yasmin Mcdonnell, Louise Mclean, and Jack Campbell. 2008. "Unjust Waters: Climate Change, Flooding and the Urban Poor in Africa." *Environment and Urbanization* 20 (1): 187–205.

Downes, Nigel, Harry Storch, Michael Schmidt, Thi Cam Van Nguyen, Can Lê Dinh, Tran Thong Nhat, and Hoa Lê Thanh. 2016. "Understanding Ho Chi Minh City's Urban Structures for Urban Land-Use Monitoring and Risk-Adapted Land-Use Planning." In *Sustainable Ho Chi Minh City: Climate Policies for Emerging Mega Cities*, edited by Antje Katzschner, Michael Waibel, Dirk Schwede, Lutz Katzschner, Michael Schmidt, and Harry Storch, 89–116. Heidelberg, New York, Dordrecht, London: Springer.

Dufaux, Frédérc, Philippe Gervais-Lambony, Claire Hancock, Sonia Lehman-Frisch, and Sophie Moreau. 2010. "First Steps in a Dialogue." *Justice Spatiale/Spatial Justice* 2.

Eckert, Ronald, and Michael Waibel. 2009. "Climate Change and Challenges for the Urban Development of Ho Chi Minh City, Vietnam." *Pacific News* 31: 18–20.

General Statistics Office of Vietnam. 2020. *Kết quả toàn bộ Tổng điều tra dân số và nhà ở năm 2019 [Complete results of the 2019 Population and Housing Census]*. Hanoi: Nhà Xuất Bản Thống Kê.

Gibert, Marie. 2014. "Les Ruelles de Hồ Chí Minh Ville (Việt Nam), Trame Viaire et Recomposition des Espaces Publics." Thèse de doctorat en géographie, Université Paris 1 Panthéon-Sorbonne.

Gibert, Marie. 2018a. "Rethinking Metropolitan Production from Its Underside: A View from the Alleyways of Hồ Chí Minh City." *Environment and Planning A: Economy and Space* 50 (3): 589–607.

Gibert, Marie. 2018b. "Alleyway Neighborhoods in Hồ Chí Minh City." In *Handbook Routledge on Urbanization in Southeast Asia*, edited by Rita Padawangi, 420–32. London and New York: Routledge.

Gibert, Marie, and Juliette Segard. 2015. "Urban Planning in Vietnam: A Vector for a Negotiated Authoritarianism?" *Justice Spatiale/Spatial Justice* 8.

Harms, Erik. 2012. "Beauty as Control in the New Saigon: Eviction, New Urban Zones, and Atomized Dissent in a Southeast Asian City." *American Ethnologist* 39 (4): 735–50.

Harms, Erik. 2016. *Luxury and Rubble, Civility and Dispossession in the New Saigon*. Oakland: University of California Press.

Hau, Ngoc. 2016. "HCM City Pumps $450 Million into Flood Prevention Project." *VN Express International*. 26 June 2016.

Huynh, Chau, Ronald Eckert, Moritz Maikämper, Barbara Horst, and Frank Schwartze. 2013. *Adapt Ho Chi Minh City: Handbook on Climate Change Adapted Urban Planning and Design for Ho Chi Minh City, Vietnam*. Cottbus: Brandenburg University of Technology Cottbus.

Katzschner, Antje, Michael Waibel, Dirk Schwede, Lutz Katzschner, Michael Schmidt, and Harry Storch, eds. 2016. *Sustainable Ho Chi Minh City: Climate Policies for Emerging Mega Cities*. Heidelberg, New York, Dordrecht, London: Springer.

Kerkvliet, Benedict J. 2018. "An Approach for Analysing State-Society Relations in Vietnam." *Sojourn: Journal of Social Issues in Southeast Asia* 33 (1): 156–98.

Lange, Marie-France, and Nolwen Henaff. 2010. "Accès à l'éducation et Pauvreté Au Viêt-Nam." Edited by Abdeljalil Akkari and Jean-Paul Payet. *Raisons Éducatives* 2010: 249–77.

Lê, Van Trung, and Tong Minh Dinh Ho. 2009. "Monitoring Land Deformation Using Permanent Scatterer INSAR Techiques, Case Study: Ho Chi Minh City." In *7th FIG Regional Conference, Spatial Data Serving People: Land Governance and the Environment, Building the Capacity*, 10. Hanoi: International Federation of Surveyors, FIG and the Viet Nam Association of Geodesy, Cartography and Remote Sensing, VGCR.

Lefebvre, Henri. 1991. *The Production of Space*. Malden: Blackwell.

Lempert, Robert, Nidhi Kalra, Suzanne Peyraud, Zhimin Mao, Sinh Bach Tan, Dean Cira, and Alexander Lotsch. 2013. *Ensuring Robust Flood Risk Management in Ho Chi Minh City*. Policy Research Working Papers 6465. The World Bank.

Long Phi, Ho, and Bach Tan Sinh. 2012. "Integrated Flood Management Strategy of Ho Chi Minh City." In *Advanced Institute on Data for Coastal Cities at Risk*. Taipei: Academy of Sciences in Taipei.

Nguyễn, Ân. 2010. "Nâng Cao Đường Để Tránh Ngập Do Triều Cường" [Raising Streets to Prevent Flooding]. *Tuổi Trẻ*. 2 March 2010.

Nguyen Xuan, Thinh, Jacob Kopec, and Maik Netzband. 2016. "Remote Sensing and Spatial Analysis for Flood Monitoring and Management in Ho Chi Minh City." In *Sustainable Ho Chi Minh City: Climate Policies for Emerging Mega Cities*, edited by Antje Katzschner, Michael Waibel, Dirk Schwede, Lutz Katzschner, Michael Schmidt, and Harry Storch, 151–73. Heidelberg, New York, Dordrecht, London: Springer.

Nhân Dân. 2016. "HCM City to Carry out VND10 Trillion-Project on Flood Prevention." *Nhân Dân*. 3 June 2016.

Padawangi, Rita. 2012. "Climate Change and the North Coast of Jakarta: Environmental Justice and the Social Construction of Space in Urban Poor Communities." In *Urban Areas and Global Climate Change*, edited by William Holt. Research in Urban Sociology 12: 321–39.

Padawangi, Rita, and Mike Douglass. 2015. "Water, Water Everywhere: Toward Participatory Solutions to Chronic Urban Flooding in Jakarta." *Pacific Affairs* 88 (3): 517–50.

Pannier, Emmanuel, and Gwenn Pulliat. 2016. "Échanges, dons et dettes. Réseaux sociaux et résilience dans le Vietnam d'aujourd'hui." *Revue Tiers Monde* 3 (226–7): 95–121.

Polese, Abel. 2018. "Vay Mượn (Vietnam)." In *The Global Encyclopaedia of Informality*, vol. 1, edited by Alena Ledeneva, 61–63. London: UCL Press.

Ranganathan, Malini. 2015. "Storm Drains as Assemblages: The Political Ecology of Flood Risk in Post-Colonial Bangalore." *Antipode* 47 (5): 1300–20.

Schramm, Sophie. 2016. "Flooding the Sanitary City: Planning Discourse and the Materiality of Urban Sanitation in Hanoi." *City* 20 (1): 32–51.

Swyngedouw, Erik. 2004. *Social Power and the Urbanization of Water: Flows of Power*. Oxford and New York: Oxford University Press.

Tấn Long, Đỗ. 2011. *Rapport Sur Les Inondations à Hồ Chí Minh Ville*. Hồ Chí Minh Ville: Comité populaire de Hồ Chí Minh Ville, centre de lutte contre les inondations.

Teulières, Roger, and Huy Nguyên. 1962. "Une Agglomération de Sampans Habités à Saigon." *Les Cahiers d'Outre-Mer* 58: 166–79.

Thayer, Carlyle A. 2010. "Political Legitimacy in Vietnam: Challenge and Response." *Politics & Policy* 38 (3): 423–44.

Tong Minh Dinh, Ho, Van Trung Le, and Le Toan Thuy. 2015. "Mapping Ground Subsidence Phenomena in Ho Chi Minh City through the Radar Interferometry Technique Using ALOS PALSAR Data." 2015. *Remote Sensing* 7 (7): 8543–62.

Tran Thi, Van, and Duong Ha. 2007. "Urban Land Cover Change through Development of Imperviousness in Ho Chi Minh City, Vietnam." In *Asian Conference on Remote Sensing (ACRS)*. Proceedings. Kuala Lumpur: Asian Association on Remote Sensing.

Vachaud, Georges, Fanny Quertamp, Thi San Ha Phan, Tien Dung Tran Ngoc, Thong Nguyen, Xuan Loc Luu, Anh Tuan Nguyen, and Nicolas Gratiot. 2019. "Flood-Related Risks in Ho Chi Minh City and Ways of Mitigation." *Journal of Hydrology* 573: 1021–1027.

Wright, Gwendolyn. 1991. *The Politics of Design in French Colonial Urbanism*. Chicago: The University of Chicago Press.

Wust, Sébastien, Jean-Claude Bolay, Franck Castiglioni, Ludovic Dewaele, Jean Niebudek, Pho Danh, Ngoc Lan Van Thi, Vinh Nguyen Quanh, Dan Tam Tran, and Ngoc Thanh Tran Thai. 2004. *Métropolisation et Développement Durable : Les Enjeux Du Règlement Planifié Des Zones d'habitat Précaire à Ho Chi Minh Ville, Entre Grands Programmes et Micro Projets*. Paris: EPLF – PRUD – GEMDEV – ISTED.

About the Author

Marie Gibert-Flutre is an Associate Professor of Geography in the Department of East Asia Studies at the Université Paris Cité. She turns the approach to 'global cities' upside down by critically exploring 'global Asia' from ordinary neighborhoods. She co-edited *Asian Alleyways: An Urban Vernacular in Times of Globalization* (AUP, 2020).

Index

 International Institute for Asian Studies

Publications / Asian Heritages

Ana Dragojlovic: *Beyond Bali. Subaltern Citizens and Post-Colonial Intimacy*
2016, ISBN 978 94 6298 064 8

Carolien Stolte and Yoshiyuki Kikuchi (eds): *Eurasian Encounters. Museums, Missions, Modernities*
2017, ISBN 978 90 8964 883 9

Christina Maags and Marina Svensson (eds): *Chinese Heritage in the Making. Experiences, Negotiations and Contestations*
2018, ISBN 978 94 6298 369 4

Yujie Zhu: *Heritage and Romantic Consumption in China*
2018, ISBN 978 94 6298 567 4

Carol Ludwig, Linda Walton and Yi-Wen Wang (eds): *The Heritage Turn in China. The Reinvention, Dissemination and Consumption of Heritage*
2020, ISBN 978 94 6298 566 7

Pierpaolo De Giosa: *World Heritage and Urban Politics in Melaka, Malaysia. A Cityscape below the Winds*
2021, ISBN 978 94 6372 502 6

Phill Wilcox: *Heritage and the Making of Political Legitimacy in Laos. The Past and Present of the Lao Nation*
2021, ISBN 978 94 6372 702 0

Penny Van Esterik: *Designs on Pots: Ban Chiang and the Politics of Heritage in Thailand*
2023, ISBN 978 94 6372 846 1

Alisa Santikarn: *Indigenous Heritage and Identity of the Last Elephant Catchers in Northeast Thailand*
2025, ISBN 978 90 4856 199 5